AND LIVING AGAIN

AND LIVING AGAIN

PRAMOD K. GUPTA

KNOWLEDGE WORLD

KW Publishers Pvt Ltd
New Delhi

ISBN 978-93-94915-41-1 Hardback
ISBN 978-93-94915-50-3 ebook

Published in India by Kalpana Shukla

KNOWLEDGE WORLD

KW Publishers Pvt Ltd
4676/21, First Floor, Ansari Road
Daryaganj, New Delhi 110002
Phone: +91 11 43528107
Marketing: kw@kwpub.in
Editorial: production@kwpub.in
Website: www.kwpub.in

Printed and Bound in India

For Mridula
and
The Will to Live

Contents

Words from a few,
Valued in Life

Harananda
Pr. Chief Security Commissioner/RPF (Retd.)
East Central Railway, Hajipur.
J 206, Corona Optus
Housing Colony, Sector 37C,
Gurugram-110001

"The best is yet to come"

Tragedies of life are transformative by nature. They push us away from the 'perspective of the herd' to use a phrase of Nietzsche, towards islands of Pythogorean silence. They are like psychic storms-- eloquent at the outset and reticent at the end. This journey through the quicksands of lonely deserts reinvigorates the ecosystem in which we have lived so far - it also readjusts the lost equilibrium between speed and rhythm.

I think every life has an inherent purpose- a dynamic directional movement. There are pauses, yet it pulsates with vitality inevitably driving us towards the higher realms of realization.

I know Pramod, the author. I can recollect that more than half a century ago we prepared together for a debate which he went on to win. We still cherish those memories. He was always inquisitive and impulsive which we all are tc some extent. And his soul always kept yearning for the unseen in the hidden corners of life.

Episodal memories never die and cognition preserves them surreptitiously in the different compartments of the mind. The book bears eloquent testimony. I hope Pramod's words will inspire many and rekindle hope in those minds anxiously waiting for the realization of their robust dreams.

Harananda

March 1st, 2023

Harananda

R.C.P. Singh,
Ex IAS & Ex Union Minister of Steel, Govt of India
At: Mustafapur, P.O.: Malti Via: Asthawan,
District: Nalanda. PIN - 803107

"It only made you stronger"

Pramod, my precious friend, and also the first with whom I knew what a bliss friendship was, has authored a book ' And Living Again'. Nothing could make me happier, particularly when he has done it during the period of convalescence from the dreaded hemorrhagic stroke which he had in April, 2021. I am thankful to Destiny. We have many unfinished tasks, some together too. Lot of plans that we made more than four decades ago took a back seat in the maze of domesticity and the service of the government and so many other things that we chose to do so far. Perhaps Pramod has to do many sensible things now. May God be with him and with us.

I know Pramod's positivity can defeat the Stroke. The fact that he has been able to finish his book while recovering is a sure sign of that. His reflections on relationships, the trauma of the illness of this magnitude and his associations with people set you thinking. His memories of experiences in the Indian Revenue Service, his thoughts on the Civil Services and the medical profession provide food for thought. I am sure he will, in the days to come, write on various subjects.

I have loved and admired Pramod during the last five decades. I don't say it enough but I do. I know things about him no one else probably does and no one knows me better than probably he does. I love the way we go right back to how we are no matter how long we have been apart and how easy it is to feel at home and safe with him by my side. We have come a long way. But we have much farther to go. I am so glad that I will have him with me the whole way.

I value knowing Pramod. I want to thank Mridula for being such a nice friend to my friend besides being his wife. I am always there with him and for him.

Rcp

March 1st, 2023

R.C.P.Singh

Vidisha Priyanka,
5125 Palm Springs Blvd,
Unit 1-107 Tampa, FL 33647. USA
Faculty, School of Mass Communication
and Advertising, University of South Florida,
Tampa, FL

"Power of positive thinking"

How do you measure the value of a human being? And more importantly, when do you realize how precious someone is to you?

Most human beings value blood ties, the warmth of the shared womb, the guiding hands of a father and the bond of siblings, but what about relationships that are born out of friendships, or shared values, or by law?

Mr. Pramod K. Gupta, who wrote this book, is my brother by law - my sister's husband; my guide - because of shared values; my mirror - because he dared to show me my true self when I was a precocious child rebelling against the world.

He holds a special place in my life, a connection that I deem almost spiritual, and a human who is one of the most valuable people in my life. So, when I heard that he had a stroke and could even die, a wave of dread and utter despair ran down my spine. It is a feeling I don't want to repeat ever again. I evaluated the value of Pramod ji in our lives as he lay in the ICU during COVID-19. I thanked my sister who reacted swiftly and decisively and probably saved his life.

In the face of his crisis, my family faced the possible loss of a human that we value more than our own lives. Not because he is our brother by law, but because he is our soul brother by some divine connection.

If I were to describe this book, I would say it is a victory of perseverance and resilience, in addition to being a chronicle of life and a process of determined recovery. His positive attitude, his Herculean efforts to gain his physical and mental abilities, his triumph over circumstantial adversities, his overcoming of personal despair, are all life lessons. Within two years since he had a stroke, he has recovered enough to write books, maintain all practical aspects of life, and deal with the environmental isolation brought upon all of us due to the pandemic.

We did not doubt once that he would recover. Because that is the kind of man he is,- positive, generous, hopeful, spiritual, authentic - a keeper. Not many people have the audacity, power and will to live life to the fullest, like the author does. And his book dares others to defy adversities, focus on self, value others and most of all, live for hope and love.

Vidisha P.

March 1st,2023

Vidisha Priyanka

Dr Pratibha Gupta,
Obstetrician and Gynaecologist, Sarvang Hospital,
Betiahata. Gorakhpur. 0551-2340176,2203971.
A-7, Awaas Vikas Colony, Betiah Hata,
Gorakhpur-273001

"So thankful to God"

I am really excited to learn that my elder brother Shri Pramod Kumar Gupta has authored a book 'And Living Again'. I wish he lives again and again. For me it is difficult to imagine life without him around. He has been a father figure for me not only by virtue of being my elder brother but by being a man of rare qualities of head and heart. I have been emulating him since childhood and learnt from him how to excel in studies. His proficiency in English and Hindi languages has been of an extraordinary level and he has been my real teacher. I still remember how in class VIII he explained to me the method to go about mastering Sanskrit.

The backdrop of the book being the haemorrhagic stroke he had in April, 2021 makes me sad. It was traumatic for us. I can't thank the Almighty enough for his being back towards a near total recovery. I am happy at the same time that he has used his period of recovery in the most creative manner. I am thankful to the doctors who took care of him. Pramod Bhaiya as I call him has always been so respectful to doctors. It was his dream and desire that I became a doctor myself.

I remember our parents, particularly our father with whom he was so attached intellectually. Had he been around he would have loved to see him write a book with reflections on life and sundry other issues. I am told he has narrated his experiences as a bureaucrat besides his reflections on issues of human relationships. I am sure coming from his pen, it is going to be a great book. I wish him best of health and togetherness with him in the years to come and many more creative ventures like this book. I am sure our mother and father will bless us from wherever they are.

Pratibha Gupta

March 1st, 2023

Dr Pratibha Gupta

Anand Kumar Gupta
Regional Manager (SBI),
RBO-5, Sangrur.

"Yet to learn so much from you"

There is no limit to human emotions. And when the emotions are infinite, one who can handle them with positivity can, in my view, be considered a complete person. Shri Pramod Kumar Gupta happens to be my uncle and I have been knowing him since my childhood. I have seen him handling emotions of happiness, sorrow, struggle, victory, defeat and trauma and I consider him to be a complete person. Born in a humble family, deprived from his mother's fullest care for reasons of her health and losing his father at the tender age of 20, he always had the dreams of touching the sky. He never compromised with his dreams. He always had a rebellious attitude towards the conservatism of the society. He always lived life on his terms. Countless emotions and experiences must be buried inside him. Surviving the stroke, he had, has been largely possible because of his will to live, besides of course the Almighty's grace.

I feel privileged to be around him. I really feel excited that he has used his time when he is recovering in putting some of his experiences in the form of a book, 'And Living Again', I am sure, will express countless emotion. His high articulation skills will definitely make it a great reading.

March 1st, 2023

(Anand Kumar Gupta)

1

Near-death

To Life Again

"It does not matter how slowly you go as long as you do not stop."

—Confucius

One can only be grateful to the cosmic force that regulates the destinies of humans and that regulates the number of breaths already decided for one, and one can only consider oneself fortunate to have survived a dreaded 'haemorrhagic stroke', particularly in these gloomy times of COVID-19 when countless many, near and dear ones, full of life, full of health, full of plans for the years to come succumbed to the quirk of fate. Like a diehard optimist, I must say it was the fateful, but not the last midnight of life. It was April 9, 2021, around 11.30 p.m. Life was as usual without an inkling of what was going to happen in the next few minutes. It was, however, a very brief 20 minutes after which for the next about four days I did not witness anything. Others who are concerned with me and were around me witnessed the misery that saw me listless, rather unconscious or subconscious most of the time. I had lost the ability to recognise faces and my responses were worrisome. I am told what followed. I was in the ICU in less than an hour of losing consciousness. That probably was a saving grace, thanks to a doctor who by chance happens to be my wife and the doctor friends who were at home in no time and brought me to the hospital. It was also the time when the second wave of COVID was at its peak and the Yashoda Hospital, Kaushambi was flooded with patients. Thanks to Mr. P. N. Arora, the owner of the hospital, the association with whom ensured my being there in the ICU where getting a bed was by all means a matter of luck.

The next four days were in the ICU. My wife must have spent those four days without any thought, with some phone calls being answered not knowing what to say. The knowledge and skills of the doctor must have vanished with the onslaught of the impending danger to a husband's survival. Something similar must have happened to my younger son. He, of course, would know it for the first time in life what it could be like. Forty-two years ago his father, who was today facing the battle for life, at his age of 20 faced an almost similar situation with his grandfather all alone. I don't know how the elder son who is in the USA must have been informed. But Providence at times does provide ways and means to fight the hardest battle. And much earlier in life I had realised that one was blessed if one had friends who were genuinely loving, empathetic, intelligent and were by education competent doctors too. While all the doctors who must have done their best inside the ICU, the physician and the neurophysician, keeping a watchful eye on the course of treatment, discussions with the treating doctors added to a smooth administration of the suitable medical option. I had my physician friend for me to make suggestions. I can understand what an onerous task it must have been for him. I will be ungrateful if I don't mention our doctor friends who have been the lifeline for us for years. They ensured that the best was done medically. Incidentally, we all are there together in a WhatsApp Group 'Ruhaniyat', named so by our radiologist friend in the group where I am the only non-doctor. Concerned and valuable messages also flew from adorable friends and doctors, famous Radiologist and Orthopaedist, which added to the support system. Other well-wishers, a noted physician and an anaesthetist friend who took the trouble of landing from far-off places, must have created the psychological and precious support environment for a hapless wife, though a doctor herself. An evolved and great friend from Noida, a few resourceful bureaucrats and more like younger brothers were there to do anything to bring me back to life, for which the doctors were doing their part. Initial minutes/hours, I am sure, must have gone towards waiting to see how the thrombotic stroke caused by the thrombus (blood clot) in the arteries supplying blood to the brain would show its severity. I was taken for the MRI of the brain more than once to watch and monitor. The clinical details, of course, are entirely in the domain of the life-savers, the attending neurophysicians and the physicians, but the little one could make out was that if the bleeding had not stopped, a surgical intervention might have been required. Statistics from Johns Hopkins suggest that 13% of all strokes are haemorrhagic. Luckily for me, the bleeding showed mercy and after the administration of the required drugs, the unconscious but breathing me was left in the manner the doctors deemed fit. For four days it was like this when they decided that with the upsurge of COVID, it was not safe to leave me at the hospital and I could be taken care of at home and the enabling facilities could be created according to needs. So I was brought home. For the next month or more my memory was not kind to me, and it is a terrifying thought to continue for a lifetime with a failing memory.

The room which we had made into a lounge for guests on the first floor was converted into a hospital room with a bed as made for a patient. A diwan was unfolded into a double bed for my wife and my son to sleep there and keep a watch on me. I discovered that my younger sister and my brother-in-law, both doctors at Gorakhpur, and my eldest nephew, a bank officer at Ludhiana, had arrived during the period of my hospitalisation. And so had my elder brother and elder sister from Patna. Perhaps this was not the time to say goodbye to them although different medical apprehensions came from a host of doctor friends, well-wishers and the immediate family. The bottom line was that for another month one could not rule out the recurrence of the stroke. So, one had to keep one's fingers crossed. The silver lining was that I had gradually started uttering words, though incoherently. I was eating food and I was answering questions without knowing consciously to whom I was speaking. Although not fully aware, within myself the fear of near death had died. That was perhaps optimism and the will to live. In retrospect, the worst was that I was not able to go to the toilet and was totally dependent on others, particularly a kind wife, for the most essential part of a human's physical existence. Well, it was going to be like this for more than a month.

I am told a male help was hired to help me for my diurnal essentials, from the toilet to changing clothes. I do not remember him at all although he was here for almost a month. That is a telling and dreadful commentary on my loss of memory. I was also forgetting to construct a full sentence either in Hindi or in English. Retrospectively comic, but so tragic while it was happening. My wife and son tell me that I started using difficult Hindi words to convey. For example, to say "keep it on the floor" I would say "ise bhoomi pe rakh do". If I had to say, "why are you sad" I would say, "tum itne vyathit kyon ho", and so on. There are umpteen such examples of the agonising fun I was creating. It is difficult to imagine how it would have been to live without memory for a lifetime.

But destiny was not going to be that unkind. My memory started unfolding some time from the middle of May 2021. I had a reasonably good memory for verses in all languages that I know, particularly Hindi, English, Sanskrit and a bit of Urdu. A famous 'nazm' of Sahir Ludhianvi, "Taj tere liye ek majhare-ulfat hi sahi" has been one of my favourites which I would have recited not less than a hundred times since my school days and won accolades and prizes for that. Lying down listlessly on my bed some day in the first week of May, I struggled to recall the 'nazm', rather long, but I could not recall except a few words from several different sentences. It was so frustrating that I cried within myself. But there was a silver lining here too. A conscious effort had begun to be my earlier self. I kept trying to recall 'shlokas' from Ramcharitmanas and Bhagavad Gita and my favourite lines from Shakespeare, Shelley and Keats. But I could not, except a few words, randomly.

Interestingly, it was Ramcharitmanas which performed a miracle for my memory. The verses with which the 'Bal-Kanda' starts read "Varnanamarthsamghanaam rasanam chandasamapi, mangalanaam cha karttarau vande vanivinayakau". Shri Tulsidas prays to and worships Goddess Saraswati and Lord Ganesha and says that without their blessings of success and prosperity the enormous and extensive task of writing the Ramcharitmanas will not be possible. Somehow, I have been reciting these lines from a very young age without a clue as to their meaning which I understood much later in life. As I was not able to recall anything from English or Hindi literature, I troubled my brain with Sanskrit. Lo and behold, I could utter these lines to myself and in the next few hours all the verses that follow came to memory. Rattling the verses to myself was a Eureka moment, a moment of fathomless happiness.

So, around the middle of May 2021, the amnesia, the loss of memory, in simple words, started gradually dying out and I started getting a new lease of life. Life before April 9, 2021 was returning mentally. A nice doctor friend explained that amnesia was only a symptom while the disease actually was dementia. It was like a fever (the symptom) and the flu being the disease. Alzheimers is one type of dementia. So, amnesia included memory loss, confusion and the inability to recognise familiar faces or places. Some of the causes of temporary amnesia include concussion, severe illness and high fever, emotional stress, etc., requiring drugs or even electroconvulsive therapy.

Although most of the time I was lying in bed with the right leg and the right hand debilitated because of the paralytic stroke, the brain was functioning now. That was enough reason to think that I was in the mainstream of life again. Being still dependent for the routine ablutions was, however, demoralising and depressing at times. In such situations only you realise what a great fortune it could be to have a compassionate spouse. Aphasia was another disorder which was the battle to be fought. Put simply, aphasia is a disorder that affects how we communicate. It can impact your speech, as well as the way you write and understand both spoken and written language. Aphasia is a symptom of some other condition, such as a stroke or brain tumour. A person with aphasia may speak in short or incomplete sentences, speak in sentences that don't make sense, speak unrecognisable words, may have difficulty finding words and may not fully understand other people's conversation. Well, despite memory showing signs of a revival, I was definitely suffering in varying degrees from all these. Memory was serving me well in these toughest times of life. I was able to recall all the lines which were dear to my heart during the last more than five decades, ever since I developed interest in literature and languages, depending on my maturity and proficiency in a language at different stages. That became a part and parcel of living the twenty-four hours of a day. Of course, the confidence of getting back to my normal self was also growing with the indomitable will to live life again. One such day I could recall the lines from T. S. Eliot (The Love Song of J. Alfred Prufrock), which always fascinated me:

> *"Let us go then, you and I,*
> *When the evening is spread out against the sky*
> *Like a patient etherised upon a table;"*

And also:

"And indeed there will be time
For the yellow smoke that slides along the street
rubbing its back upon the window-panes;
there will be time,
there will be time
to prepare a face to meet the faces that you meet;
there will be time to murder and create
and time for all the works and days of hands
that lift and drop a question on your plate;
time for you and time for me
and time yet for a hundred indecisions
and for a hundred visions and revisions,
before the taking of toast and tea.
In the room the women come and go talking
of Michelangelo."

Confined to my room, rather the bed, recalling verses which find place in several diaries and notebooks maintained for the last almost five decades, I was telling myself each moment every day that I will not be like this and it was probably a very temporary phase, howsoever difficult. On April 21, 2021, I suddenly discover that a physiotherapist, young and reasonably confident, starts coming and helping me with my crippled limbs. Till now there was another physiotherapist, a young lady who has been treating me. I recall her only vaguely. I only recall that I could not remember her name.

My new physiotherapist told my wife that I should recover substantially but he also said that it was less than a month after the stroke which was too early to say anything and that he would need to evaluate during the next couple of months to be able to say something which would be sensible professionally. With him the first about 15 days were eventless for me for the simple reason that I don't recall anything. He tells me that I was able to lift neither my right leg nor the right hand and that he was keeping his fingers crossed. Then suddenly he discovered movement in my leg and he felt enthused to follow his treatment protocol. There has been no looking back since then. He also told my wife after two months that I was going to be completely cured, as good as I was earlier if not better. So, the physiotherapy continued, initially for an hour every day and after a year extended to two hours daily. It continues till date. With my physiotherapist a new kind of relationship developed as months passed by. It was a relationship of trust and positivity. He became a great friend and a family member. Not only that he was energetic, hardworking and disciplined, his positivity was something that distinguished him from most others. With him around there was hardly a day when one was left with any doubt that one will not be alright.

So, after a little more than a couple of months, sometime from the end of May, one was in bad shape with the paraplegia of the right limb but the fear of near death was gradually disappearing. It was because the most crucial part of the human body called the brain was healing. It is only in a sickness of this magnitude that one realises how everything is in the 'mind'. Sometime after a year, i.e., in April 2022 I found that the limping gait was improving but the improvement was discernible only to somebody who was to see me after at least 3 months. Again, it was positivity which was making one sure about a total recovery. And I must say that a diehard optimist, which my physiotherapist was, can really change the way you look at things. Although a fiercely optimistic person myself, it was he who kept hopes alive for a more than total recovery. One had to have patience with time. Mentally, I set a target of two years.

"Your body can stand almost anything. It is your mind that you have to convince."

I had become extra active with the mobile phone, although operating with the left hand. For the first time I realised what a great discovery it was. The flip side of it apart, the way it can keep one close to the world is amazing. In a situation like I was in or for anybody who cannot handle multiple means of communication because of physical constraints, it can at once become a substitute for newspaper, television, theatre, etc., for everything from which you derive information and entertainment. So, from June 2021 onwards, having regained mental faculties substantially, I was coming closer to the outside world. This was giving a feeling of "living life twice" or "living life again".

Through the mobile phone and the internet, the first inspiring, though tragic, story that I came across was that of Sandeep Singh, an ex-captain of the Indian national hockey team. A full back of the team, he was a penalty corner specialist. He has been dubbed as the 'Flicker Singh' in the media for his specialisation of the drag flick, one of the fastest in the world. He was the youngest player ever to play at the Olympics in Athens in 2004. He was seriously injured on August 22, 2006 when he was 20 years old after being hit by an accidental gunshot in the Kalka Shatabdi Express train, while on his way to join the national team due to leave for the World Cup in Africa two days later. He was paralysed and was on wheelchair for more than a year of his life. His fairy-tale comeback to the field is too inspiring an incident. He started walking in a year from the incident and regained his place in the team in 2008. He retired from Hockey in 2016 and now serves as the Sports Minister in the state of Haryana. Sandeep Singh also has a biopic, titled *Soorma* based on his roller coaster life as a hockey player. Having come across the story of Sandeep Singh, which was a great generator of hope towards recovery, I saw the movie *Soorma* on Netflix.

While Sandeep Singh's story was a great story of hope and the resolve to get well and forget the paralytic stroke as a story of things that happened, the scenario in the outside world was getting extremely depressing because of COVID. While somebody dying in the USA or UK or elsewhere in the world was sad news, it was devastating to witness the fatalities back home, right by your side. Sometime in the month of June 2021 browsing my mobile phone I found that dear friends Vinod Dua and Chinna Dua, celebrities in their own right were in the hospital, in rather serious condition. Chinna Dua succumbed to the virus soon, probably on June 11 which I remember because I had called both Vinod and Chinna a day before, my pitiable health condition apart. My call to them had gone unanswered. Chinna losing the battle for life was unnerving. It at once reminded me of the fragility of life. Although I had known them for a number of years, it was during the years since 2016 that I had been interacting with them at an intellectual level. The current political situation, music, Hindi and Urdu poetry and friendship with a substance were the common subjects we often discussed. Both of them were gifted singers. A very nice memory with them is of January 2017 when my elder son visited from the USA and I had organised a dinner at Hotel Royal Plaza, along with all arrangements for a musical session. They enthralled everybody when they sang "Nigahon Nigahon mei dil lene wale" from *Kashmir ki kali*. Chinna had an impeccable sense of fashion—everything that was typically feminine and Indian. Widely known in Delhi for her Sarees, 'potlis' (small purses/bags) and 'bindi', she once told me that she was a little concerned about who was going to keep the huge number of sarees she had collected over the years. Another nice memory is that of an evening at India Habitat Centre, Lodi Road in 2018. It was part of the Urdu Literature Festival, known as Afreen. Chinna's rendition of Urdu nazms (songs) was enthralling and Vinod's talk on the identities of Hindi and Urdu languages in poetry was brilliant. The most memorable time as friends was an hour-long conversation as recently as in February 2020 at an evening organised by Duleep Bhatia, a common friend, as part of his son's wedding celebrations. Fortunately, none of our common acquaintances were there to waste time on pleasantries and meaningless gossip. Our discussions ranged from left politics on the Jawaharlal Nehru University (JNU) campus to Dushyant Kumar, the celebrated poet. Being an alumni of the JNU and having been politically active myself as a student, it was of interest, a little disappointing though, for me to learn from Vinod that he felt that the leftist leanings of any group need not be questioned at all. My take on the issue was that various groups of students would do much better if they respected the views of others and under any circumstances violence or hooliganism had to be dealt with by the university administration. Political leanings or philosophical commitments need not crystallise while at the university. It should be in the stage of evolution and take shape while in the social and national life outside the university. There was hardly any disagreement on Dushyant Kumar's poetry. His inimitable 'ghazals', particularly the ones contained in *Saye Me Dhoop* published in 2008 can only be admired for the revolutionary zeal and the extraordinary diction. "*Kahan to taya tha Chiragh har ek ghar ke liye, Kahan Chiragh mayassar nahin shehar ke liye*" were the lines with which we said goodbye to that evening. That was destined to be the last proper meeting with Vinod and Chinna. I could see here and there on the social media that Vinod was rapidly losing on health after Chinna's death. It was not very long after Chinna's death that Vinod too breathed his last in December 2021, even though a few months ago he had recovered from COVID after a prolonged hospitalisation. I am told he had developed some problems with his liver. Two creative lives were lost.

On the March 31, 2021, taking a stroll on the roof of the building which housed the office of the CREDAI (Confederation of Real Estate Developers Association of India) of which I was the Director General-cum-CEO, I had an hour-long conversation with a very dear friend, Vijay Jhindal. He was always there for me in all my pleasures and pains. A couple of years younger than me, Vijay was an extremely successful entrepreneur and businessman with his affairs running in more than a dozen areas. He had made a good fortune for himself. Extremely humble, and rubbing shoulders with the powers that be of the present regime, he was a highly educated person, being a

Chartered Accountant, an LLB, a Company Secretary, etc. But COVID spared none. Till May 2021, I was practically cut off from the world. Sometime in the beginning of June, I recalled that Vijay was to come to me for some professional advice in April. I was surprised, and a little hurt too, that he had no time to check on me during the time I was struggling for life. Then I received a call from a friend in Mumbai who wanted to come to see me, and he came the next day. He is substantially connected with the film world. So, after my illness the discussion switched over to movies and the gossip of Bollywood. In the course of our conversation, he suddenly mentioned that he was missing Vijay Jhindal. It has been more than two decades of my association with Vijay and more than a decade with this friend from Mumbai and I never knew that they knew one another so intimately. He told me that he knew about my intimacy with Vijay but purposely never mentioned it. The greatest shock was to follow when he told me that Vijay left us for the heavenly abode sometime in the month of May 2021 itself. The COVID devoured him. My hemiplegia paled into insignificance and I found it almost unbelievable for the next few minutes. It was so unbelievable that I later confirmed it with his co-brother at Jaipur who happened to be a senior colleague in the Indian Revenue Service and a very dear friend. Moments of parties at Vijay Jhindal's sprawling house in Delhi, my meeting a few bigwigs of the present political dispensation with him and various functions at the FICCI auditorium suddenly flashed through the memory lane. The fragility of human life and the cruelty of COVID had assumed fearsome proportions.

Having neither seen the newspapers nor watched the news channels properly on the TV for nearly three months now, I thought of updating myself with all the news, particularly the ones relating to COVID and the disaster unleashed by it. Even though the hemiplegia restricted my movements, and I was myself going through a phase of self-pity, I decided I would go through the newspapers of the last three months to know what all had happened. Time by and large had stopped for me after April 9, and it was my wife's face only which was reminding me that the world was beautiful and I ought to get back to my older self to see it again. My wife also, to keep me away from all the negative news, had been maintaining an obvious reticence since April. I decided to start using my mobile phone so that I could search things and find answers to my queries through Google. Well, once I started doing that I was instantly drowned in a plethora of depressing information regarding critical illness and deaths in the second wave of COVID which had engulfed the country sometime in April 2021, which by and large coincided with the stroke I was suffering from. I learnt about a host of civil servants who had succumbed to COVID in the second wave. A number of erstwhile colleagues of the Indian Revenue Service, colleagues from the Indian

Administrative Service and other services lost their lives. The list included a good friend, although out of touch for quite some time, A. K. Singh, IAS who was posted as the Chief Secretary of Bihar. Vijay Kumar, IRS too breathed his last and when his wife, a distant relative of ours, called my wife, I at once thought she had called to check on me. She was absolutely unaware of my having undergone a stroke and she had called to inform me about Vijay, and that she wanted to meet us. It was all like a series of tragic tales.

But more tragic pieces of information were to follow. Two friends of the Intermediate at the prestigious Science College, Patna were to say goodbye forever. One Dr. Ashok Pathak had already left us in 2020 just when the COVID had started. A friendship of the age of 15 in 1974 away from home in the college hostel has its own memories to unnerve you when you hear that your friend of that tender age had left the world. Sixty cannot be an age to die. I and Ashok were roommates at the hostel for some time. That had further cemented the bond of friendship which sustained through the years. Coming from an extremely modest background, Ashok had the unflinching desire of cracking the medical entrance and becoming a surgeon to earn name and money too. He needed money to bring his family in a condition to enable his brothers to pursue their studies. He successfully did that. He never compromised with his focus on studies and competed for medical entrance and finished his MBBS by topping the University and securing honours in several subjects. He then did his Masters in Surgery to become a surgeon. He settled at Begusarai probably because he wanted to be closer home to take care of his extended family. In the initial days of the IRS when I was posted at Patna as an Assistant Commissioner of Income Tax, I frequently visited Kahalgaon and Bhagalpur—my home and my in-laws' home. Invariably, travelling by road, I used to make a stopover at Ashok's place at Begusarai which was on way. There are endless memories. It was not the time to go. It was too soon for that.

Equally sad was the fact of Bharat Mishra, a friend since 1974 succumbing to COVID in the second wave. Bharat too was together at the hostel at Science College, Patna whose news of death came to me long after he was no more. It was his wife who had called from his number which was obviously saved by me. I could not have imagined that it was his wife who would call me to inform me of Bharat's demise. She was weeping profusely over the phone crying foul against the doctors whom she perceived to have made a mess of the treatment protocol. She also accused a friend and a doctor at the same time, holding him responsible for his death. It was difficult to agree with her or make a comment on the medical treatment, but I could fathom the hurt and the agony. Bharat was a very senior Engineer with the NTPC and was rather unhappy with the lack of transparency in all that was happening about his promotions etc. He had told me a year ago to see if I could do something through the bureaucracy to ensure justice to him. I could do little for which I feel bad, worse perhaps because he is no more. I still cannot believe that Ashok and Bharat are no more.

Near home I was looking for Arvind Sharma, a young man in his 40s who had been visiting me almost every fortnight during the last more than a decade. I was a little surprised that even after three months he had not bothered to check on me because I was finding it unbelievable that he would not come to know of my condition from common acquaintances. Nobody was picking up his mobile phone even though it was ringing each time. So I got in touch with a common friend only to be told about the worst. We had lost him too, to COVID. On any health parameter it was difficult to believe. A man of austere habits, he never even took tea and was addicted to his morning walks and Yoga. From the background of a landlord, he had huge agricultural holdings at Patna and nearby. Dabbling in politics, with the background of being a nephew of an ex-Congress President of Bihar, he had recently made a huge investment in house property in South Delhi and shifted there from trans-Yamuna. Always worried about his son's education who was still in school, he had grandiose plans of sending him to the USA for higher studies after school. I always used to tell him that his son should at the moment concentrate only on his Class X studies and the idea of the USA in Class XII itself need not be discussed with him. Alas, there will be no occasion to listen to him and counsel.

There seemed to be no end to the misery caused by COVID and the casualties having already taken place. It was more disconcerting because all this was happening closer home. For the encashment of some matured National Savings Certificates in the name of my wife and the payment of LIC premium I looked for Vivek Agrawal, the guy who had been around me for these services during the last 20 years or so, only to discover that he too was no more. He would have been hardly 50 years of age. With such people who have been there advising you on Life Insurance and other investments at early stages in life you develop a bond which may or may not be emotional but nevertheless important, and as humans with a heart you feel they had a place in your life which only they occupied. Similarly, my man Friday for my and my family's computer needs during the last 25 years, Anil recently lost his life to some ailment. He was like a family member by now. Around 50 years of age is no age to leave the world. Anil has only added to the sadness.

The COVID thus had become the most dreaded killer since March 2020. In our lifetime we had not seen or even heard of such wrath of nature. But tragic deaths took place even without COVID. For me, personally, a great jolt was received in the form of Sanjeev (Kumar Singh) who lost the battle for life, not because of COVID, but because of Dengue at the famous Medanta Hospital at Gurgaon on

October 16, 2020. It was shocking to say the least. He has been too close and I can claim that nobody on earth knew his weaknesses and strengths more than I did. I knew him from Samastipur, Bihar and met him first in 1975. I had gone to Samastipur from Patna where my father was posted. A simpleton from the village, his mother was a teacher of Hindi in the school where my younger sister was studying along with his younger sister. A few months later he came to Patna and managed to get admitted into college. Subsequent years are a story of his hard work and good fortune. His entire family used to hold me in high esteem which I really value. Being a professor of History at a college at Samastipur, his father used to ask me a lot of things whenever we met at Patna and when I was studying History at JNU, Delhi. He was enamoured of the professors at JNU. Sanjeev was a man of extraordinary grit and physical prowess. Way back in 1979 when we were just 20, he beat up hooligans on the road who tried to harass me. Later when he came to Delhi and had no room to stay, common friends Shekhar and Satish came to his rescue and that perhaps facilitated his competing for the Civil Services. He later proved to be an excellent police officer in the Madhya Pradesh cadre and later at the National Investigation Agency. He was a fitness freak and had responded to the 'Fitness Challenge' of the Hon'ble Prime Minister Shri Narendra Modi through a Tweet and a video uploaded in 2018 when he was 58 plus. The video had become viral in the circuit of the civil servants and deservingly so. As we grew older and got preoccupied with our personal lives, our meetings became infrequent. We had reservations too with his family members whom we found not going well with us on either intellect or on genuine emotions. Be that as it may, Sanjeev's departure from amongst us was a reminder that life was uncertain and that we ought to make it simpler.

By now it has been almost a year of the stroke. It has been an eye-opener in many respects. It has been a kind of litmus test for the relations you valued and cherished for years. It was questioning your wisdom in understanding people and particularly friends, a word we use so liberally. It is around this time that I came across some information about Sharon Stone, the celebrity star of Hollywood. I had seen the celebrated movie *Basic Instinct* in 1995 (it was a 1992 movie). I was a little curious when I read that she had a massive stroke in September 2001. She bled for days rather than hours and medically then it was a rare brain bleed. Her cerebral haemorrhage lasted for nine days as she informed herself in a conversation with Willie Geist. Any known risk factors for stroke were totally absent in Sharon Stone's case. She never had migraine, high blood pressure or diabetes. There was no family history of stroke either. She didn't smoke. But yes, she was under mounting emotional strain due to a crumbling marriage and the looming custody battle for a newly adopted son who was a toddler. She was only 42 years of age in 2001 being a March 1958 born. The massive stroke that she suffered cost her not only her health, but her career, family, fortune and global fame. She has written a book, *The Beauty of Living Twice* wherein she has chronicled her efforts to rebuild her life. Over the course of the pages of the book she talks about her pivotal roles, her life-changing friendships, her worst disappointments and her great accomplishments. She reveals how she went from a childhood of trauma and violence to a career where she had similar experiences. She has herself said in her interviews that people were "brutally unkind" after she suffered a stroke. Sharon Stone says she took off from acting for two years although it took seven years for her to recover fully. In her book Sharon Stone has recalled her trauma of the stroke which I would quote here—"when the room is so silent and no one's running around trying to fix you, that's when you realise how near death is and how serious everything is." Further, "you write about the light, the feeling of falling, seeing people who had passed." She gets pensive and says, "I found that I wasn't the only one who'd this kind of experience. It's so profound. And I know that scientists feel that it's a scientific thing that happens. And spiritualists believe that it's a spiritual thing. Personally, I am with Albert Einstein, who believed that it is both." I was tempted to read the book. So, I just picked up my mobile phone and ordered it on Amazon. I have been a booklover but very selective. Good language always fascinated me. But whatever the diction or story, Sharon Stone's story felt like mine. Providence was kind to make me a survivor too. Whatever we may think or say, the fact remained that the only absolute truth was death. The rest—love, ambition, pride, values of all kinds was to be taken with a pinch of salt. Nevertheless, once the fear of near death was dwindling and all other emotions had started bothering, the desire to delve a little deeper into the changed situation in terms of bonds with friends and so-called ones even though they were decades old, empathy of the close relatives and the dilemma of doing something for a face for the outside world was asserting itself. The book arrived by courier the next day and within the next few days I finished reading it. As rightly described by someone, the book *The Beauty of Living Twice* was a book for the wounded and a book for the survivors. I was definitely feeling wounded on many counts and I was a fortunate survivor. I found many references to relationships in the book to be like something happening to me. All that only confirmed to me that adversity of this magnitude could only bring you closer to the realities of your worldly existence. Contraption of a few glasses of wine and accompanying food which could be called gourmet's delight, and meaningless discussions conditioned by our egos, keep us in a false world. We remain so happy in a make-believe world that we start thinking it to be real. More often than not we say goodbye to the world having lived with falsities where even self-contentment was "make-believe". Well, it may not be desirable to wish that we need to have a near-death experience to perceive the true relationships in terms of empathy but it is not a totally worthless proposition. The world after experiencing a down slide in terms of your material utility is so exciting and revealing in terms of understanding the "make-believe" that constitutes life. But life biologically and with a sound mind is important. I really lament and feel so sad that destiny made a comedian like Raju Srivastava give up life at the age of 58 when he was still regaling the world. I wish he would come back. I am sure his observations would have been more incisive had it not happened and he would have produced a new level of comedy. When we live in a make-believe world, we pretend that things are better, different, or more exciting than they really are, instead of facing up to reality. I am sure tearing into make-believes can really produce a different level of comedy.

It is a rather painfully long period to heal after a stroke. The National Institute of Neurological Disorders and Stroke informs that recovery time after a stroke is different for everyone—it can take weeks, months or even years. Some people recover fully but others have long-term or lifelong disabilities. With the right amount of rehabilitation, a person's speech, cognitive, motor and sensory skills can steadily be recovered. Although just 10% of people fully recover from a stroke, 25% have only minor impairments and 40% have moderate impairments that are manageable with some special care. It was a pretty long period in my case for the recovery. This is one and a half years after the fateful night when I had the stroke and I am still struggling with the hemiplegia of the right leg and the right hand. Hemiplegia is, broadly, paralysis on one side of the body. It is a condition, caused by a brain injury, that results in varying degrees of weakness, stiffness (spasticity) and lack of control in one side of the body. My physiotherapist, however, would always correct me to say that I was no longer suffering from hemiplegia and that it had now shifted to hemiparesis. Hemiparesis is characterised by weakness on one side of the body. A person with hemiparesis might not be able to move his arm, or may feel tingling or other odd sensations on just one side. Hemiplegia is paralysis on one side of the body.

Even though it is a long road to recovery, the body, after a few months, starts giving indications regarding the extent of recovery. If deformities don't take shape, there are reasons to be happy and hopeful even though there may be a very slow and insignificant progress in gait or the movement of the hand or fingers. The importance of patience comes into play at this juncture and a positive attitude may work wonders. After six months I myself thought that in the next fifteen days or so I would be back to my normal self but it was not going to happen like that. In fact, I had told the CREDAI (Confederation of Real Estate Developers Association of India) management where I was working as the Director General-cum-CEO after my superannuation from the Indian Revenue Service that I should be fit enough and in a position to join in the next one month. But the painfully slow progress of recovery made me change all my plans. I was still happy that I was able to think of plans in life after the near-death experience. I was in regular touch with my neurophysician to let me know how my brain was healing. After two more MRIs in the fifth and sixth months, my neurophysician told me that there was nothing to worry about the brain and that the clot formed on account of the bleeding had healed. So, one had to wait with time and physiotherapy. Practically now physiotherapy, the passage of time and my own determination to get well were the three factors on which my recovery rested.

The role of physiotherapy and the physiotherapist is crucial for recovery after things are alright with the brain which can be seen only by the neurosurgeon or the neurophysician. So, it was Dr. Indrajit Saxena, my physiotherapist, who was going to be the most important person around for me. He still is when it is 18 months now of the stroke. A young man, around 40 years of age, Indrajit is handsome, slim, fit and extremely amiable. A diehard optimist, Indrajit would never allow any negativity to take over. All these traits make him an extraordinary physiotherapist to take care of me. His general awareness has a good level. What is strikingly special about him is his indomitable and positive spirit. In fact, I started addressing him as Mr. Positive after a few months. I developed a special bond with him. After all, he was spending almost two hours every day with me. He was kind and considerate and agreed to come home for my treatment. So, from 2 to 4 p.m. every day, I was with him and at his disposal. As regards the treatment protocol, he was convinced that what he was doing was alright, but he remained non-committal if any advice came from any neurosurgeon or physician or orthopaedic surgeon who visited me, being my friends. He used to convince me that a conservative approach was the best and any interference by machines was best avoided. While he used to compliment me on my general condition of health and my youthful look, he never minced words in conveying that age was not on my side. He said that it could take time but a sure recovery was indicated beyond any doubt. That all the limbs were moving, that no deformities had developed, that I was able to walk, limping though—all these were indications to feel happy about. It was just a question of time as he always said and the time also could be a day, a month or two months. Perhaps it was the calcaneus in my case which was taking time to heal. The calcaneus (heel bone) is the largest of the tarsal bones in the foot (hind foot) below the three bones that make up the ankle joint. Other bones are the Tibia (shinbone) and the Fibula (smaller bone in the leg). The other problem was the right hand where the fingers, even though healthy in look, were not able to hold things. There was a serious problem of grip. All these days I have been doing everything using my left hand, including writing. I was told that movement of the fingers of the hand came in the category of 'fine' movements and it is the last to get fixed.

The physiotherapy was making sense and within myself I was getting restless sometimes, and greedy all the time for a total recovery. I was sure by now that the last one and a half years had made me a different person, who was going to take life differently. I had planned to visit my elder son and the two sisters-in-law in the USA which I postponed to April 2023 with a positive hope that I would be like before by then. I did not want to use the wheelchair at the airport or inside the aircraft so that the memory of the stroke did not impinge upon the US trip.

Advice and suggestions on my condition and additional steps to be desirably taken for a quicker recovery never ceased to pour in from concerned friends and well-wishers for which I am grateful to them. Sometime in September 2021, a very dear friend, Mr. Tarun Bakshi, who had been keeping a watch on my progress suggested that there was no harm in taking a chance with Acupressure. Tarun Bakshi himself keeps going to famous Spas and Health Centres and he has some idea of the efficacy of the therapies administered at these Spas. I agreed and my physiotherapist also had no objection to it. Mr. Bakshi had fixed a renowned Acupressure guru too who would visit me at my house thrice a week. Acupressure as an exercise and a treatment for fixing beleaguered limbs seemed to be good but I felt in a couple of months that it had little effect in my case. So, I discontinued it. Mr. Bakshi then suggested that there was no harm taking a chance with Acupuncture too for which one of the most renowned therapists in Delhi was one Dr. Raman Kapoor. A specialist in Acupuncture, Dr. Raman Kapoor is a qualified allopath too. He is associated with Gangaram Hospital at Delhi. He runs his professional establishment at Greater Kailash in Delhi. I discussed with my physiotherapist who was firm in his assertion that Acupuncture as a therapy may be effective but it was not needed in my case. He was humble, however, to tell me that he had no problems if I went for therapy. So I did. It was six days a week. Half an hour of Acupuncture and the time taken in commuting included, it was two hours of involvement every day. With due respect to the therapy and the therapist, I did not find any substance in Dr. Kapoor's assertions on the efficacy of Acupuncture. I am not a doctor and thus my comments may not be credible, but I was a sufferer being the patient, and quite an educated one, and I am sure if anybody sought my opinion I would suggest in the negative for the therapy for somebody having problems with limbs after a stroke. For about three months I wasted time, energy and money on the rigmarole of Acupuncture. All that I did was that I exchanged pleasantries with Dr. Kapoor every day and discussed bureaucracy and politics with him which hardly was of any interest to me at that stage. So I called off and said goodbye to Acupuncture after three months. I, however, never compromised with my physiotherapy. It was the month of March 2022 now. I also took a firm resolve not to waste time any more in experimenting with therapies and depend entirely on physiotherapy

"The comeback is always stronger than setback."

and my physiotherapist. The physiotherapy was showing very slow but sure signs of improvement. But once more that resolve was to be broken. A very concerned family friend and a man connected with many stalwarts in the medical field and himself running a fairly big medical establishment, Mr. Pravin Gupta came for a periodical visit and suggested that there was a miracle man in Ludhiana who was a practising physiotherapist and he was going to invite him with his team for a few sessions. I could not say no to him. In the next couple of weeks, he arrived and made me do some exercises. I found it very harsh and unscientific. I had to politely say that a second session could be waited for because I was already going through a physiotherapy regime. Keeping in view the concern and the efforts of Pravin Gupta, I had to profusely thank him and buy time on the plea of duplication.

A last suggestion to expedite recovery came from a young doctor, a bariatric surgeon who is in my neighbourhood, being the son-in-law of the owners of the Meenakshi Hospital. He one day came and informed that one Dr. Sachin Kandhari, a neurosurgeon known to him, was running a state-of-the-art hospital known as IBS hospital at Lajpat Nagar, New Delhi for neuro and spine treatment. He said that the team of doctors there had made very significant advances in Neuromodulation.

On his insistence I agreed to visit the hospital first and then decide if I would like to join the treatment. I spoke to Dr. Kandhari and sought a time to see him. On the appointed day and time, I visited the hospital along with Dr. Vikrant who knew Dr. Kandhari. Dr. Kandhari was a smart and impressive person. Other doctors saw the condition of my debility and made their evaluation. I was suggested a plan of treatment which was basically physiotherapy with the aid of robots. I found the whole plan of treatment rather cumbersome and clashing with the physiotherapy at home. I decided I wouldn't go for it. I was getting confident and hopeful of the physiotherapy at home. It was March 2022 now and the next month it was going to be one year of the stroke on April 9. Not unhappy, though, but limping was restricting movements outside. The right hand was still dysfunctional although no deformity was discernible. I used to be socially quite mobile but not being able to go out was not bothering me much because I was equally comfortable sitting at home. In fact, I have been primarily a home loving man. My problem was that I was finding it a little sad to tell a friend that it was not possible for me to join for lunch or dinner. So I found it to be a worthwhile idea to start venturing out even though limping and having difficulty in riding the car. One such occasion arose because of a phone call from a revered and affectionate senior who had been my boss too when I was the Chief Commissioner of Income Tax, Uttarakhand (headquartered at Dehradun) and he the Principal Chief Commissioner of Income Tax, UP (West) stationed at Kanpur. He wanted to meet me over dinner at Delhi Gymkhana Club. I decided to go for the first time after almost a year. Another very close common friend, a junior colleague, presently posted at Mumbai as a Commissioner, was contacted by me to ascertain whether he was coming to Delhi on the weekend. He was and so the programme was firmed up. It was to the best of my memory March 26, 2022. We assembled at the Gymkhana Club,—myself, Mr. Abhay Tayal, the senior colleague, and Neehar Ranjan Pandey, our younger colleague. We chose to sit in the Chinese restaurant of the club. After a year it was like opening to the world for me. We had shared hours together on official issues and witty and humorous gossip in the past. So it was like a kaleidoscope of official life recalling many incidents from our functioning as senior officers of the Government. One unmistakable conclusion that I could draw was that the Government was a leviathan and too impersonal. Tragedy, nevertheless, is that we spend a lifetime connecting with it in a manner and making it all-consuming. The dinner was extremely enjoyable.

April 9, 2022 marked the first anniversary of the stroke I suffered. The limping continued. The right hand was still in a state of dysfunction. But I was feeling healthier. My memory, my reflexes and my general perception of my own health were positive. I was enjoying my roof garden like before. This garden was my wife's creation. Her obsession with the garden had made it the most important corner to derive not only some aesthetic pleasure but a lot of lessons also were there to be drawn from the life cycle of different plants and flowers. Why do some flowers only bloom for the day? Why do rains bring smiles and shine to the leaves? Why do some plants keep strutting even in the sweltering heat of 45 degrees? Perhaps the morale to live again after decay could be best defined as Life. If one observed the plants and leaves around closely, one could feel a connectivity with the plants too. The perception of that connectivity was the essence of life and relationships, including the ones with the plants.

Another occasion to venture a trip outside arose next month, i.e., in May 2022. Good friends and junior colleagues, Amitabh Kumar and his wife, Lekha, called up to say that their son's wedding was happening on May 16 at Jaipur. We have many common friends. I found out that a very dear friend, S. D. Jha, was also planning to go. So was another great friend P. C. Mohanty who was to come from Bhubaneshwar. So I was left with no doubt that I should go. I decided to undertake a road journey to Jaipur though I was a hater of road travel in India. During the last 20 years I have always travelled by flights as far as possible. We left for Jaipur in two different vehicles but together. My driver kept a small stool so that I could ride the vehicle smoothly. The 5 hours' journey to Jaipur was smooth with no pain in the leg or the knee. That was a discovery to rejoice. With a wheelchair it turned out to be a nice and enjoyable stay at Jaipur. Meeting a host of friends was a nice feeling. I was now getting confident and greedy to connect with the outside world by being at places. An old desire was to spend a night at Oberoi Amarvilas, Agra because I am told all the rooms there have a view of Taj Mahal. I have been to Agra so many times in life, countless in fact. In recent years as the Principal Chief Commissioner, I stayed at most of the places but Oberoi was left out. I was scheduled to visit Agra and stay there on April 9, 2021 but destiny willed otherwise and I spent that night in the ICU of the hospital. I again made a day's reservation for May 15, 2022 and went to Agra in the same manner as Jaipur. It was a really enjoyable time with Mridula's (my wife) company and support, quite in keeping with the frequent holidays we were used to. The view of the Taj Mahal from the room was breathtaking. So was the food which was a gourmet's delight.

Next day we checked out and visited Mr. R. N. Agrawal, an elderly person and a known industrialist. Going to his sprawling house and meeting the members of his extended family including the youngsters of the next generation was a nice experience. I felt more comfortable than with my own extended family. What I felt very nice was that there are still people who hold you in high esteem for honesty and integrity and a humble and respectable behaviour with the members of the public while you are in a position of authority. I remember meeting him once more than three years ago as Principal Chief Commissioner of Income Tax at Kanpur. Harassed by a junior officer for punishable reasons, he narrated his problems and I instantly issued instructions to resolve the issues. It was resolved the next day. While he was leaving my room, I could see an expression of relief and amazement at the same time on his face. That was satisfying for me indeed. On our way back to Delhi we also visited Vrindavan and had a 'darshan' of 'maa Katyayani devi' who is considered a powerful deity.

My elder brother's 50th marriage anniversary had fallen in May 2021 but any family celebration had to be postponed because of my illness. I told my brother as well as my nephews to happily go for it and that I would also join the celebrations at Patna. I was gathering courage and confidence to travel by flight after April 9 last year. So, on May 30 we left for Patna by an Indigo flight. I could travel to Patna without any embarrassing inconvenience. The wheelchair was of course used at every stage. East Delhi has the privilege of having one of the finest temples known as the 'Hanuman Balaji Temple'. I have been a regular visitor to this temple for the last more than two decades. In fact, before the COVID struck there was an unfailing regularity on my part in going to the Yamuna Sports Complex almost four days a week, and to the Balaji temple every Saturday after my morning walk. The temple had recently undergone extensive renovations and it had become a place worth visiting, the religious significance of it apart. The man behind all this is one Mr. Vinod Kumar Bindal. He has been like an elder brother during the last more than two decades although our first interaction was between a Chartered Accountant and an officer. A meritorious chartered accountant of high competence, his commitment to the temple is unflinching and praiseworthy. In the month of July, I decided to visit the temple and did so on the 12th of the month. The beautification of the temple and the creation of facilities there has been beyond belief. Besides the sanctum sanctorum, a lawn on the roof and a state-of-the-art auditorium and so many conference rooms make it an academic place. With nice and clean sitting places and a huge verandah for eating and the convenient toilets, the place is an example among temples. Religiosity of the place apart, thousands of people being served food of a high quality which you or I would love to eat, makes it a really secular place.

Yet another trip was coming our way. A very dear friend owns a beautiful house in Kasauli, Himachal Pradesh, who keeps going there frequently. For the last couple of months he has been asking us to make a short trip to Kasauli which, as he said, had undergone a transformation in the last decade. My last visit to Kasauli was more than a decade ago and, therefore, I felt rather tempted. We decided and the next morning we left. I felt very appreciative of the fact that the roads had diametrically improved. It took a little more than 5 hours to reach Kasauli. I had my accommodation at the Army

Club, infrastructure at Kasauli in the form of hotels being poor. We had a relaxed evening at the club itself. There is a point from which Shimla is visible. The next day was spent at my friend's place. His house was beautiful and very aesthetically done. We had a sumptuous lunch. But by the evening, we felt that we had not much to do at Kasauli and that simply enjoying the coolness of the place was not enough reason to stay there. Because of my problems with my right limb and my movements being restricted, we thought it was better to go back home. So, we left Kasauli for Delhi at 9 p.m. to reach home by 2 a.m. It has been one and a half years now since the fateful day—April 9, 2021. I am still struggling with my gait. I am still longing to write. I have been a reasonably good sportsperson who would love badminton and football to billiards ever since childhood. I was appreciated for my good handwriting always. My debilities were giving me a gnawing feeling and a "drowsy numbness used to bewail my senses", in the words of P. B. Shelley. On an optimistic note, I would tell myself, "if winter comes, can spring be far behind?" I was not unhappy, though. After all I had come closer to my older self so far as my mental faculties were concerned. The hope of a second stint at life had become alive and it was definitely going to be qualitatively different, probably more satisfying, richer and poised. I was increasingly realising the truism contained in the saying that life was nothing but all that happens while we are making so many other plans. After all, one was blissfully unaware of the fact that a brain stroke could be one such thing to happen. It was still merciful. It did not kill like an obstreperous monster. It did not create a situation where the eternal Shakespearean dilemma could be remembered:

'Life is but a walking shadow,
a poor player,
That struts and frets his hour upon the stage
and then is heard no more.
It is a tale
Told by an idiot,
full of sound and fury
signifying nothing.'

Well, that which does not kill us only makes us wiser and stronger. So, after one and a half years and its experiences and realisations, if one was going to live life again one ought to remember that there are only three cardinal facts of life—blessings, losses and lessons. There were blessings and enough of that to have escaped death. There were losses—the time lost in convalescence, the worries and the trauma it would have caused to those in whose life I had a place of significance and for whom my being there mattered and the least important being the financial loss because I was not willing to go back to the lucrative job I was doing being the CEO and the Director General of the CREDAI. The lessons indeed are most important—the lessons in the dynamics of human relationships. Those who stayed with me with empathy and concern are great eye-openers. In persons in whom I thought there was love, it was non-existent. And there was a surfeit of it where I thought Love did not matter. Huge corrections were needed in the errors of judgement over the years. Sometimes one needs to distance oneself to see and understand things more clearly. I genuinely feel there is not enough time to waste for fun devoid of emotions. There is hardly enough time to love the people who love you. Dear Past, thanks for all the lessons. I am perhaps ready now.

2

Who Are Friends

"Truly great friends are hard to find, difficult to leave and impossible to forget."

I think the most casually and loosely used word, and used rather too often is 'Friend'. The dictionary defines a friend to be a person that you know and like (not a member of the family), and who likes you. Friendship is defined as a state of enduring affection, esteem, intimacy, and trust between two people. In all cultures friendships are important relationships throughout a person's life span. A Google search would suggest that a friend is a person on whom you can confide in almost anything and everything. These are the people with whom you share a strong bond of trust, mutual affection, selfless love, companionship, typically one exclusive of family or sexual relations. But the most convincing of the definitions of a friend or friendship that I found, particularly in the aftermath of the stroke, was, "Friendship isn't about whom you've known the longest. It's about who walked into your life and said, 'I'm here for you', and proved it." There have been too many fun-filled and good times in life spanning more than 60 years. It has been good luck at the best. There has been a haemorrhagic stroke once which has been cataclysmic. But escaping the worst has been providential and a moment to celebrate. All the celebration has been a reminder of the faces, of the words, of the physical help and of the time spent with who actually were there, who could be there and who actually could be called a 'Friend'. Was he/she the one with whom you were, for decades, sharing great food and wine or was he/she the one who rarely met you and he/she was there when you were struggling for life? That I think should be the litmus test for somebody to be called a friend. However mighty one may be, whatever paucity of time may be there because of preoccupations, if one does not have the natural calling to see you in the ICU of the hospital, he was never a friend. Of course, the acquaintances, the admirers for any reason and the people who interacted at any stage with courtesy for official reasons are to be considered better than so-called friends. They had at least the semblance of some empathy.

Mridula's (mine too, in an independent capacity) doctor friends have been unforgettable. With a high level of education, being qualified and accomplished medical professionals, they have been matchless as friends. Dr. Deepa, the busy gynaecologist at Yashoda Hospital, was an angel in those difficult moments. Our hearts go out for her and we feel indebted as a family. That I had to live might have been ordained by destiny but she definitely left no stone unturned by supervising the ongoing medical treatment and holding my wife's hands whose medical faculties had taken a back seat because her husband was clamouring for life. Being close family friends, we had spent so many evenings together at home with recitations of Urdu poetry by me and Dr. Deepa's qualitatively superior singing. As a matter of my personality trait and my unflinching proclivity for music, I never minced words in admiring her singing. I was moved when my wife told me that she even hummed my favourite songs to resuscitate me. By some celestial alignments you come across such friends in life. To add to my good luck, we had Dr. Sanjai, Dr. Deepa's husband and equally dear friend, to watch the medical proceedings and discuss issues with Dr. Sumanto, the attending neurophysician inside the ICU. Sanjai was my saviour in more ways than one. He kept a close watch on the initial medical interventions which were crucial. Dr. Sanjai, in my view, is an excellent physician who has an academic bent of mind on issues which may be the crux to sail through the initial stress of the physician. That also means having a sense of responsibility which only a 'friend' can have.

Our dear friends Dr. Nidhi, a brilliant radiologist, and her husband, Dr. Gaurav, the accomplished pathologist, were there for their inputs and concern. So was present Dr. Richa Singhal, another accomplished gynaecologist and her husband, a professionally smart paediatrician. Mridula as a doctor has tremendous trust in Dr. Richa Singhal's wisdom. Dr. Naresh Gupta, our neighbour and lifeline for years and his wife Sunitaji were also around. So, this group of ten with me in the ICU was, for a change, there at the Yashoda Hospital instead of our drawing room where our general meetings used to be held with reasonable frequency. It must have been very depressing there. For me it was a matter of gratitude and I won't ever forget it in this lifetime.

Dr. Shweta Garg, an anaesthetist, was also present on the fateful night at the hospital. So was her husband, Amal Garg, a junior colleague in the Indian Revenue Service. Amal Garg, an accomplished singer, has been active in charitable activities and runs an NGO for the upliftment of the less privileged young children. He is a recipient of an international award for his charitable activities. I am extremely grateful to stalwarts in their respective medical fields, Dr. Harsh Mahajan and Dr. Yash Gulati, the radiologist and the orthopaedist respectively. Harsh, I am told, had spoken to Mr. P. N. Arora, the owner of Yashoda Hospital, immediately after he received news of my condition. He then drove to Delhi to reach the Yashoda Hospital as soon as possible. Yash also made it to the hospital despite his busy schedule as a doctor, and his pursuits of music and poetry. Harsh and Yash only reinforce the trust in the goodness of human beings and the calling of a cherished friendship. I also feel grateful to Dr. Vandana Garg, an accomplished physician at the Max Hospital and a good friend who came to the hospital to see me. These were the doctors to whom no words can convey my gratitude. But there were a few more 'friends' who were not doctors by qualification but were there for the comfort of my wife. R. D. Gupta, a very considerate friend by disposition, was there. So was O. P. Singh, the IPS Officer and the ex-DGP of UP. So, I must think I have been fortunate to have so many 'friends' who genuinely thought they should check on me without any loss of time when I was in a crisis and when there was a question of life and death. It is not very usual. These many people meant too many 'friends' in the truest meaning of friendship. I can't forget to mention Sanoj, our manfriday at home, who has been with us for the last more than 25 years. He stays with us with his family at the ground floor of our house. He has always stood like a son in all the crises we have faced. He was always around me during the period I was in the hospital doing sundry errands and praying for me. Our driver Rajesh too kept awake for nights looking after me. This is the story of the night when I was listless having left a wife who always thought I was too strong to be in a situation like this. All these years she had been planning to deal with any medical emergency happening in Kaushambi to somebody near and dear but in her remotest imagination she did not ever think it could be for her husband. A medical phenomenon is probably the greatest leveller. It can humble the mightiest and the weakest alike. But destiny was probably only putting me to test, a very tough test, and perhaps tougher for those who genuinely loved me.

A thought that always crosses my mind is that what bliss it is to have people around you in the category of 'friends' true to the connotation of the word. It is greater bliss if they are sharp and intelligent with their minds and are doctors. A professionally competent doctor who has a friend's empathy is looked for in the weakest and the most vulnerable moment of life. All others may be lovable but the doctor transcends all emotions for the simple fact that he/she has the training and the ability to try to bring you back to life from death. I have been fortunate in this respect. Right from my childhood I have seen a doctor being remembered in the most difficult moments. Hence I developed an unflinching reverence for people practising medicine. I always felt that mediocrity should never be allowed in the study of medicine and that socially and financially the medical professionals deserved a much better reward. It is not without reason that somebody said that the word 'doctor' before their names is not just a prefix. It is actually their super power. They need to be justifiably congratulated on their calling in terms of their career which offers the combination of intellectual and moral interest which is found in no other profession. Doctors are a group of people who have more opportunities to do good in a day that others don't have even in a lifetime.

"Over time, you realise that some people aren't worth it anymore."

They enjoy the privilege of people letting them into the most intimate aspects of their life and each day they go back home with a satisfaction that they have done something valuable and they are maturer in terms of their understanding of human beings. It is rightly said that it is the medical professionals who see the weaknesses of humans. As against this, the lawyers look at the wickedness and the theologians look at the stupidities. I often tell my doctor friends when they turn up late for a party that they missed the party for saving a life or alleviating somebody's pains. We came in time and drank more.

"The life so short, the craft so long to learn", said Hippocrates. The doctors learn their craft through the long and hard way. And that craft puts them in a situation, more often than not, when it could be said that "somebody who was before you, did not lose faith in God, he only transferred it to the doctor and the medical profession". Hippocrates also said that the love of humanity is only there where the art of medicine is loved. And there is one more beautiful quote from some philosopher who said, "nobody ever looks ugly with a white coat on their body or a stethoscope around their neck." The words for the medical profession and professionals as above may sound like an overstatement and exaggeration to some people.

With Harananda (1972)

With R.C.P. Singh (1976)

Out lifelines – from right to left Dr Nidhi, Dr Naresh Gupta, Dr K.K. Singhal, Dr Richa Singhal, Dr Mridula Gupta, P.K. Gupta, Dr Sanjai, Dr Deepa, Mrs Sunita Gupta, Dr Gauras is missing

Sujata, Tim, Clarisa, Vidisha, Kunal, Erika, Sara, Nihit and Linda

The reasons for that are not far to seek. But let us have the reflections on "who is a friend" first. I owe my life to friends in a substantial manner who were doctors, who empathised and were there on the fateful night when I was not even in a position to tell them "I want to live. This life has been beautiful." But there have been friends, not medical professionals but who have been healers of a different but equally great level. I have mentioned a few but I can't afford not to mention a few more. Anurag Mishra, a brilliant engineer working freelance on cybersecurity and Sanjiv Jain, an Engineer having become an expert in Stocks, have been like younger brothers, and it has been sheer good luck of mine that decades ago they came in touch with me for reasons ordained by Providence. If they found the vibes of an elder brother in whatever I might have said to them or done for them is again my fortune. I don't deserve any credit for that. Vishal Bakshi and his wife, Suparna, the vivacious duo always soothed me in the difficult phase. So did Rakesh Nangia, the dynamic finance professional who has his definitions of a friend's concern absolutely in place. Mr. Shishir Priyadarshi, the high-profile IAS officer and a Geneva based World Trade Organization executive, has been affectionate as ever. So have been Mr. Sanjeev Tripathy, the 1972 batch IPS officer, and his mature and sensitive wife, Neeta Tripathy, who at the earliest opportunity had the empathy to connect with Mridula and spend a couple of hours with us at home. I cannot but feel grateful to Vijayshree, the young and

"The more I find myself, the more people I lose."

dynamic lady from Dehradun, always active in sundry cultural activities, who did not miss to see me. Yamini, a young and lively IRS officer of the 2005 batch was not a surprise but with my not very old association she only reminded me that retirement from Government Service meant little if you had a heart to connect with somebody, particularly when you have undergone the crisis that I did. I feel grateful to Kishan Khadaria, the competent and well-connected professional from Mumbai, who was to come and see me once the COVID subsided to reasonable levels. In fact, he gave me the sad news of the demise of Vijay Jhindal, my friend at Delhi in April itself, whose reticence had been bothering me for a few months. Dr. Rajiv Agrawal, the eminent cardiologist at Meerut, spent a few hours at home which was a great mood elevator in the state of sickness. Ameeta, Mridula's friend from childhood, and her eminent physician husband, Dr. B. K. Singh visiting from Dhanbad, was reassuring of the nice feeling of friendship. Mr. Tarun Bakshi, an industrialist of repute, extended all help and support which was so kind of him. His wife, Anu Bakshi, a woman of substance and imbued with a highly developed aesthetic sense, was so supportive all the time. Mr. Kedar Nath Mittal and his wife, Aarti Mittal, from Dhanbad, who have always stood behind us like a rock were there always, reminding us that time and distance never mattered in relationships of heart. The presence of Mayank Jyoti, the illustrious officer of UP Government and his wife Smita was also a great source of strength for my wife. It would be ungrateful of me if I don't mention Lava, our cute dog who came near my bed for months, looked at me as though she was assuring herself of my welfare. It is not just human beings who express genuine emotions.

We forge umpteen relationships in our lifetime. Other than kindred, we loosely call everybody a friend. That's the reason 'friend' has become the most abused word. "Who is a friend" probably is more difficult to understand than if we become a little negative and attempt to see "who is not a friend" and decidedly so. Although it generates unimaginable sadness, life throws unmistakable signs, particularly in a crisis of the magnitude a stroke can create. We spend years trying to absorb the obvious and convince ourselves of the reality of a relationship unfolding. Let me give actual, not hypothetical, situations from experiences of life.

We meet so many people in our life from the time we start going to school. We go to college and ultimately enter our lives as officers, doctors, lawyers, businessmen, etc. We forge relationships of togetherness and friendship. Some become very intimate relationships in terms of frequency of interaction. For years we remain under the impression that we share mutual respect and concern. We party together in happy times. We are by and large helpful too for sundry issues arising in life. Then one fine morning a haemorrhagic stroke makes you helpless. The minimum that genuine empathy demands is that you see your friend in such a crisis. It is possible that you may not be back in life. If your friend does not have the desire to be with you in such a crisis, the years of so-called friendship becomes a waste of emotions. Alas it has happened to me. I still can't believe how a person, big or small in terms of status, whom you thought would be the first person to help you sail through the crisis, can't find time to see you. Worse still if he or she is in the same country and the city. But this should probably be a lesson only and no source of regret. After all this is how life is.

Somebody whom you find very intelligent, full of life, energetic, witty (although out of proportion sometimes), well-placed in terms of career and fun-loving can always be an ideal friend if you meet him in your 30s. But in India there is an imaginary or real reason to feel better-equipped to handle problems of life, unwarranted though, and created by a failure of the systems, if you are connected with people in good positions in the government. So, the tendency to befriend such people in life becomes a matter of strategy for those who may be otherwise very nicely placed in life themselves. There is absolutely no issue about such personality traits because your emotions for a friend are unruffled by his thoughts and priorities as long as your foundations of friendship with him are not affected. Alas, it happened with me too after more than three decades of nice feelings for somebody whom you, like a fool, always considered to be a dependable friend. I may not be perfect as a friend but have always been respectful to friends. Why else would I make a plan to visit such a friend (so perceived) when he relocates abroad, undertaking a 14 hours' flight. Why else would I give him a benefit of doubt when it is even alleged that he made lewd overtures to one of the dearest persons to you of the other gender. Life indeed creates situations when you are compelled to feel like a fool that you might have been.

You may know somebody from a very tender age when you are in school. He as well as you as you do well in terms of making a career or entering a career. You naturally become great buddies because of studies, sports, music etc., which were areas of common interest as small boys. For a few years connectivity is lost but later on, entering the same career, the association is renewed. As the connection renewed emanates from childhood's togetherness, it makes you so happy. The families also meet. Your spouse is a simpleton with no complexes of temperament and egos of a respectable career. His spouse also is intelligent although without a career of significance. In many traits, like conversational skills, she is better than her spouse. So the friendship of wives also flourishes. She always occupies a high place in your life so much so that she develops a trust in your maturity in assigning a place to somebody based on goodness of conduct. She often enquires about her husband's erring behaviour, particularly in matters of other women and his incomprehensible bad temper. I, of course, could not make any comments or offer suggestions on these because of the husband being a great friend and her being in life primarily because of him. Over the years, my friend's general reputation of conduct in public life nosedives to an abysmally low level and presumably an inferiority complex grips him because of my rising reputation, primarily because of a reasonably good public speaking and appreciation by superiors. Such a situation obtaining with what is going on inside the human mind creates distortions in reactions to happenings in life. Such a person, to assert his identity, creates falsities so far as his image in public life is concerned. But the unfortunate part of this is that he has to do it with his spouse and, to make it credible, he has to vilify his friend,—somebody who has helped him in the most difficult moments of life and whose wife has been a lifesaver as a doctor for him. I ignored the world when the other well-wishers indicated that he was the one who created difficulties for me because of his innate inferiority complex. To bring an allegation on the most consistent friend without any evidence and an opportunity to ask basic questions on the absurdity of accusations obviously can't make sense to anybody with any wisdom or with any semblance of wisdom. What can you do except feel sorry for yourself for having wasted so many years with and for such nincompoops. There seems to be truism contained in what Peter Ustinov wrote: "I do not believe friends are necessarily the people you like best, they are merely the people who got there first."

"Someone asked me if I knew you. A million memories flashed through my mind but I just smiled and said I used to."

But nothing can speak more poorly of yourself when you, in the prime of your life, compromise with character, ethics and mediocrity while letting somebody enter your life as a friend. Any compromise on matters of ethics can have long-term repercussions on the quality of our living as a group if you are mindful and conscious of it. Moreover, ill-gotten money in your profession or job gives an ill-placed confidence and you tend to forget that just because you made money does not make you better or even bring you at par with those compatriots who initially excelled and chose to do things as a career which has been a matter of social prestige. Making money by hook or by crook does not alter the facts in any manner. Unfortunately, such people get more satisfied in terms of their ill-placed ego when bright people in terms of their student days' performance start holding them in awe for their money. Such people later start finding glamour in high-end alcoholic beverages and business class travel in an airline. Their spouses become objects. With no worthwhile education and a career, they lose self-respect and choose to become 'yes' persons for their spouse. Such people start interacting and socialising with people to serve some selfish interest which helps make them more money and dismiss them from life once the purpose is served. But can one, or should one, lament all this after decades? One has to pay the price for one's own errors of judgement.

The sickness—and the period of convalescence after that—has been an eye-opener in many respects. The severity of the stroke, the struggle between life and death in the initial few days and the rather long period of recovery made it clear that everything in life was so uncertain that one must keep living so long as one was alive. Not a moment needs to be wasted without a meaningful utilisation of time which may include deriving pleasure from the most mundane of activities. The period of convalescence on the one hand gave me reasons to be grateful to Providence for allowing me to live life again, and on the other, it allowed me time to reflect on life in its nuances. So far as relationships are concerned, the understanding of the most loosely used word 'friendship' was so essential to the remaining years of life. While what is stated here may be purely subjective and a reflection of my thought process, one thing that most will agree with is that life and relationships are serious issues. One need not accept anyone else's definition of life and relationships. One needs to define it himself. Probably "Who is a friend" is a more difficult question than "who is not a friend". One can't of course wish to undergo the agony of a stroke to try to understand "who is a friend" but it will be advisable and emotionally preferable if one could understand "who is not".

Some of the persons who have been in my life and are dear to me, and whose comments of a personal nature are taken with deference by me, have often remarked that I tend to be emotional at times and that others' maturity should not be presumed. My take on the issue is that one should never mince words in expressing what one feels. The last couple of years have only given the wisdom that the process of elimination should keep going on continuously till the last breath. After a year of the stroke, I had shared the following message with a select few:

- "My dear ..., Today is the fateful day of last year when I went to the hospital struggling for life. One year has changed my perceptions of life—for the better. Has made me simpler and realistic. Has made me realise that a person like you whom you meet by destiny can be so valuable for your being. All these years of career, family etc., are offshoots. I am not infallible but your being there gave meaning to my existence. It was ordained by destiny. I am much better in terms of my physical health, but of course there seems to be a long way to go to be like earlier. Sometimes I get depressed, but what keeps me going is my own will and extraordinary human beings like you and your love and concern. I want to live beaming with life for a few more years with you all around. So, I should be fine in the days to come. Thank you so much. Pramod."

- I did not expect a reply to this but I wanted to see the feelings in the form of reaction, if any, forthcoming from the select few to whom I had sent the above message. These select few have been those people who, I thought, had a special, enduring and dependable relationship with me. I did receive responses, in some cases instantly. In some cases, I received cryptic replies but definitely overwhelming. In quite a few it was an outpouring of sentiments. From a few minuscule few whom I thought were my 'friends' and who were connected at the level of heart, it was absolutely disappointing. So, after a year of the life threatening trauma it was an eye-opener again. I was wondering how, during the last more than 35 years, the persons whom I thought were those who thought as one with me, at least in a crisis of the magnitude of a stroke, turned out to be the ones who were 'friends' only for happier times. I also reached the unmistakable conclusion that people's perception of your usefulness was the key determinant in most relationships. Resultantly, if you started reflecting on the situation you had to feel amazed as to how you should only think of a very few who could probably help you face life. Being realistically philosophical, the fact remained that you were alone and anyone who connected at a plain with you with genuine empathy and was emotionally respectful was the one who was God's gift. One person like this was better than hundreds who connected with you for their perception of your power and your position. So, the process of elimination continued, although it was too painful to discover that out of the plethora of people with whom one visited places, sang, drank, made plans of fun, helped in crisis situations, only a few had the heart to respond. I was afraid the numbers of those who could extend meaningful support would reduce to single digits. When it was one and a half years, I again sent the following message, after eliminating a few to whom I had written earlier. It was like this:

- "Dear ..., I am sure you are doing fine. Life has been a roller coaster for me—it is indeed so for all in varying degrees. That I have survived the stroke I had, now (today) 18 months of that, has been a blessing of destiny in a certain way. This period of convalescence has been a period of reflections, an eye-opener kind of an experience. All that one has learnt is that we keep striving for a myriad of things, and we forge umpteen relationships many of which die down with bouts of fun because of their superficiality, and the fact remains that we are essentially alone. Yes, some who connect with genuine emotions of closeness and some substance do generate some nice feelings. You are definitely one I always value, for whatever reason. Limping still, but I think I am gradually moving towards

> health, and the next few months should see me fully fit, hopefully, although I have selectively started moving out with my limping with the right leg and some debility in the right hand. Often think of you. Best wishes always. Pramod."

The message was a real outpouring of emotions but genuine and heartfelt. It evoked responses of nature and magnitude which were not exactly what I had thought. But I felt happy and satisfied that the chosen persons to whom I had sent the messages by and large fell into my definition of friends. I am grateful to them. In one and a half years of my isolation of a kind had made me redefine with clarity the essential three limbs of friendship. The first was 'superficiality' (or the absence of it). Though it was a little late in life to understand and internalise, the fact remained that you could afford to continue to be superficial till the time everything was going well, and there was no application of mind to the issues of the heart. The second limb, according to me, has been 'substance'. Why do we need to find substance in friendship? What is substance? Well, substance, put simply, could be seen as those things which are not purely mundane and not necessarily spiritual. Substance is something which has an intellectual and also emotional content. If emotion which makes you feel the pains and pleasures in the same vein of the person you call your friend is absent, I think that the time you spend with that person is absolutely mechanical. How can there be a meaningful connection in a purely mechanical relationship? The third limb, 'closeness' flows from the existence of substance in the relationship.

"In order to love who you are, you cannot hate the experiences that shaped you."
–Andrea Dykstra

The foremost importance in friendship is that of trust. It is a very important, rather vital trait or component in friendship. Trust could be associated with dependability, reliability and honesty. Trust is the building block for the foundation of a house. The entire house of friendship could collapse without this block. Trust is built most effectively by being consistently reliable over a period of time. Another important trait required in friendship is loyalty. Loyalty is standing by your friend through losses and wins. It makes the bond between friends stronger and strengthens the bond. It is also one of the fundamental building blocks. However, it should be important to remember that the allegiance to a friend should not compromise who you are as a person and your morals, and it also should be remembered that loyalty is about people who stay true to you behind your back and just not to your face. One needs to be honest too in friendship. And honesty would mean being real to your face and real behind your back. Respect for others' opinions and beliefs has to be another bedrock of friendship. The free flow of communication is another essential ingredient of friendship. Absence of it may not ensure a long-lasting friendship. This is one of the reasons why great friends of a very young age cease to be friends as they grow because the years would have created the difference in intellect.

Jealousy is one reason why most friendships go to rocks. When jealousy is present in a relationship there is bound to be some negativity because a person's jealousy leads him to do horrible things. Everyone gets jealous sometimes which is not unnatural to human beings, but it becomes destructive when one cannot see past one's jealousy. It ends up clouding one's decision-making. When people are jealous, people become competitive and lose sight of their love and care for one another, and this can become a potential reason for destruction of friendship. Signs of jealousy surfacing in friendship are unmistakable if observations are made carefully. Any good news, particularly of one's achievement, is reacted to with negativity. The jealous person always tries to go one-up or outshine by any means. He always finds it hard to celebrate the achievements of the other person with sincerity. When a friend is constantly judging his friends by his choices, he is not a good friend since he makes his other friends feel insecure and doubtful of themselves. When there is a judgement in friendship one constantly feels afraid to be honest. Friendship should always be a free environment. Being over-possessive of people can stem from the fear of losing a person, or it can emanate from a person's insecurities. Contrary to the belief that this occurs in other relationships, it happens in friendships. Sometimes we confuse being over-possessive with being protective. Being over-possessive is feeling as if you own that person. Being protective means simply looking out for your friend and wanting the best for him. Over-possessiveness is definitely a negative emotion. Then, another serious issue is that of competition between friends. While a little competition can be healthy, a lot of competition could be disastrous. An occasional friendly fun can be good for friends. It helps motivate friends to reach their maximum potential, creates memories and provides entertainment. Although, when you base your friendship on trying to be better than your friend, it isn't healthy. A friend who is constantly losing may feel deflated and sad if the friend who is winning all the time is the one suggesting constant competition. They might find pleasure or satisfaction in your failures. You also can't help but feel ashamed when someone who is supposed to support you takes pleasure in your shortcomings. It is important to be observant of how you feel after spending time with a friend. If he or you constantly feel frustrated and inferior, it might be time to break up. Friendship can never be competitive. When you feel like you are in a friendship with yourself, and your friend does not put in as much effort as you do, and they don't value you as much as you value them, it is another dangerous situation in friendship. In a one-sided friendship the communication, organising programmes involving time and money and efforts fall on one person. The other person only comes to you when he needs something. Sometimes this can happen for lack of communication. An effort can be made by talking to your friend about how you feel. That will require honesty. If the situation does not improve or you see no effort on the part of the other person, you are probably in a one-sided friendship and it is time to call it a day. A sure sign that indicates you are in a one-sided friendship is that your friend never opens up. You are the one who is always vulnerable and constantly baring your soul and the other person does not reciprocate.

Well, the thoughts and perceptions on friendship as above are entirely on the basis of my personal experiences. Needless to mention, there may be differences of opinion and wiser perceptions. Life in any case is eternal learning. All said, we need to develop a mind which learns to ignore rather mind and we need to make a heart which never hurts. We need to make a touch which never pains. And we need to make a relation which never ends. But we need to remember that once you feel uncomfortable, that's a sure sign to quit. Any delay may cause an avoidable hurt.

3

Remembering My Father–Babuji

"Thinking of you"

"You were my Father,
That mattered most,
Nothing mattered more.
No matter how old I am,
I always need you.
I don't want to say in grief,
That you are no more.
I want to be thankful
That you were.
For long
I didn't believe in heroes,
Now after so many years
I think you sure were one.
So unflinchingly strong,
Amidst all your tribulations.

I think about you
When I am happy.
I think about you
When I am sad.
Even though it hurts,
But I would give anything
To relive your memories
Again & again.
I did say to you
That I loved you
But I didn't know then
What a son's love was.
Now that you are away,
I can't waste time.
I want to say
I love you
Again & again,
A myriad of times.
Till my last breath".
(In Memoriam—My Father)

June 30, 2020

"बाबूजी"

"क्या कहूँ,
वक्त अबाध गति से चलता रहता है।
सच है कि गुजरा वक्त वापस नहीं आता
पर वक्त नश्वर होता है
नक्षत्र में टूटे तारे की तरह

ज़हन में कैद हो जाता है।
बयालीस वर्षों की यादें भी
जहन की परतों में
बिल्कुल ताजी सी लगती हैं।
खुश था छोटी सी उम्र में
जब पिता के पैरों पर बैठा था,
बहुत रोया था मगर
जब उनके पैर मेरे कंधों पर थे।
कैसे सुधारूँ गुस्ताखियाँ अपनी,
कोई अब कुछ कहता ही नहीं।
कभी डरते थे जिनकी डाँट से,
अब उनकी खामोशी सताती है।
वो प्यार, वो गुस्सा, वो मशविरे,
सबकी बेइंतहा याद आती है।
यूँ तो अब "गूगल" आ गया है,
पर वो अंग्रेजी की "डिक्शनरी"
अब भी साथ रखता हूँ।
पता नहीं कब पूछ दें
किसी शब्द के मायने,
हमेशा तैयार रहता हूँ।
यूँ तो अब सब कुछ है
आपकी बहू, आपके पौत्र, धन
पर फिर भी सब वीरान लगता है।
आप जो पास नहीं
असुरक्षित ये जहान लगता है।
अपनी संतान की
खुशियों का इंतजाम करके,
आप बस सो गये

मेहनत तमाम करके।
सच कहूँ
आप मेरे पास हो
मैं आपसे बातें करता हूँ।
मेरी जिंदगी की इमारत में
ईंटें नहीं, आपका खून है।
आपकी आवाज
जो मेरे ख्यालों में गूंजती है,
मेरा सुकून है।
आपकी खामोशी
मेरा संबल है।
आप मेरा साहस हो,
आप स्वाभिमान हो,
आप मेरी पूँजी हो,
आप मेरी पहचान हो,
आप मेरी इज्जत हो,
आप मेरी शोहरत हो,
आप मेरा अभिमान हो,
धरती को भी जीत लूँ,
पर आप मेरा आसमान हो।
मेरी हर साँस
आपकी शुक्रगुजार,
मेरी हर धड़कन
आपकी कर्जदार।

जून 30, 2020

That fateful evening of June 30, 1980 is indelibly etched in my memory. We lost our father pretty early in life.

A person has many facets, so had my father. All that I recall is a father who was doting. When he left us, I was 20 and studying for my postgraduation in History at the Jawaharlal Nehru University at New Delhi. My father had superannuated from the Government of Bihar as a class 1 officer on September 30, 1979. He was in the process of shifting to Kahalgaon, Bhagalpur, Bihar which is his place of origin. We had a modest house at Bakerganj, Patna, too. He wanted to spend time with us. He, therefore, called me to Patna from Delhi in the month of June 1980. My younger sister was studying at Patna in her second year of Intermediate. So, we all assembled at Patna around June 20. The top floor of the house had a small apartment for ourselves. The rest of the house consisting of two floors had tenants. We were having a wonderful time devoted to conversations regarding our studies and general exchange of views on contemporary subjects. My father was a very enlightened man and his general awareness and knowledge of history, geography and science was formidable. I had also added to my knowledge of things and my interpretational abilities during the last few months that I had spent at JNU. So it was a very stimulating time intellectually and a very cherishable time as a family. My younger sister spent most of the time with her books preparing for the medical entrance examination of the year.

My father had made a rule for us, particularly my sister, that he would take us for a movie once a month.

He also enjoyed watching films. So he planned to take us to the nearby movie hall "Rupak" which was at a walking distance of 5 minutes from our house. The famous movie of those days, *Aasha* starring Reena Roy and Jeetendra was running there. The film had this famous song:

"Sheesha ho ya dil ho
Aakhir (toot jaata hai)
Lab tak aate aate haathon se
Sagar (choot jaata hai)
Sheesha ho ya dil ho
Aakhir toot jaata hai
Kaafi bas armaan nahin
Kuch milna aasaan nahin
Duniya ki majboori hai
Phir taqdeer zaroori hai
Yeh jo dushman hai aise
Donon raazi ho kaise
Ek ko manao to duja (rooth jaata hai)
Sheesha ho ya dil ho
Aakhir toot jaata hai
(Baithe the kinare pe
Maujon ke ishare pe)
Ham khelein toofanon se
Is dil ke armaanon se
Hamko yeh maloom na tha
Koi saath nahin deta
Maajhi chod jaata hai
Saahil (choot jaata hai)

Sheesha ho ya dil ho
Aakhir (toot jaata hai)
Sheesha ho ya dil ho
Duniya ek tamasha hai
Aasha aur nirasha hai
Thode phool hai kaante hai
Jo taqdeer ne baante hain
Apna apna hissa hai
Apna apna kissa hai
Koi lut jaata hai
Koi (loot jaata hai)
Sheesha ho ya dil ho
Aakhir (toot jaata hai)
Lab tak aate aate haathon se
Sagar (choot jaata hai)
Sheesha ho ya dil ho"

Everything in the afternoon was so enjoyable. About 15 minutes before the movie would have come to an end, Babuji asked us to leave because he was feeling very uncomfortable and was having an unbearable pain in his head. We left and started walking towards our house. Within the next 10 minutes we reached home and my father was on the bed, restless. He was gradually losing coherence in speech. The caretaker of the house and some other tenants also gathered. We decided to take him to the Emergency of the Patna Medical College Hospital. One of our tenant's Ambassador car was available and with great difficulty we were able to transfer him from the second floor of the house to the car. When we reached the hospital, we were told he was no more. That one moment of life is etched in my memory. I was in a state of vacuum and I was not able to comprehend what had happened. So was my sister. It seemed somebody had robbed me of everything and a small child was left in the world without any idea of what was to be done next. In the next half an hour we were on our way back home. With the help of the tenants we brought back the body of our father on the ground floor of the house. I don't know how the news spread but some distant relatives gathered in half an hour. A couple of elderly persons from our elder sister's in-laws' house at Danapur had also gathered. To my relief and surprise Mr. Anil Sharma, then President of the Patna University Students Union, my senior colleague and a very respected person in Patna, suddenly appeared there, having come to know about what had happened. So did Harananda, studying at Delhi and having come to Patna for the summer vacation. He was like an elder brother and his father Mr. B. N. Sinha was a good friend of my father. And then came Sanjeev, who was then doing his graduation at Patna. I don't remember how my elder brother at Kahalgaon, Bhagalpur was informed. It was the others who were taking decisions for us. Sanjeev and Anil Sharma decided we had to go to Kahalgaon which involved a road journey of at least 8 hours by road. It required permission by the police to carry somebody who was not alive. Anil Sharma was the only person who had the confidence to talk to the Senior Superintendent of Police, Patna and obtain the required permission. He did that. He also hired a car for us to travel to Kahalgaon. Sanjeev was an exceptionally confident guy and a rare friend who volunteered to accompany us. He was to become an IPS officer seven years from then. And he proved to be a very brave and exemplary officer. Even God was magnanimous to a great soul like him. I am indebted to him for his gestures.

We left Patna for Kahalgaon the next morning. My father's head was in my lap and his feet in my sister's. Sanjeev shared the front seat with the driver. The endless journey began. We hardly talked on the way except for sharing the inconveniences of the journey and dealing with them. We stopped for a few minutes at four or five places. It was by evening, before it became dark, that we reached Kahalgaon. The house was full of people from all over Kahalgaon and villages nearby. Kahalgaon itself is not a village as the name would suggest. It is a fairly populated town and a subdivision administratively. It was a heart-rending scene at home. I could fathom the popularity and the love of the people in the neighbourhood that my father enjoyed. He never ignored people with whom he had grown up, irrespective of how they were placed in life. My elder brother obviously took charge of everything at Kahalgaon. My mother was in a listless state. Next morning, we started our journey from home for the bank of the Ganga for cremation with the two sons and Sanjeev lifting the carriage. I was reminded of so many beautiful mornings that I had spent with my father on the bank of the Ganga. The Ganga at Kahalgaon is extremely beautiful and it is regarded as holy because it is Uttarvahini there and people carry the Ganga water from the neighbouring Sultanganj in the month of Shravana to be offered to Lord Shiva at Deoghar. The last rites at the Ghat, as it is called, took about an hour after which the pyre was lit. A chapter of life had come to an end, particularly for me, without any knowledge of how things were going to move in life from that moment. With my brain having become dysfunctional I was trying to figure out how I was going back to JNU and how was I going to ensure my sister's career ahead. My elder brother was there but I was the one who had to take the crucial decisions about our careers. It was almost night by now and I forced some strength on myself to think about the future course of action in life during the night. Perhaps I was too young and the harshest reality of life had shown its face to me. The protection, the pampering and the unconditional support of the strongest person in my life was lost. Nothing could make me lonelier. We were at home in the next half an hour. I could see my grieving mother, both my sisters and my elder brother-in-law, who was very supportive. I took Sanjeev with me and went for a stroll. My expressions were no longer with me and I could not even find words to thank him. I only asked him whether he wanted to go because I found him tired. He had shaved his head like a son. That is something I can never forget or undervalue. The gratitude I owe to him can't find an expression in words. He told me that he would go to the railway station and would leave for Patna if he got a train. I gave him a silent and tearful goodbye. I came back home to feel further depressed in the depressing scenario prevailing there.

My elder brother briefed me about the rituals to be observed during the next ten days or so. He had to do the most of it which of course he was willing and committed to do. I am thankful to God for at least an elder brother being around. I told him that everything that he said was fine but the future course of action regarding my plans of going back to Delhi and my sister's studies for her medical entrance examination needed some thought and I would revert to him by the next day. It was easier said than done because I had the apprehension that he might not agree with everything that I would tell him. Anyway, I bought time for the night to reflect, plan firmly and inform. Then I retired to one corner of the house, feeling sadly forlorn.

The next morning I had firmed up my plans. I told my brother I would leave for Delhi in a week's time because the University had reopened. Moreover, I also wanted to admit our sister in a coaching institute with a hostel to stay. She would otherwise have unnecessarily got further depressed because the Entrance examination was a few months away. I gave no option to my brother for any suggestion. He also was nice to agree. The next morning we left by the Upper India Express. On reaching Patna I found that my closest friend then, R. C. P. Singh, had also reached Patna on hearing about my father. We stayed at our house at Bakerganj entering which gave a depressing, rather eerie feeling because it was my father's memory everywhere with whom we were spending a great time hardly a week back. Nevertheless, I along with RCP started our search for the best Coaching Institute and a girls' hostel. Finally, we found that the best place for the girls to stay was a hostel near Patna College run by a socialite Mrs. Sushma Ashok Sinha. The renowned coaching institute Ram Mohan Roy Seminary was nearby. We got the admissions done and put my sister in the hostel. I had taken some money from my brother and RCP gave me the balance required. I gave a tearful hug to my sister and left for Delhi with RCP. It was a new life now with priorities to be fixed again regarding career. There was none except RCP who stood like a rock with me. He left no stone unturned to make me concentrate and prepare for the UPSC Civil Services and keep my postgraduation on standby. Even otherwise we were always together but now onwards RCP ensured he never lost sight of me. Our rooms in the hostel at JNU were also in visual range. That's an unforgettable association.

My sister competed for the medical entrance with flying colours. When the results came, I was informed by a friend from Patna by way of a telegram. I was in Delhi. That was the fastest communication possible then. It was even otherwise a great thing, but happening as it was with our father not being around gave a unique feeling of happiness mixed with indescribable sadness. A battle was won. There was a similar feeling when I competed for the UPSC Civil Services and joined the Indian Revenue Service in 1984 in preference to the Indian Police Service because my father, right or wrong, was of the firm belief that wearing a uniform had the potential of creating a regimented mind. He was otherwise a great admirer and advocate of an efficient policing and Police as an institution.

My conscious and effective association with my father actually lasted for nine years from 1971 to 1980. I was in class viii in 1971 and my father had come on transfer to Daltonganj in the Palamau district of Jharkhand (then in Bihar). Coming to Daltonganj became a life changer for me. My father was an extremely intelligent man academically. He was not only a very learned man in Science subjects but was equally proficient in languages—English, Sanskrit and Hindi. Initially I thought I was thinking so because he was my father, but when I compared him with my schoolteachers and my father's officer colleagues, I used to find a clear difference in intellect. Years later when I came to JNU and met learned professors of the country and myself grew in intellect, and even now when I have myself finished my journey in the bureaucracy, having rubbed shoulders with the who's who of Indian intelligentsia at different places, I can say that without any doubt. I often used to think he should have been a professor of English or Physics or an ICS officer. In fact, I even asked him once as to why he did not exercise better career options, to which his reply was 'family needs'. Being a question of a very personal nature, I did not consider it proper to talk about it.

We had come to Daltonganj on my father's transfer from Biharsharif in the Nalanda district of Bihar. If I recall, my father's energies were sapped by sundry domestic issues. My elder brother and sister were married while my father was posted at Biharsharif. My mother whom I loved so much but never expressed in so many words, was not well during this period. She had to be hospitalised on multiple occasions. I was too young to help my father in any way. But I could see his running around and the physical pains that he had to undertake. He was a man who was extremely loving to his wife, but physical sufferings of a person whom one loves genuinely take away the carefree and nice moments from life. I am sure he must have been undergoing tremendous mental agony too. The work at his office at Biharsharif was also too taxing. He had to handle it all by himself. In fact, during the years after 1971 my mother could never recover fully. I remember my father's occasional gestures of love to my mother. Those were very poignant moments. After 1974 when I left home for the hostel, my meetings with my mother became limited to vacations when I came home, wherever my father was posted till his retirement and at Kahalgaon after that. I have a feeling of guilt that I did not take enough care of my mother which I should have done, at least after I joined service and finished my training period in 1986. One may love parents greatly but that is not all. Poetic expressions of love are admirable but not enough. I remember she was so happy when I got married and was so proud that her daughter-in-law was a doctor. She herself was a very pretty woman and if we are reasonably alright to look at, the genetic credit goes to my parents and substantially to my mother. I wish I could have cared more and could be in her service for the years after 1986 till she was alive. Forgive me 'Ma' for my failings. If there is a life again, be my mother and let me be with you and for you.

At Daltonganj, my father's instincts of a teacher came to assert. He was comparatively at peace. Two of his children, my elder brother and my elder sister were married off and they were no longer staying with us. So, three of us were with him—another brother who was elder to me by two years, myself and my younger sister who was in class V then. Not that I had shown any special trait as a student till I was at Biharsharif, but I used to stand first in the class and the teachers and the principal of the school always treated me as a good student. My father was happy about it. He made a very strict regime of discipline for us at home. He would ensure that we got up by 5.30 in the morning and got down with studies. Then we had to reach the school by 10 a.m. and come back by 4 p.m. We were supposed to go out to play and come back by 6 p.m. We had a reasonably big bungalow with lots of space to play. In winters we used to play badminton at the court made in our house itself. Friends used to assemble there. From 7 p.m. to 9 p.m. again it was study time for us. My father was always around while we were with our books. He would advise us that anything to be learnt by heart is best done in the morning. Similarly, it was preferable to study Mathematics in the morning hours. He would often ask me words from the English language, their precise meanings and their usage. He would insist on my making sentences using the words. He also ensured that we studied Sanskrit and mug up the Sanskrit verses. He made us learn Sanskrit verses from the Ramcharitmanas and Bhagavad Gita and many poems in English, besides the ones in the school textbooks. Out of many from Shakespeare, Wordsworth and others, the one I had kept on my table was by Kalidasa (original in Sanskrit). I still remember that which was as under:

"Look to this Day,
for it is Life
the very Life of Life.
In its brief course lie
all the verities and realities of your existence:
the Bliss of Growth,
the Glory of Action,
the Splendour of Beauty.
For yesterday is already a dream
and tomorrow is only a vision;

My Father

My Mother

but today, well-lived,
makes every yesterday
a dream of happiness
and every tomorrow
a vision of hope.
Look well, therefore, to this Day.
Such is the salutation of the Dawn."

—by Kalidasa

Off and on, my father used to check whether I remembered each word correctly. The result of all this was that in the next one year I had made a substantial addition to my vocabulary. He would also ensure that I was studying the Science subjects with perfection and was not losing marks in school examinations. By now I had become a star kid in the school.

A great thing to happen at Daltonganj was a few students whom I met at school. One was Sanjeev Ratan Mishra who was a year senior to me at the school. His elder sister, Aruna Mishra was senior by two years and studying at the local girls' school. They were children of the local Divisional Forest Officer. They were extremely bright. Sanjeev was almost a genius, particularly good in Mathematics and Science. I learnt later that Aruna competed for the entrance examination of the All-India Institute of Medical Sciences and became a doctor. Sanjeev went abroad, probably to study Engineering. Our personal and family friendship lasted for a few months and we lost touch later for reasons I don't recall. Perhaps our fathers did not have points of interaction to sustain a longer friendship. But the person who changed me and my life was Harananda, two years senior to me at the school. He was the son of Mr. B. N. Sinha, who was the District Education Officer. They stayed close to our house. Mr. B. N. Sinha was a very affectionate person and quite learned. Languages used to fascinate him. He was a natural choice as a friend for my father. During the next one year it became almost a daily affair to meet and interact with them on sundry issues. My father and he would ask questions from English and Hindi literature and words, spellings and their usage. Often, we used to have dinner together. Life for me was becoming a journey towards gaining knowledge.

Harananda was the real life changer for me. He is the one about whom I can write pages. He was the star student at the school, scoring almost cent per cent not only in Science subjects, but even in subjects like Social Studies, Sanskrit, English and Hindi. His creativity in writing poetry in English and Hindi was unbelievable. In retrospect, I find it like a mystery to think that a boy at 14 or 15 could have that level of proficiency in languages. I heard of Shakespeare and Wordsworth and Kalidasa and Bharatendu Harishchandra for the first time from him. He inspired me to read good books beyond what was to be read for examinations. He had a very nice handwriting. He became a favourite of my father too. He knew Urdu besides being proficient in English and Hindi. I too got interested in Urdu language because of him. I still recall that for the first time I heard about Sahir Ludhianvi from him. His father got a book titled 'Aamantran' published which was a collection of poems written by him. I still retain a copy of that book. So, he became my teacher, effectively. I have no hesitation in stating that much of what there is in my personality which could be called creative is owed to two persons—my father and Harananda. I treated him as an elder brother and still call him Bhaiya. The next year, in 1974, he left for Patna for his intermediate. It is my privilege to keep in touch with him till date. With my father no more and uncle Mr. B. N. Sinha also having left for his heavenly abode, I wonder how fast the time flies. It is difficult to believe that we ourselves are now in our 60s and even our children who have come of age now are younger than the times I am recalling. Someday soon, I plan to meet Harananda Bhaiya and tell him how much I owe to him.

Daltonganj in the Palamau district of Jharkhand (then in Bihar) was quite a beautiful place surrounded with forests. It is famous for the Palamau (Betla) National Park nearby, which is known as an abode for elephants. My father often used to take us there. These visits were like family picnics. We used to go in a jeep, stay there in the Forest Department's guest houses and visit the forest in the night in an open jeep with flashlight. In a couple of hours, we used to come across herds of deer and elephants.

The accompanying forest guard would advise us about the technique needed to maintain calm and watch the elephants. These jungle visits are etched in my memory and I am reminded of my father whenever I go back to my memories. Another district close by was Hazaribagh which was famous for tigers. Babuji took us there also so many times. It had a beautiful guest house in the middle of the jungle. It was a unique experience to be inside the jungle for the whole night in the comfort of the guest house. But unfortunately we could never come across a tiger. These visits unmistakably showed the zest and love my father had and his concern that his children should see and enjoy places. Most importantly, he made these trips also very educative because he would keep asking us to describe the beauty and the magnificence of the jungle in English and also in Hindi, correct us, particularly me, on our expressions. After each trip there were additions to my vocabulary. On coming back, he would sometimes ask me to write an essay on the trip. He would then make corrections and make suggestions on the betterment of expressions.

He was not oblivious of the fact that as children we may be desiring to see movies. He himself used to enjoy watching films in cinema halls. So, he made a rule that once a month he would take us for a movie. He religiously followed it. There were two cinema halls at Daltonganj. He showed us several movies in those halls. He would always sit with my mother inside the hall and talk to her. These movies, for me, were significant lessons in creative writing. I was always given a homework to write an essay on the theme and the message conveyed through the movie seen last. I still remember that we had seen a movie *Kucche Dhaage* starring Vinod Khanna and Kabir Bedi and I wrote an essay in the pre-Board examination of class X because a question included in the examination in English Paper I asked for an essay on the film last seen. My essay was appreciated by the teachers and the Principal even called me to his room to pat me. A similar thing happened once more and I remember I wrote an essay on the movie *Dushman* starring Rajesh Khanna, Meena Kumari and Mumtaz. That essay also brought a lot of appreciation because each word in the essay was taught by my father. These were great morale boosters and sources of confidence to a student of class IX or X. That a child's growing up can be made so creative and educative was a reflection on my father's indulgence with his child. It did miracles for me. Now, in retrospect, I feel the difference it made to my level of knowledge and my interest without which I might have become a good student with bookish knowledge but definitely not the one who was a little different.

In all these comparatively happier moments of life I noticed that my father used to get very high fever with shivering once every three or four months. The temperature used to go so high that he would lose coherence in thought and speech for a few hours. Those used to be frightening moments. I used to sit by the bedside at his feet not knowing what to do. I don't remember any doctor coming to our house to see him but he would keep some medicine which he requested to be given to him. He used to be fine in a couple of days. On my query, he told me he that he had a problem of filaria and the high temperature was a result of the filarial attack. There was nothing to worry. I was not convinced but I was too young to probe further. He ought to have consulted a doctor and I am not sure whether he did. Anxiety on this score found a place perennially in my mind.

I was at Daltonganj till 1974 when I passed my matriculation with fairly high marks but below the expectations of my father and my teachers. They were expecting I might top in the state but the ranks up to 10th were mostly grabbed by the students of Netarhat school. My father was happy though. He decided to send me to Science College, Patna for my intermediate. It was the usual trend those days. Most of the bright students, on the basis of the Matriculation results, would go there only. It used to be a matter of prestige. It was painful to leave home but I was excited too because of the independence I was going to have. Any child of 15 would find it exciting. I got to stay in the college hostel which was a great thing because it was only the top few on the basis of marks who would qualify for the hostel. The rest had to make private arrangements, or were day scholars. At Science College I suddenly realised that all were so brilliant. The monopoly I enjoyed at the school was no longer there. Most of the students were hardworking and Physics, Chemistry,

Mathematics and Biology were their obsessions. Almost all were preparing hard to compete for the top medical and engineering colleges of the country. There were some who were planning to change disciplines after intermediate for other careers, the most important and sought after being the Civil Services.

I was slightly different. I had developed interest in debates and elocution and was actively participating in competitions while at school. A high point reached was the first position and the award for being the best speaker in the debate competition organised in 1972 on the occasion of the silver jubilee of independence. It made me a known face at Daltonganj and my father so proud. Credit for this in substantial measure goes to Harananda who always inspired me to participate in debates and always helped me prepare well. At Science College also one such major occasion came. I got selected to represent Patna University at an All-India Debate at Banaras Hindu University. I was the youngest participant to be selected. Two were selected from each university. The other person selected from Patna was a student of postgraduation. A total of 25 universities were to participate. My father was pretty happy when he was informed after 3-4 days through a letter by me, the only way to communicate those days. We left for Varanasi a day before the appointed date for the debate. All arrangements were made by the Banaras Hindu University for our stay and food. We were put up in the Law Faculty Hostel. BHU has massive and grand buildings but the quality of students, as we could make out from their conversations and the mannerisms, leaves much to be desired in a University of national stature. The Institute of Medical Sciences and the Engineering College on the campus, of course, have the best of students because the students in these colleges come through a rigorous All-India Entrance Examination. We reached the BHU Auditorium the next morning at 9.30 a.m. and the debates started at 10 a.m. It was the biggest gathering so far which I was going to speak to. The subject of the debate was "What is superior and more important—liberty or equality". I had to speak for liberty and the other participant from Patna was to speak in favour of equality. One by one all the participants from different universities had finished speaking by 5 p.m. Results were announced in the next couple of hours. That was a great moment because we could not believe that our team was adjudged to be the best team. Our happiness was unbounded.. It knew no limits. We received a huge trophy. A postgraduate student from Institute of Medical Sciences, BHU was adjudged as the best speaker. In sheer excitement of the glory, we came back to Patna to be greeted by the Vice Chancellor of Patna University the next day. It was so satisfying. I was feeling more confident as a speaker. My father was so happy with me that he came to see me at Patna within the next few days. He hugged me, a hug I can still feel after nearly five decades.

A great personal tragedy was destined to strike us the next year in 1976. My elder brother, two years older than me, who had gone to Kahalgaon/Bhagalpur to study, died there under mysterious circumstances. For all of us it was a tragedy which was difficult to absorb. I can imagine what a great tragedy it must have been for my father who lost a smile on his face during the months that followed. He was a reasonably bright student and very affectionate, at least to me and my younger sister. He had of course very little communication with our eldest brother. He used to write affectionate letters to me, some of which I have retained till date. I came back to Patna crestfallen. My father got transferred to Samastipur and he shifted with my younger sister and my mother. My studies too got affected. After my Intermediate, I shifted to Patna College for my History Honours. In 1979, after my graduation, I shifted to JNU for postgraduation, visiting Samastipur and Hazaribagh (my father's last posting) in the vacations. My father maintained his regular touch through his letters, always motivating me for the UPSC Civil Services after the age of 21. This is what it had been till the fateful day in 1980 when destiny was at its cruellest. My father had shaped my personality by June 30, 1980 to handle the world on my own.

The loss of my father was definitely the most traumatic event in my life. I still can't forget the pain. But now, when I am myself 63, and it has been more than 42 years, I don't want to say in grief that he is no more, but I want to be thankful to my destiny that he was there and he took meticulous efforts to shape me into a person that I am. I am so grateful Babuji. A few lines by Kelly Roper match my emotions:

"The time we had, Dad,
Wasn't nearly enough
To pack in an entire
Lifetime of love.
There are so many questions
That I need answers to,
But now that you're gone
There's no way to ask you.
But there are still photos
To remember you by,
Each time I look at them,
I still want to cry.
They say grief is easier to bear as time goes by,
But that doesn't stop me
from wondering why?
Why my dear, sweet dad
Was taken so soon,
When he was my guiding star,
My sun and my moon.
There are no answers
To a question like this,
So I will cherish your memory,
And morn the years we'll miss."

4

Mridula

> "If I had to dream up the perfect woman, she wouldn't even come close to you."
>
> —Cory Matthews in '*Boy meets World*'

"Mridula" is a name which has been a part and parcel of my life since June 15, 1986, more than 36 years now, because of the institution of marriage. She is my wife. I have known her since 1982. I must say there has been a romantic inclination between us ever since we met. Eventually, the thought and the decision to embark on a life together through marriage was a conscious exercise. Luckily, we have no significant reasons to regret till date. We have on and off reflected on life and handled the issues in life applying mutual wisdom. We have taken conscious efforts to shun mediocrity in whatever we have done and handled setbacks, reconciled with realities and respected one another as a matter of principle and habit. I have made her sad sometimes by my actions. She also has done that, rarely though. But these have been of no consequence because we have always analysed the reasons for the apparent sadness. We always believed that an unexamined life was not worth living. These examinations have invariably shown us the paths to tread.

It should be worthwhile to reflect a little on these frequently used words—wife, marriage and romance. A wife, as all definitions would suggest, is "a married woman, especially when considered in relation to her partner in marriage". A wife can refer to the husband as her spouse, and the husband can refer to the wife as his spouse. The word comes from the Latin 'sponsus' meaning 'to pledge' or 'promise'. Wife is used to refer to the female partner in a marriage. The Bible describes a wife as "one flesh with her husband". This is not just physically, but in the totality of who you are, your husband, and you are one. This means that we carry one another's burdens and celebrate each other's victories. There is nothing sweeter than to be a praying spouse and see the Lord working in his/her life. As per Proverbs 18:22 (KJV) "Who so findeth a wife findeth a good thing, and obtaineth favour of the Lord". Bible verses about wives tell us about the importance of marriage and the blessing that a wife can be for a man. In fact, the Bible says that finding a good wife is evidence of finding favour with God.

A commonly accepted and encompassing definition of marriage is "a formal union and social and legal contract between two individuals that legally, economically and emotionally unites their lives". In other words, marriage is a legally and socially sanctioned union, usually between a man and a woman, that is regulated by laws, rules, customs, beliefs and attitudes that prescribe the rights and duties of the partners and accords status to their offspring (if any). The books of Sociology define marriage as an institution to satisfy physical, psychological, social, cultural and economic needs of men and women. The primary aim of marriage is the regulation of sexual activities through a stable relationship, which otherwise may cause social disruptions. Marriage has been defined as an institution for admitting men and women into family life, legitimising offspring and establishing other rights and obligations of husband, wife and children.

Romance is a story of love between two people, often containing exciting events. This is the shortest definition of romance on the internet. Romance in a relationship is a feeling of love for, or a strong attraction towards, another person, and the courtship behaviours undertaken by an individual to express those overall feelings and resultant emotions. Romance as juxtaposed to love also needs to be seen. Love is a deep liking and adoration towards a few people we have in our lives. Love makes us go to great lengths for the people we love. Romance, on the other hand, may or may not transform into love. A relationship that is only based on it is bound to end sooner or later. Men tend to define romance sexually. Women more commonly define romance as words and behaviours that represent that they are loved, cherished, valued, respected and desired. Although there is some carry-over between the two definitions, they're still not the same.

With this brief conceptual background there will be enough clarity in my story of knowing Mridula, talking to her, feeling for her and sharing her pains and pleasures. I met her first in 1982 at Bhagalpur where she was studying for her MBBS. I was then at JNU, Delhi but used to visit Bhagalpur because my younger sister was also studying at the same medical college. In any case my hometown was Kahalgaon which was just 30 kilometres away from Bhagalpur. Mridula was a class friend of my sister, Pratibha, whom we called by the name Cheena. In fact, they were very close friends.

The difficult phase of life was continuing. The little respite and happiness had arrived in the form of my sister competing for the medical entrance. My studies and preparations for the Civil Services Examination were going on but uncertainties of career were always there at the back of mind. These uncertainties had assumed fearsome proportions after my father's death.

I have been a fairly flamboyant man/boy since childhood. I never shied away from meeting older people, including my father's friends, who were mostly officers. I was fairly popular too among my peer groups. As regards the girls, the natural curiosity and excitement expected in a young boy for girls was also present inside me from a very young age. I never missed any opportunity to try to impress the other person, including a girl, by whatever worth appreciation I had in me. That mainly included everything noticed, appreciated and complimented for. And all this came very naturally to me. Artificiality had not touched me. Perhaps this was a result of the little extra that my father and Harananda inspired me to learn while at school at Daltonganj. Although we were in a small town like Daltonganj to start with, that was enough for a fairly rich exposure in terms of interactions with boys and girls of good intellectual capacities commensurate with age. Even till date, when I have superannuated from a rather sought-after career, I find in retrospect that a few people I interacted with at Daltonganj, like Sanjeev Ratan Mishra and his elder sister Aruna Mishra and Harananda, were exceptional. They were not just brilliant in Science subjects—enabling them to become a technocrat and a doctor from reputed institutes of national level—they were proficient in English and Hindi languages which made impressive personalities out of them. Harananda was almost a genius and now at 65 he is a motivational speaker with a large number of followers. A journey further to Patna and JNU, Delhi only exposed me to a larger world of talent and brilliant students and girls from a metropolitan background, and indeed from the whole country. JNU was a real game-changer in terms of interactions with the members of the fairer sex. Coming from a smaller place like Patna it was a cultural change. The special thing regarding JNU was that it had a large

"I've tried so many times to think of a new way to say it, and it's still I love you."
—Zelda Fitzgerald

number of girls studying there and they were from all across the country. Even the Centre for Historical Studies, where I was studying, had almost 40% girls as colleagues. The smart, the very good looking and scholarly among women were also there in large numbers. I had the privilege of one of the most learned and attractive personalities, Prof. Romila Thapar, as my faculty adviser. I have seen a minuscule few in the country during the last more than 40 years or so with greater command over expressions and better accent in spoken English.

It was in the backdrop of this physical and mental condition and disposition that I met Mridula for the first time at Bhagalpur. My younger sister had adequately introduced her to me. I found her very impressive. The conversation mostly happened about our careers and also her family. She told me that she had passed her Intermediate from I. T. College, Lucknow. Most of her relatives were there as they were basically from there. Nanaji, who was a doctor, had migrated from Burma where he was the Chief Medical Officer of the Burmese railways. World War II forced them to leave Burma. Her mother, the most famous doctor of Bhagalpur, had landed up in Bihar after her marriage. Her father was from Bhagalpur with huge landed properties in the Santhal Parganas. He was

Mirdula 1983, 1984

Mirdula 1984, 1985

Mirdula 2022

Mirdula 2019

With Mirdula 2019

With Mirdula at Goa (2017)

Mirdula, Pattaya (2016)

With Mirdula at Kaushambi (2022)

otherwise a professor of Agriculture and at that point of time he was on deputation with the Government of Bihar in the Department of Agriculture. There was a remarkable simplicity about Mridula combined with a very high level of self-confidence. I was happy that I met an accomplished girl. That was all.

As 1982 progressed my results for the Civil Services examination came. I had taken the examination with an avoidable hurry. Nevertheless, I was finally successful but with a rank that was not likely to get me a service that I would have liked. It was a little depressing. But I also felt confident that with a little focus I would clear the examination the next time. Now I had to decide what to do next. I had to leave JNU. Luckily, job options were available. I finally decided to move to Kolkata and join the General Insurance Corporation of India and write the Civil Services again from Kolkata itself. I did that. During the years between 1982 and 1984 I used to visit Bhagalpur rather frequently, once in a fortnight on an average. Naturally the occasions to meet Mridula also became frequent. Initially, it was a pleasure only because it meant meeting a girl who was bright in studies, smart, good looking and coming from an illustrious family, yet wearing admirable simplicity. To add to my pleasure, she used to wait for me at the Ladies' Hostel after confirming my programme with my sister. She was both a hosteler and a day scholar. She would ensure she was at the hostel the day I went.

"If I go a million miles away / I'd write a letter, each day and every day / 'Cause I know that nothing, nothing / Can ever change that love I have for you."

–Sam Cooke

During the next two years, intimacy with Mridula grew. But it was intimacy only between two people. I was intimidated when I learnt that Mridula was quite sought after by the boys at the college. That was the first sign of my liking for her which could be said to be more than friendship. For the last couple of months, I have been subconsciously comparing Mridula with the girls who have been friends at JNU and also colleagues among the women folk at the National Insurance Company at Kolkata. I must say that I always found her more accomplished in totality. The crucial moment came when one day I received a letter by post at Kolkata from her. That was the decisive moment in our relationship. Thoughts and attraction in the subconscious took a concrete shape and I was sure it could be called nothing else but love. Mridula's letter was very decisive in its assertion. Her expression of love had no ambiguity. She had a very good command over language and her vocabulary was fairly rich. Emotions were genuine. I was struck with a feeling of romance. But it was love which had overtaken me. I told myself I must reply to her letter in words which should precisely convey what I was feeling.

My results of the Civil Service Examination for the year also came in the meantime and I cleared it with a fairly good rank. Now it was a question of a couple of months to leave Kolkata. I decided I was going to visit Bhagalpur umpteen times before I left. It took me more than a week to find words to reply to Mridula's letter. I replied with literary assertions of my liking and adoration. I nowhere used the word 'love' but conveyed it quite effectively. Later, after a few years, Mridula told me that she was very upset at my delayed response and it hurt her self-respect but she was sure that if the feeling of love remained unexpressed it would lead nowhere. If I said 'no', she would have been crestfallen but, as she said, she would have still felt that I was a nice man and I ought to have known that a 'woman' like her admired me. I really was overwhelmed by this thought of hers. It only further added to my adoration for her.

I was reading *Doctors*, the celebrated novel by Erich Segal. It has been one of the finest books of fiction I have read in my life. The other two have been *The Class* and *Love Story*, by Erich Segal again. And I have also loved *The Godfather* by Mario Puzo. *Doctors* takes us into the lives of the Harvard Medical School's class of 1962. This stunning novel reveals the making of doctors—what makes them tick, scheme, hurt and love. *Doctors* brings to vivid life the men and women who seek to heal but who must walk through fire. At the novel's heart is the unforgettable relationship of Barney Livingstone and Laura Castellano, childhood friends who feel the love between them and their friendship ripens into passion. In my present state of mind, I was often comparing Mridula with Laura Castellano.

I soon visited Bhagalpur. It was a different state of mind this time. My sister was doing fine. She was intelligent enough to know that I had developed that special feeling for Mridula but she never discussed that with me. She was very happy at these developments. She considered Mridula to be an ideal girl and wanted to see me happy. I am grateful to her for that. I spent a lot of time with Mridula on this visit. Finding a friend like her was a great thing to happen. Our conversations, I feel in retrospect, were of a very superior level. I found that she had ambitions, but they were not all-consuming. She was a medical student studying enough to become a good doctor and she had varied interests. She was a music lover and herself a reasonably good singer. She had culinary talents and she used to experiment with varieties of food. She had an immaculate sense of dressing up. So, she encompassed all the traits which probably make a desirable person, particularly a woman. I could conclude that she was a very balanced person I had ever met. She was neither like an overtly cerebral girl battling for her medical degree nor like a bubble-headed ordinary girl whose only goal in life was an engagement ring. Now onwards I was in love with her and worried about deserving her.

The times since late 1984 were different for me. I had one more person in my life, and a very important person to think about. Mridula, now onwards, was always part of my thinking process. I came back to Kolkata with an added dimension to my existence. Parting from her at Bhagalpur last time had pangs, but there was no suffering. I had found my love. The last visit to Bhagalpur was quite eventful. Mridula had taken me to her house where I met her parents. Her mother was a smart lady talking mostly in English. I later learnt that she was originally from Burma. She was born and brought up there. The family had migrated to Lucknow during World War II. It was after her marriage that she landed up in Bihar. Her father was a Professor of Agriculture. He was a very handsome man and had a beautiful handwriting which I could see from a file lying at the table where I was sitting. They were very progressive in their thoughts. They had an inter-caste marriage in the late 1950s which itself was more than enough to show how progressive they were. Even in our generation an inter-caste marriage was something which was resisted by families. Mridula's mother was an eminent gynaecologist and she was almost a household name in Bhagalpur. It was a very cordial and decent first meeting. I was not sure whether they knew how I had entered their daughter's life. I also noted with a sense of appreciation that Mridula was absolutely unaffected by her parents' profile, particularly of her mother. In fact I, having lost my father, had become a little shaky in my interactions with socially important people. But it was so comfortable interacting with Mridula's parents.

I came to Kolkata and resigned from the National Insurance to join the IRS. My friends and colleagues at Kolkata gave me a rather emotional and fun-filled farewell. It was a great time spent with them and I still keep in touch with some of them. I joined the National Academy of Direct Taxes at Nagpur on December 26, 1984. My friendship with Mridula, or our mutual love to be correct, flourished through letters. Our creative writing was at its best. Every day at 11.20 a.m. during the first break from classes, the probationers used to run to the Academy post office to check for letters, if any, from home. The frequency of my letters from Mridula was such that the colleague probationers used to be envious. In fact, many of them used to say that someday they would like to meet the girl who was writing letters with a frequency which was unbelievable. They were surprised and impressed when they came to know that the girl in question was a medical student.

I came home in the month of June 1985 for my sister's wedding. It had to be solemnised at Kahalgaon. Mridula insisted on being with us and took her parents' permission to spend a week with us for her friend's wedding and landed at Kahalgaon. It was a great time in all respects for me. Her craving to see me and talk to me was unmistakable to observe for me. I only felt grateful and irresistibly close to her. She sang songs at home and we had a wide variety of subjects to discuss whenever we could steal time. I resolved to get married soon and discussed it with her. It was a firm 'yes' from her side. I told her I would divulge the plans soon to my family.

In the month of December we had our All India trip (Bharat Darshan, as it is called for the probationers of the All-India Services). I was at my creative best during those three weeks of Bharat Darshan. I described each place I visited to Mridula in a style that Mridula loved. In fact, the little skill and the penchant for English and Hindi languages played an important role in my love life. It had made me noticeable to Mridula, and on further interaction it became a source of fatal attraction for her. Mridula has kept my letters safely in nice albums and I can see how I remembered her 37 years ago while at Goa, Mumbai, Chennai, Mahabalipuram, Pune and so many other places. We got married in 1986.

It has been a blissful life with Mridula. For everything that I did and which made her happy, I am thankful to her zest for life. For everything in my personality that she might not have liked, I am thankful to her for having graciously ignored them. I have never seen her shortcomings because I have been a diehard lover. We have together handled struggles of career, pains inflicted by circumstances and people who have been unkind and all the sufferings of life. We created the best of times that we could do together. We saw the world together, travelled extensively and socialised lavishly. Sometimes in life, happiness found a place which was too much. Sometimes it was too little. I always found the good things about Mridula and admired her for it. Although she is my wife, the way she handled this adversity which came in the form of a stroke to me has conveyed the strength and endurance she has. Even this period of convalescence has been worth living. I have forgotten what it feels like to live alone. I didn't know her before 1982 and now I don't remember not knowing her ever.

5
The Family

> "The greatest thing in a family life is to take a hint when a hint is intended and not to take a hint when it isn't intended."
>
> —Robert Frost

We all know what "Family" connotes. To enter the pages of sociology is not required to define it. A pedantic exercise to try to define would be a meaningless exercise. The fact remains that when a significant event arises, the family, whether we relish it or not, necessarily comes into play. One is lucky if there is a family to extend meaningful support in such situations. Getting struck by a medical tragedy like a haemorrhagic stroke is definitely a momentous event. It surely decides who is there for you. It gives enough and sure signs of unconditional support if one is lucky to have some people to extend that. I have definitely not been unlucky. Yet I would like to expend a few words to understand what is generally understood by 'family'.

Family is defined as a group of persons united by the ties of marriage, blood or adoption, constituting a single household and interacting with each other in their respective social positions, usually those of spouses, parents, children and siblings. If one is to give a deep meaning to the word it could be said that family means having someone to love you unconditionally in spite of your shortcomings. Family is loving and supporting one another even if it is not easy to do so. It is being the best person you could be so that you inspire your loved ones. Family can provide you enormous positive energy and can make you conquer many things. A family gives stability in various ways. It is said that family is the foundational institution of society ordained by God. The family is a fundamental institution of human society. In the scripture 1 Timothy 5:8, it has been said that "If anyone does not provide for his relatives, and especially for members of his household, he has denied the faith and is worse than an unbeliever." Those are strong words given to us by our Lord. Families and children have always been close to the heart of the Lord. In the Psalms 127:3-5 it is said that children are a heritage from the Lord, offspring a reward from him. Like arrows in the hands of a warrior are children born in one's youth. Blessed is the man whose quiver is full of them. They will not be put to shame when they contend with their opponents. The reality of life, however, may also make us think that family does not necessarily mean blood family. There are many blood families that are very negative and have no family love towards each other at all, while there are friends who are intensely loyal to each other to death. Ultimately, family means closeness, love, and respect for each other.

I have devoted a chapter on 'friends' separately. Friends are valuable and may be greater sources of happiness and a stronger support, but let me go by the traditional conceptualisation of family. I have venerated my parents who gave me birth. Unfortunately, I lost my father when I was a little over 20 only. I miss him always for all that he did for me. However, the fact that he was my father who took care of me as a father is enough reason for holding him in the highest esteem. The same feeling is there for my mother also. I will not repeat an enumeration of my father. I have a guilt feeling for life that I could not act like an ideal son for my mother who, despite her health issues, so many times made me feel how selfless and sacrificing a mother could be. Although I was firmly settled in life, to spend time together with her, being at her service and making her happy by the pampering of a son remained a desire only. I lost her and I always feel I could not be the ideal son for a mother. There is no way I can do anything now. I just want to say "I love you Ma". I don't know whether there is a rebirth. Had there been one, I would like to live for a hundred years with her and for her.

My siblings include an elder brother, an elder sister and a younger sister. I had the misfortune of losing an older brother pretty young in life. His loss pains me. My elder brother and sister are ten years older than me and the younger sister is 4 years younger. I did not have much interaction with my elder brother for very long. When I was past 12, he had settled in life and gone away from parents. He is a nicely settled man with a flourishing family. His two sons and a daughter are doing well in life. I can see that he enjoys his family bliss. He has always been a great support. After my father's death, when I was pursuing my studies at Delhi, he became the saviour of the situation. His presence mitigated many insurmountable difficulties which would have been debilitating. During this present crisis caused by the stroke also he has been very supportive by his physical presence. The management of family properties after my father's demise was facilitated by his presence. He knew how to handle these issues.

My elder sister was married when I was still in school. She has been a homemaker although she was pretty good in studies. It seems my parents never gave a thought regarding her career. She is now in her 70s and fairly well settled in life although we lost our brother-in-law a few years ago. He was a nice man, at least very caring for us. My sister and brother-in-law only have daughters who are well settled. The two eldest have been quite bright as students. Not surprising that they could become professionals (a doctor and an engineer). I have very fond memories of my elder sister. She had a mother's instinct, at least for me and my younger sister. I can never forget that she used to wait for us for lunch or some food when we came back from school. We must have been at very early stages of school and she herself might have been in high school. She would always protect us when parents were angry for any reason.

I have been an elder brother to my younger sister in a real sense. It may be also because we were the two who were staying with our parents. Initially not very sincere with studies, she suddenly became a hardworking student after her class VII. There was no looking back for her after that. Standing first in the class always, she became an adorable child in the school. I helped her at home with her studies. Even my father used to teach her. She had a flair for language, particularly Hindi. She was very good at Science subjects. She passed her Matriculation with flying colours and came to Patna for her Intermediate. I was already at Patna doing my graduation. Her Intermediate was marred by my father's sudden demise. But next year she reorganised herself and competed for the Medical Entrance Examination. She is now a famous doctor at Gorakhpur. Her identity has an added feature besides that of a doctor. She got a book of her Hindi poetry published about a year ago. Now she is a poetess acknowledged widely. She has been a great well-wisher and a great friend. She has been an equally great friend of my wife. We have shared all the pains and pleasures together. She is married to Dr. Arun Prasad Gupta, a very hardworking and empathetic surgeon whose success as a doctor is admirable. He has been a great support in all crises. In the present adversity also, he was one of the first persons I looked for once I regained consciousness.

My younger sister is Dr. Pratibha Gupta whose nickname is Cheena. She has three daughters who are my friends in their independent capacity. The eldest two stayed with me for quite some time when they came for studies to Delhi. The eldest is Tanvi who is a gynaecologist now. She works as a faculty at Christian Medical College, Vellore. The next is Pallavi who graduated from Delhi University. She then moved to the USA, did her MBA. She fell in love with an American boy who is wonderful in his simplicity. They are happily married and settled in the USA. Their wedding was solemnised with the Vedic rites as well as Christian customs. We organised the wedding at a Goa beach. I acted as the best man in the wedding. The third is Curie, a sweet girl, now an Engineer, presently working at Hyderabad. My nephews are also friendly. Both of them are State Bank of India officers. I always had greater personal bonding with the elder nephew. He was a great support for Mridula when I was lying in the ICU at the hospital after the stroke.

Mentioning my sisters-in-law (wife's sisters) too for me is mentioning my family only. The eldest one Mamta is a professor. Married to a doctor, she is an embodiment of simplicity. Two sisters younger to Mridula are in the USA and they are American citizens. Sujata is a doctor with a postgraduation in gynaecology from the Institute of Medical Sciences, BHU. She has further done her postgraduation from the USA also in paediatrics. She was exceptionally bright as a student. She topped the Medical Entrance Examination of Bihar. The next is Vidisha who is a journalist. She had worked for the *Times of India*, Delhi before she moved to the USA. Both the sisters-in-law possess rare empathy. In fact, I depend on them in more ways than one. Vidisha, the youngest, has a unique gritty personality. Unfazed by sources of stress she has the extraordinary quality of dealing with any problem as and when it arises.

Sujata's two sons were born and brought up in the USA. I remember the elder one's birth in the year 1993 because I made my maiden trip to the USA for the occasion. At that time she was in Mobile, Alabama. It was an exciting trip with Mridula as I was exploring the USA and Europe for the first time. I travelled across France, the United Kingdom and Switzerland with substantial time spent in the USA. Paris was romantic. The visits to Lido and Moulin Rouge were great youthful escapades. I have visited Paris later also but the memories of the first visit are matchless. London was like home. Although we stayed in a hotel near Piccadilly there were many Indian friends visiting. Exploring London with them was very interesting. More often than not, I got a feeling that I was in India, of course a much cleaner, and orderly one. Switzerland was beautiful. Lake Geneva's expanse was a wonder to watch.

The peak at Mount Matterhorn was iconic. We had no time to see Monte Rosa, Finsteraarhorn or Piz Bernina. It was too cold in Switzerland. A walk around the old town in Geneva gives an idea of its beautiful history. The shops and cafes down the narrow hilly streets enable you to savour the Swiss style of life. Like in Paris, there are many galleries as well as museum sights in Geneva. In the USA we visited seven stations. Not depending on any help, I had booked Visit USA air tickets from India itself. The USA was massive, gigantic rather. New York and Chicago were fascinating in their different ways. A visit to New Orleans in the Louisiana state was memorable. It is located along the Mississippi river in the south-eastern region of the USA. A cousin of Mridula was doing his MBA there. Rahul acted as a great host. Himself an achiever academically, he had the unique distinction of having cleared the SCRA and IIT JEE with high ranks. Having toured extensively, we reached Mobile and spent more than ten days there.

What impressed me most was the egalitarianism in the spirit of American society and the dignity of labour. I was amazed when the surgeon who operated upon Sujata for the birth of her child came for dinner to her house and the nurse Sister Gloria also came along. The dinner was organised to celebrate the birth of the child. The surgeon and the nurse were interacting as though they were equals in terms of their status. The surgeon, I was told later, was a highly paid person which is usual in the USA. This kind

My Father and Mother

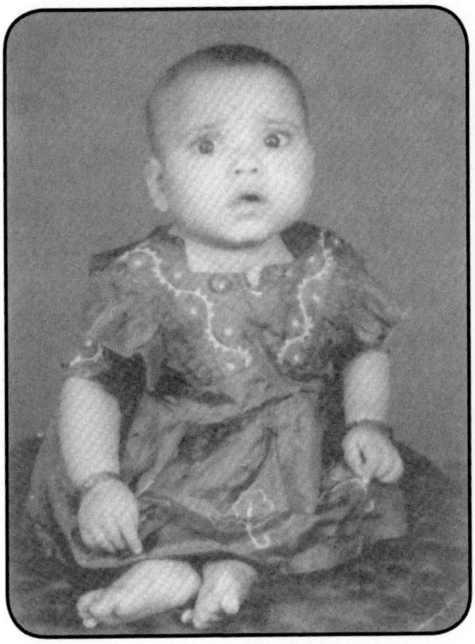

My Sisters – Pratibha and Prabha

My Father and Me

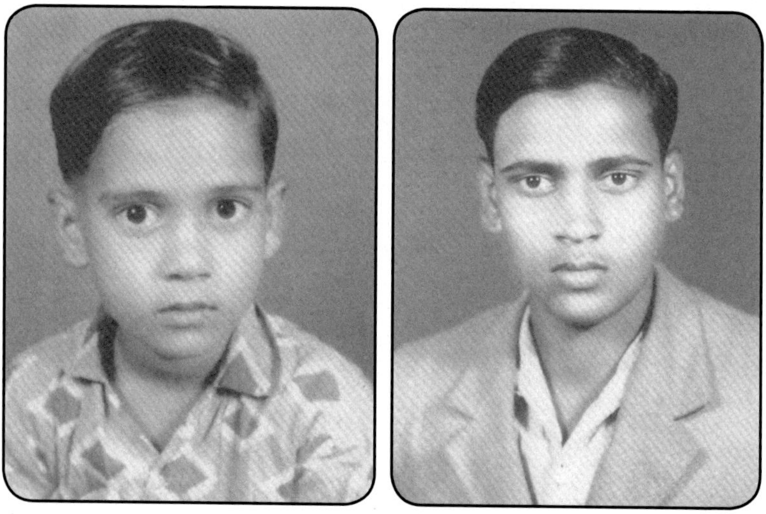

My Brothers – Ajay and Vijay

My Sons – Prerit and Prakhar

My Sons – Prakhar and Prerit

Myself – Mridula – Prerit – Prakhar

Mridula – Myself

of a social situation is unthinkable in India even though we claim that we swear by socialism, the word 'Socialist' having been brought in the Indian Constitution by the 42nd Amendment Act of 1976. Perhaps the economic levels of people and a massive population are the reasons. But there are attitudinal issues too. We have lacked genuine commitment to the right values socially. We may criticise the West by branding them capitalists but we need to be a little more realistic to the situation obtaining at home. Befooling ourselves in perpetuity is by no means wisdom. Since 1993 we have travelled through the world, the USA several times, but the memories of the maiden trip have been memorable.

Apoorva and Kunal, Sujata's sons, now grown- up men in their 20s, impress me. My interactions with them have been limited but they are humble and down-to-earth. They are respectful to elders. Despite being Americans, they have definitely imbibed the desired Indian values to a great extent. Now as an engineer and a psychiatrist, both of them are doing well for themselves.

My description of family would be incomplete if I don't remember my mother-in-law and father-in-law. They are no more. We lost them in 2006 and 2005, respectively. My mother-in-law, Dr. Sarla Ram, from the late 1970s till she was alive, was definitely the most famous and noted gynaecologist of not only Bhagalpur but of the entire Eastern part of Bihar. A virtuous lady with a compassionate heart, I have rarely seen doctors who are so honest and

"The informality of family life is a blessed condition that allows us all to become our best while looking our worst."

–Marge Kennedy

committed to the profession. She had a large heart. Even an untruthful mention of poverty made her waive the consultation fees. Many people used to take undue advantage but she never minded. A little uncomfortable with Hindi because of her Burmese background, she had adapted to local behaviour patterns and language with ease. A very affectionate mother, she had all the childlike qualities of craving to watch a movie or having good food. She was extremely loving to me personally and used to treat me like a very important person which, in fact, was embarrassing at times. It was because I was a bureaucrat and a son-in-law at the same time. I, of course, always behaved like a son and she appreciated it. She should have lived for a few more years. I miss her and feel fortunate that she was my mother-in-law. My father-in-law was a Professor of Agriculture. He was a handsome man. He was on deputation to the Agriculture Department of Government of Bihar for a number of years. Coming from a rich agricultural background, he was quite progressive in his thoughts. The decision to get married to a girl of a different caste from Lucknow in the 1950s more than adequately shows that. He had a beautiful handwriting. I spent many evenings listening to his experiences of life. He was proud that his wife had a great name and was able to earn substantially. Such appreciation for a wife during those times was very uncommon. I wish I could have enjoyed his being around for a few more years. My in-laws always gave me a feeling of support and strength irrespective of whether I needed them or not.

The family relationship that substantially determines one's life in the 30s and onwards is the one with your children. It is as vital as it was with parents. It's a reversal of roles. This phase can be bliss, not so great or even painful, depending primarily on destiny. A friend of mine is a very sound man intellectually and his wife too is equally accomplished in terms of career and she is a great mother. They once told me a word of wisdom. They said there was no textbook which could tell you the rules of ideal parenting. There was no formula which could be applied and you could make a child ideal. There was no method by which children could be made respectful, compassionate, confident in a positive way and empathetic. So different persons may do their best for their children according to their wisdom but the results in all cases may be different. The Hindi movie *Baghban* depicts a very realistic situation. With all the academic accomplishments, a boy, when he grows up, may be of no use in your old age including when you die. Another boy may not be so great an achiever academically but he may be a gem of a person and a son giving a godly status to parents. A son may not be bothered about parents' health at all while another may be always concerned with that. A son may have fallen into bad habits and he may not think it proper to hide from parents to avoid their hurt. Another son may be too conscious and will always ensure that the parents are not hurt. A son may enter into a competition with his parents only trying to match them if the parents are achievers in worldly terms. He often does not realise that a father or a mother may be achievers for the world, but for the son they are just parents and the son's love and respect can only guarantee happiness. Beyond an age, the sons may stop sharing difficulties in career, marriage or finances, little realising that it is the only selfless relationship in which the parents can go to any lengths to help. Friends may be good but they have their other priorities also besides the friendship with you. Their emotions may not be permanent. Moreover, parents only can derive genuine happiness even by achievements of their children which may be insignificant. These are the reasons why we see children of deprived parents, poor parents and uneducated parents becoming achievers and ideal sons and the sons of the privileged parents, financially and otherwise, lag behind. Therefore, the moral of what is seen happening around is that one should do the basic duty as parents and shun any expectations. If there is financial security created by you, hold on to it till you are alive. Pray to the cosmic force to be kind to you in terms of health till the last breath of life. And you will be exceptionally fortunate if your spouse and you are on the same page in terms of love and concern till the last moments of life.

I am blessed with two sons—Prerit and Prakhar. They are quite intelligent. For me it hardly mattered if they were daughters. For me, the children were great gifts of providence. When they were born it made me and Mridula so happy that all other nice moments of life paled into insignificance. Looking at them itself was happiness par excellence. Even trying to excel at our job and profession became a lesser priority for me and Mridula. I still remember the first day of their school. They cried and ran to us. The teacher then had to do a lot of cajoling to take them back to their classes. Times flew. The major part of their schooling was in Delhi. For the younger son the entire period of schooling was in Delhi while for the elder one it was at Dhanbad till class I. They did reasonably well. The elder one became a little more conscious for better results after class VIII. The younger one on the other hand was an all-rounder with keen interest in sports, particularly basketball. Having done their class XII, they entered prestigious colleges of Engineering and Law respectively. The elder one became an Engineer and the younger one a lawyer. The younger one, Prakhar, showed an inclination to pursue stand-up comedy as a career. I am happy that he is trying to make a place for himself as a stand-up comedian. He runs a comedy club known as Happy High in Delhi. The elder one went to the USA and he is definitely doing very well professionally. That makes me feel good and proud of him. They have come of age now. Their reactions on issues which concern the parents are at times a little incomprehensible. Their views on issues like family ties, family concerns, love, marriage etc. are far from clear. Irrespective of what they think and do, we love them infinitely. For them we can compromise even with our emotions. They are no longer children. We don't want to force anything on them. We can always ensure we are there when they need us. We feel happy at times. We are hurt too at times. But these things are all in life. They are nice and intelligent young men and worrying beyond a point serves no purpose. As long as the breath is ceaseless, one has to keep going. The stroke had shaken me last year. Now I hope I should be my normal self in the next few months and the remaining years in life are healthy. Yet I feel I am racing against time. I want my sons to shower their entire love right away. A beautiful poem came to my notice. It is worth reading.

"When I'll be dead,
Your tears will flow,
But I won't know.
Cry for me now instead.

You will send flowers,
But I won't see,
Send them now instead.

You'll say words of praise,
But I won't hear,
Praise me now instead.

You'll forget my faults,
But I won't know,
Forget them now, instead.

You'll miss me then,
But I won't feel,
Miss me now, instead.

You'll wish
You could have spent more time with me,
Spend it now instead."

It is often said that one should keep no expectations from children when they grow up. That is fine. But it applies to parents who have to depend on their children for financial support or even unreasonable emotional support or are physically debilitated. If one is fortunate to be in a position to be a giver for all time, this suggestion becomes meaningless. The minimum emotional expectation is rather healthy in my view. It keeps one going with the bliss of the family. Children must be responsive to parents' reasonable expectations. If children can be responsive to casual friends and acquaintances there is no reason why they should not be so for the parents. I think if destiny has been kind to them to have made them capable, they should be doing their best to take care of the needs too of their parents, particularly when age or health is not with them.

In relationships other than that of the family one should definitely have no expectations. A friendship may be enjoyable or old; it has the potential of losing its charm without any substantial reason. There are complexes never being apparent. There could be a competition never expressed. There may be jealousies so common among civil service colleagues which I have witnessed. Ultimately, it is Family which inherently has more chances and the highest possibility of seeing you through rough weather. Just love it. Preserve it.

6

The Indian Revenue Service–35 years

> "Little else is requisite to carry a state to the highest degree of opulence from the lowest barbarism but peace, easy taxes, and a tolerable administration of justice: all the rest being brought about by the natural course of things."
>
> —Adam Smith

Thirty five years out of sixty practically covers the whole life span. It is all the more significant because these thirty five years constitute the prime of youth and end with entering the last phase of life which may be long, and not so long if the destiny to inhabit the earth is not kind. In any case the phase of thirty five years leaves one to reminisce, to feel happy about or even to regret. In retrospect one reflects on one's own evolution. Being a part of the Government or Government service one realises that there were limitations and the evolution was not all encompassing as such. Whether it was worth it or not may be largely subjective. There are more than twenty class I services and a few class II services to which recruitment takes place through the Civil Services Examination. The examination itself is fairly hallowed, particularly in parts of the country. Some services are more preferred for historical reasons and also on the basis of social perceptions. But these are all very subjective in terms of positives and negatives that one witnesses in the course of the career. I have my own take on the issue. I will deal with the issue separately. With rank 156 in the Civil Services Examination I had a fairly good choice of services available to me. I chose to go for the Indian Revenue Service. The IRS or the Civil Services generally may or may not be a great career choice. The IRS, however, does provide a good career option. I have no regrets. Times when it was good, it was wonderful. Times when it was not so good or even bad, it was an experience. In the paragraphs below I just want to share my experience in the IRS. To any outsider the narrative may not be of great interest. In fact it may be a little boring too, but I do hope it will provide a bird's eye view of the service's profile and an insight into the negatives and positives too.

The brush with the IRS started at the National Academy of the Direct Taxes, Nagpur. I reached Nagpur from Kolkata by the Geetanjali Express on the December 16, 1984. I was required to go to the Director General's office to complete the joining formalities. It was late in the afternoon by the time I reached Nagpur. I, therefore, headed to the administrative building housing the DG's office. There I met two fellow probationers or trainees as we were called. They were Ajay Chauhan from Delhi and Santosh Kumar Sandhu from Punjab. Both had the smartness to strike a friendship instantly. So the initial moments were very cordial. They had finished the joining formalities and that facilitated the process for me and made it very smooth and quick. It was a few minutes of work to fill up a few forms. What was most enjoyable was walking to the hostel block which was a little more than a kilometer. Those ten minutes taken in the journey were hilarious. They had a strong wit and a refined sense of humour. As first friends in the Academy our association sustained and it has flourished till date. Sandhu, after three years joined the Indian Administrative Service and Chauhan superannuated as the Principal Chief Commissioner of Income Tax, Bhopal holding jurisdiction over Madhya Pradesh and Chhattisgarh.

The entire period of probation spent at the Academy was probably the most enjoyable period in the entire career. We had on-the-job training for three months in between. I had it at Patna. We were seventy probationers in the batch with eleven ladies. They were from all parts of the country and from divergent fields of study. The hostel for the probationers was quite comfortable and each probationer had a single room with an attached toilet. The hostel had a music room and a room for billiards. The dining hall of the hostel was well equipped and reasonably good food was served. The mess was managed through a committee called the Mess Committee. The committee had a secretary from among the probationers. It was headed by a President who was elected and this election used to be a festive affair. Many probationers used to be keen to become the President. There were not enough facilities for outdoor games those days but there was enough space on the campus to convert into football grounds and make badminton courts. The Facilities for sports were developed in the subsequent years. Five years after our probation period when I visited the Academy I found the Academy to be an entirely changed place. It was already a sprawling campus and a lot of facilities like playgrounds, a new mess and a few new hostels were created. It was nice to see the Academy in such a beautiful shape because it had become home for us. Subsequently I visited the Academy at least four times for short training courses including the one called the Middle Management Course. It was a treat to the eyes seeing the Academy flourish. But I feel the CPWD could have done a much better job with the same expenditure.

The best part of the life at the Academy was the friendship one forged with the fellow probationers. Acquaintances turning into intimacy in 20s or early 30s mean a lot. The confidence of being class I officers of the government and fanning all over the country is a unique privilege of All India services and particularly those services which have an interface with the people. One gets a feeling at a young age that any problem anywhere in the country can be dealt with. When systems are not in place in the government and one feels harassed that even the work which is a matter of right does not get done in the normal course, it definitely becomes a privilege. Unfortunately though, this is regarded as one of the advantages of being a class I officer where your intervention can probably get a job like this done. We may say so many things and talk about the shortcomings including corruption in public life in the developed world, but one thing is indisputable that the activities which impinge on the lives of the people on a day to day basis happen without hassles. Friendships forged at the Academy have withstood the test of time. Some of course became closer for reasons of intellectual predilections, similarity in terms of habits, homogeneity of spouses, etc. They have been a source of strength.

The schedule of the classes at the Academy was rather tough. The subjects taught were Income Tax Law, Wealth Tax and Gift Tax Law, Accounts and other Taxes broadly. Coming from a background with no exposure to these subjects one could not afford not to be attentive in the classes. One had to study for frequent home tests. The entire period of probation was broadly divided in three semesters. At the end of each semester there was a Departmental Examination and it was mandatory to clear the three departmental examinations for confirmation in the service. Those who could not do so at the Academy were given extra chances to clear the examinations later. So broadly the schedule of studies at the Academy was not very busy. I personally found the subject of Accounts very uninteresting.

Young and full of enthusiasm generally, the probationers, however, never missed an opportunity to create moments of fun and merriment. Some fond of alcohol, those interested in billiards and those who were keen lovers of music had their own groups of friends to spend their evenings together. There were a few very good singers among probationers. I, being an ardent lover of music and an unfailing admirer of good singers, became a natural friend to two batchmates, Rajiv Anand from Mumbai and Vishwas Rattan from Haryana. Both were very nice ghazal singers. Rajiv Anand used to leave me spellbound by his rendition of ghazals sung by Mehdi Hassan. It was a great shock and pain to lose Vishwas Rattan who had a cardiac arrest in 2012 while posted in Mumbai. We used to have long music sessions at frequent intervals. I often used to recite poetry of Sahir Ludhianvi and Faiz Ahmed Faiz. They were always appreciative of my small contribution to the musical evenings crafted by their singing talents. Some of us were very keen to be at the sports ground in the evening after the classes. We used to play football in a makeshift ground for the purpose. Badminton was my great love. So weather permitting some of us used to play badminton too. P. C.

Mohanty from Orissa and Ashok Sinha from Bihar were very keen sports persons. Ashok Sinha was a fitness freak. He had by far the best physique in the batch.

A very nice opportunity came for me to speak some time in the month of April, 1985. It was the occasion of what was known as the Probationer's Talk. Probationers were given the option to choose a subject to speak on and they had to face questions from other probationers. I always found occasions of public speaking to be very enjoyable and exciting. I chose the subject 'communalism' because it was highly debated in the national media and I had spoken about it before an intellectually vigilant group of students at JNU. My sources of study on the subject included 'Communalism and the Writing of Indian History'. It is a very stimulating small booklet and deals with communalism having crept in the writing of Indian History. It is authored by the leading historians of ancient, medieval and modern Indian history being Romila Thapar, Harbans Mukhiya and Bipan Chandra respectively. All the three have been professors at JNU and their erudition is formidable. I am a great admirer of all of them. Professor Romila Thapar has been my faculty advisor at JNU. I have learnt a lot from them and they have provided a framework to approach an issue for an analysis. It has substantially added to the intellectual part of my personality and I am grateful to them. I am afraid in other universities in the country this was hardly possible. Professor Thapar had an immaculate expression and I, till date, have not met a comparable speaker. However, I found her a little intolerant in arguments. I could never become her blind follower. The basic flaw in their version of Indian history that I found was that it alienated many Hindus who might otherwise support a secular policy. Obliterating the vast differences between Islam and Hinduism by a stress on syncretism and 'composite culture' drains Indian history of much of its meaning. Their view that communalism took its modern form during the colonial period is tenable but more complex analysis is required than is provided in their writings. The 4th Earl of Minto was called the father of communal electorates for legalising communalism by the Morley-Minto Act in 1909. The All-India Muslim League and the Hindu Mahasabha represented such communal interests, and the Indian National Congress represented an overreaching 'nationalist' vision. However, things changed substantially after 1947. In the changed situation our thought process also needs to change. With a growing population and an assertive minority a fresh look at the issue is required. In my view the abolition of communal parties is essential to curb communalism so that religion and politics can be kept separate. Imparting secular education and banning communal teaching, whether by minority or majority, is also required. Developing the attitude of tolerance towards other religions with the help of mass media is also something on which the government has to be proactive. Loyalty to socio political groups by political parties has to be shunned. Appeasement of minorities for political gains should not receive support of the people. I could speak with conviction in the 'probationer's talk'. It was well received. I had to face an alive audience and face questions which only made me happy. I felt rejuvenated intellectually for the first time after leaving JNU. The fellow probationers were too nice even to congratulate me. It was a day away from Law and Accounts which most of the probationers felt happy about.

Another great occasion to enjoy came in January 1986. The probationers belonging to all Group A services are taken for an Industrial Tour for three weeks which is also called the 'Bharat Darshan'. The tour is roughly for three weeks. The probationers were divided in three groups and one part of the country was to be selected by each group. I chose south-west India. Favourite friends among the probationers were also in the same group. The whole trip is a memory forever. I think so much youthful fun with friends was rarely witnessed in life till then. The added source of confidence was that we were senior officers of the government. The whole trip was funded by the government and we had to contribute a pittance. We visited Mumbai, Pune, Goa, Chennai, Hyderabad, Ooty among other major places. Our train reservations were centrally done. The trip from Goa to Mumbai was by ship. And the trip from Mysore to Ooty was by bus. For me the greatest thing about the trip was that Mridula was always in my thoughts. I used to write a letter to her every day from each place that we visited. It was a wonderful romantic feeling. I became sure during the trip that I was in love. In fact I made a plan in my mind that I was going to tell her that I wanted to marry her immediately after the training period was over. I also planned to meet her parents in this regard. In the Industrial trip we were taken to one corporate organisation's office, mostly the manufacturing premises at each station. We were explained the manufacturing process and how the company was functioning generally. The top functionaries of the company used to talk to us. We were also invited for lunch and the visit concluded with a vote of thanks to the hosts.

There are too many nice memories from the Bharat Darshan. We were all these days thinking that IRS, IAS, etc. were terms everybody would be knowing. To our utter disbelief at Mumbai the driver of the cab in which we were travelling enquired from us about what we were doing. We replied with a vague sense of pride that we belonged to the IRS. His further query was which company it was. It was very disappointing and a bit of a shock too. We realised that the presumption of self-importance was funny and meaningless. A nice moment for me came at Ooty. We visited the premises of the Hindustan Photo Films. Their photographic films are sold under the name 'Indu', which means 'silver' in Sanskrit (silver halides are used in film). We were invited for lunch which was very elaborate and delectable. I was asked by my fellow probationers to offer a vote of thanks. In my brief speech I used the word 'sumptuous' for lunch. The word was liked so much by my batchmate K. M. Prasad that he even now after 35 years mentions this. K. M. Prasad has been a very affectionate friend and recently superannuated as the Member, CBDT. The trip to Ooty from Mysore by bus was very exciting and full of fun. Our friends Rajiv Anand and Vishwas Rattan made the journey memorable by their singing. They sang a song 'Sun Saheba Sun' from the film *Ram Teri Ganga Maili* which we had watched at Nagpur before leaving for the trip. We could not have imagined it could be sung so well. At Goa we had gone for lunch at the restaurant OCoqueiro where Charles Sobhraj, the escaped criminal and serial killer was nabbed by the police. The restaurant had become very famous because of this. Their dish Chicken Cafreal was loved by Charles Sobhraj. It is a wine-marinated chicken dish brought to Goa by East African immigrants. We also had a taste of it. The visit to the Salar Jung Museum at Hyderabad was a great delight. The Salar Jung family is responsible for its collection of rare art objects from all over the world. The family is one of the most illustrious families in Deccan history, five of them having been prime-ministers in the erstwhile Nizam rule of Hyderabad-Deccan. The visit to Raja Dinkar Kelkar Museum also

"Taxation is the price which civilized communities pay for the opportunity of remaining civilised."

–Albert Bushnell Hart

known as Kakasaheb Kelkar museum at Pune was also equally fascinating. The museum has a vast collection of artefacts and more than 21,000 antiquities. The on-the-job training happened in the last quarter of 1985. We were to give preferences for the place and that was to be allotted on the basis of rank in the civil list. I opted for Patna and four officers could only be sent there. I had no problem because I was fairly high in the Civil list being 3rd in the batch. Four of us reached Patna. S. D. Jha, my batchmate was also with me. We were left to fend for ourselves in terms of our stay and food. We stayed at our house at Bakerganj, Patna. The house was occupied by the tenants except the top floor which was a compact small flat. We cleaned the house ourselves and settled there. For our food we used to depend on the nearby restaurants. It was not bad. We were excited because it was the first time after a year of theoretical training we were going to see how the Income Tax Department actually worked in the field. We reported at the Central Revenues Building of Patna and called on the local Commissioner who was a smart and suave person, but he hardly involved himself with us. Within a few minutes he disposed us of. We were to report to officers of the Deputy Commissioner level for our training. One officer was assigned the responsibility of training each one of us. The officer to whom I was supposed to report belonged to the 1979 batch. He gave me a few files and asked me to go through the Profit and Loss Accounts and Balance Sheets, understand and discuss with him after a few days. I did

With Finance Minister Smt. Nirmala Sitaraman at Varanasi (2019)

Outreach Meeting at Noida (2018)

UP (West) surpasses its tax collection target for 2018-19

FEATHER IN THE CAP It is the only income tax region in the country to achieve the collection target

Preety Acharya

NOIDA: The income tax department of Uttar Pradesh (west) has surpassed its target for tax collection for financial year 2018-2019, even as the national target falls short. The target for UP (west) was set at ₹28,855 crore and ₹29,099 crore have been collected as tax during the financial year 2018-19.

The national tax collection target for 2018-2019 was set at ₹12 lakh crore but the government has collected only ₹11.18 lakh crore. The tax collection of ₹29,099 crore was achieved after refunding around ₹7,080 crore. Out of the 19 income tax regions in the country, UP(west) is the only region to achieve its target. Officials said that a total of 91 surveys (raids) were conducted in the region following which an undisclosed income of ₹160 crore was recovered.

"We have been holding meetings with the taxpayers and professionals in the finance world to increase our reach. It is very important to spread awareness on the importance of paying taxes to have a better connection with the taxpayers," Pramod Kumar Gupta, principal chief commissioner of income tax, UP (west) and Uttarakhand, said.

According to senior officials, a total of 26,000 Non-Resident Indians (NRI) and foreign establishments have invested in UP (west) but only 2,600 such people and firms pay tax. The department has been trying to increase its base of international taxation by reaching out to NRIs and firms from abroad who have invested in UP (West).

"We have been trying to reach out to a maximum number of NRIs and firms who have invested in UP (West). The huge gap between the number of registered PAN cards and the actual number of taxpayers in the region has to be reduced. Right now, only 10 percent of the total NRI taxpayers pay taxes," Anupama Anand, Commissioner, International Taxation, said.

UP(WEST) SURGES AHEAD

The national tax collection target for 2018-19 was ₹12 lakh crore but the government has collected only ₹11.18 lakh crore

Taxpayers attend an interactive session with income tax officials on Tuesday. Sunil Ghosh/HT

UP West (2018-2019)

Target	₹28,855cr
Collected	₹29,099cr

91 raids were conducted in the region unearthing undisclosed income of ₹160cr

A total of 26,000 Non-Resident Indians and foreign establishments have invested in UP(West) but only 2,600 such people and firms pay tax

There are over 20 lakh taxpayers in UP(West)

Within Noida (2018-2019)

- The target for Noida was ₹1,005 cr and the department has collected ₹1,014 cr
- Income tax officials had conducted 11 surveys unearthing undisclosed income of ₹23.38 cr
- Legal proceedings have been launched in 28 cases
- 36,218 new assessee have been added
- Approximate 2.5 lakh taxpayers in the district

I-T dept's efforts to reach out to taxpayers prove useful as Noida also crosses target

Preety Acharya

NOIDA: The Income Tax department of Noida has collected ₹1,014 crore tax against the target of ₹1,005 crore for financial year 2018-2019.

According to the officials, the target has been achieved following efforts by the department to reach out to a maximum number of taxpayers.

Officials said they have been organising various events to spread awareness among them.

The income tax officials conducted 11 surveys(raids) in 2018-2019 and following which an undisclosed income detected of ₹23.38 crore was detected.

Officials said that they initiated legal proceedings in at least 28 cases.

According to officials, 36,218 new assessees have been added in the same period.

There are approximately 2.5 lakh taxpayers in the Gautam Budh Nagar district.

The income tax department has reportedly been getting in touch with various gram panchayats, residents welfare associations and trader's associations to spread awareness on the importance of paying tax.

"During such sessions, taxpayers are informed about the importance of paying taxes on time. Taxpayers can also clear their doubts and discuss their issues. Their issues will be resolved on the priority basis that's why we have been trying to reach out to various organizations and resident welfare associations in order to spread awareness," Raju Tayeng, the principal commissioner (assessment), said.

The income tax department held an interactive session with the taxpayers of the Gautam Budh Nagar on Tuesday as well.

Principal chief commissioner of income tax, UP (West) and Uttarakhand and the principal chief commissioner of income tax (Exemptions) Pramod Kumar Gupta along with other senior officials took part in the session.

"We have been focusing on the assessment work to increase the number of taxpayers. We have surpassed our target because we have been trying to get in touch with various sections of the society," Gupta said.

Local residents took part in the session expressed the need for more transparency between the taxpayers and the income tax department.

"We feel that Chartered Accountants and other finance professionals try to misguide us at times, so it will be a great help if we can have better communication and more transparency with the income tax department to avoid any hassle," said Shishir Gautam from the Noida Entrepreneurs Association who attended the session.

Hundreds of residents had attended the session.

Officials had got in touch with various resident welfare associations to spread awareness about the session.

नोटबंदी के दौरान प्रदेश में एक करोड़ से अधिक नगद जमा करने वाले 39 लोगों पर इनकम टैक्स विभाग कसेगा शिकंजा

उत्तराखंड में 414 लोगों ने जमा किए पांच अरब

हिन्दुस्तान /22/3.

देहरादून : वरिष्ठ संवाददाता

नोटबंदी के दौरान उत्तराखंड में 414 लोगों ने पांच अरब रुपये बैंकों में नगद जमा किए। इनमें 39 लोगों ने अभी तक इनकम टैक्स विभाग के नोटिस का जवाब तक नहीं दिया है। इन पर 31 मार्च के बाद आयकर विभाग कार्रवाई की तैयारी कर रहा है।

मुख्य आयकर आयुक्त पीके गुप्ता ने बुधवार को पत्रकारों से बातचीत में यह खुलासा किया। उन्होंने बताया कि उत्तराखंड में नोटबंदी के दौरान ढाई लाख रुपये से ज्यादा बैंक में जमा करने वाले कुल 3255 मामलों में नोटिस जारी किए गए।

इनमें 414 मामले ऐसे पाए गए, जिन्होंने बैंकों में एक-एक करोड़ रुपये नगद की रकम जमा की। 50 लाख से 1 करोड़ रुपये तक नगद जमा करने वालों की संख्या 400 है। जबकि ढाई से 50 लाख रुपये नगद जमा करने वालों की संख्या 2161 है। उन्होंने बताया कि इन सभी की जांच की जा चुकी है। एक करोड़ रुपये से अधिक जमा करने वाले 39 मामले में आयकर को कोई जवाब नहीं मिला है। जबकि ढाई लाख से अधिक जमा करने वाले कई मामलों में नोटिस का जवाब नहीं मिला है। नगद जमा करने वाले 50 फीसदी मामले संदिग्ध हैं। इन मामलों में आयकर विभाग 31 मार्च के बाद कार्रवाई करने जा रहा है।

आयकर विभाग के मुताबिक एक करोड़ रुपये अधिक नगद जमा करने वालों में पेट्रोल पंप संचालक, निजी नर्सिंग होम संचालक, रियल एस्टेट कारोबारियों की संख्या अधिक है। इनके पिछले वर्षों के रिकार्ड के साथ ही नोटबंदी के दौरान नगद लेन-देन के मामलों की जांच की गई। खास बात यह है कि नोटबंदी में नगद जमा करने वालों में 90 फीसदी मामले राज्य के मैदानी क्षेत्रों के हैं।

मुख्य आयकर आयुक्त पीके गुप्ता। • हिन्दुस्तान

- 31 मार्च तक जवाब नहीं देने पर सर्वे और छापों की कार्रवाई करेगा आयकर विभाग
- एक करोड़ रुपये अधिक नगद जमा करने वालों में पेट्रोल पंप संचालक, निजी नर्सिंग होम संचालक शामिल

राज्य में एक लाख नए करदाता

राज्य में पिछले वर्ष के मुकाबले आयकर दाताओं की संख्या 1,03,881 बढ़ी है। पिछले साल राज्य में इनकी संख्या 5,17,940 थी, जो अब 6,21,821 हो गई है। सबसे ज्यादा वृद्धि नॉन कॉरपोरेट सेक्टर में हुई है। यानी आम आयकर दाताओं की संख्या में 16 फीसदी की वृद्धि दर्ज की गई है। मुख्य आयकर आयुक्त पीके गुप्ता ने बताया कि राज्य में 11 हजार करोड़ रुपये का आयकर लक्ष्य था, जिसमें से 10,300 करोड़ रुपये कर के रूप में जमा हो चुके हैं।

सर्वे में सरेंडर हुए 33.61 करोड़

आयकर ने इस साल अक्तूबर के बाद राज्य में 22 सर्वे किए। 12 सर्वे गढ़वाल और 10 कुमाऊं क्षेत्र में हुए। इनमें 33.61 करोड़ की आय घोषित की गई। इस पर 10 करोड़ का टैक्स तय किया गया और चार करोड़ रुपये जमा भी हो चुके हैं। बाकी रकम 31 मार्च तक जमा होने की उम्मीद है।

यूपी निर्माण निगम मामले में जांच पूरी

मुख्य आयकर आयुक्त पीके गुप्ता ने बताया कि यूपी निर्माण निगम से जुड़े [illegible] प्रकरण की जांच पूरी कर दी गई है। मालूम हो कि इस मामले में एक आईएएस अफसर भी जांच के दायरे में आए हैं और इस मामले अफसर को भी नोटिस जारी किया गया है।

अफसरों के क्लब पर आयकर सख्त

नौकरशाहों के क्लब सिविल सर्विसेज संस्थान पर आयकर ने सख्त रुख अपनाया है। मालूम हो कि 'हिन्दुस्तान' ने 6 फरवरी के अंक में 'अफसरों के क्लब ने आयकर बचाने को छूट वाला [illegible]' शीर्षक से रिपोर्ट प्रकाशित कर मामले का खुलासा किया था। मुख्य आयकर आयुक्त पीके गुप्ता ने कहा कि यह मामला अपील में चल रहा है और उन्हें 31 मार्च तक मामले का निस्तारण के लिए पत्र लिखा गया है।

I-T is planning for action against CSR irregularities

I-T commissioner Pramod Kumar Gupta warns in Aurangabad

LOKMAT NEWS NETWORK
AURANGABAD, MAY 6

Many scams are taking place in the name of Corporate Social Responsibility and the Income Tax (I-T) department has concentrated on such rackets. Many people will be trapped in the next six months, said principal chief commissioner of Income Tax Pramod Kumar Gupta in a press conference here on Monday.

The CC was in the city to attend a public relation programme organised by the Institute of Chartered Accountants of India (ICAI) Aurangabad and the Directorate of Exemptions of IT Department. The programme was organised for charity organisations at ICAI Bhawan. Gupta interacted with the media persons after the programme.

He said that at present TDS scam is taking place in the entire country. The department has conducted preliminary survey in Uttarakhand and Uttar Pradesh and 20 more surveys will be conducted. After confirmation, letter will be sent to all the chief ministers through the finance ministry.

The commissioner added that many hospitals inform about expenditure of funds for research and now such information will be

Principal chief commissioner of Income Tax Pramod Kumar Gupta speaking in the public relation programme in Aurangabad. Also present are Ganesh Bhalerao, justice Shrikant Bhosle, Sardar Singh Meena, Rohan Achaliya and Sandeepkumar Salunkhe.

verified. There should be no irregularity and research should be conducted as per the provision. Aurangabad Tax Practitioners Association is going to provide free advice and guidance about the I-T related problems. I-T commissioner (exemption) Pune Sardar Singh Meena, Aurangabad's joint charity commissioner Justice Shrikant Bhosle, additional IT commissioner Sandeepkumar Salunkhe, Aurangabad CA Association chairman Rohan Achaliya, Ganesh Bhalerao were also present.

Tax professionals hold a major responsibility and their participation is very important as they guide people and give them better advise. Progress is impossible without trustworthy balance sheets and we are keeping an eye on every such thing. Everybody should follow his duties, commissioner Gupta appealed.

Only 2,000 trusts file returns

There are in all 70,000 trusts in Marathwada while 30,000 are in Aurangabad. Despite it, only 2,000 trusts were filing their returns. However, after uploading their details on computers and appealing all of them, 7,000 of them were de-registered, informed Shrikant Bhosle.

U'khand collects ₹10k crore as income tax, 10% hike from last financial year

Yogesh Kumar
@timesgroup.com

Dehradun: In the current financial year, the income tax (I-T) department has collected over Rs 10,000 crore — a hike of 10% in comparison to last year. Uttarakhand has also registered 1.3 lakh new taxpayers across the state for the first time after demonetisation and the implementation of GST.

Chief income tax commissioner (Uttarakhand), Pramod K Gupta said that the revenue collection's jump was due to the series of outreach programs carried out in Uttarakhand. "The special focus was on tax widening in Uttarakhand and our department has achieved the figure of over 1.3 lakh that is phenomenal. I hope more people would be added and the revenue collection increases further."

File photo

State has also registered 1.3 lakh new taxpayers this year

Gupta added the revenue collection target of Rs 11,000 would be met within the month end after the last advance tax payments details are received. As of date, he said, Uttarakhand has 6.21 lakh income tax payers, including firms and individuals. Like previous years, the Oil and Natural Gas Company (ONGC)'s share of I-T revenue collected in Uttarakhand, is 69% of the total.

Gupta added that the noncorporate section (individual) revenue collection share is 16.29 %. Gupta said that 22 surveys were carried out in Uttarakhand covering firms and professional. "This year, our teams in Kumaon and Garhwal had detected Rs 33.61 crore undisclosed income and Rs 4 crore penalty was collected," he said.

The IT department continues to scan the details of the bank accounts which had suspicious deposits after the demonetisation in 2016. "In total over 3,255 bank accounts were under the scanner due to the high-value deposits—ranging from Rs 2 lakh to over Rs 1 crore—which are checking as per their ITRs," he said.

As per the conservative estimates, over Rs 400 crore were deposited in different accounts in Uttarakhand after the demonetisation and the IT department's probe into the individual case is underway.

IT dept to maintain close vigil on charitable trusts

TIMES NEWS NETWORK

Aurangabad: Citing that the charitable trusts are falling short in delivering on the expected lines, the income tax department will start maintaining a close watch on charitable trusts across the country.

The senior income tax authorities expressed concern over a huge amount of tax evasion and the misappropriation of funds, with the connivance of corporate houses paying Corporate Social Responsibility (CSR) and the trusts receiving them.

Principal chief commissioner of income tax (exemption), Delhi, Pramod Kumar Gupta said that a lot of the work on the social front that the government fails to do or the government does not have adequate resources and infrastructure for the same, the charitable trusts are expected to do but considering the experience so far, the charitable trusts have failed to deliver on the expected lines, due to which the IT department will be keepig an eye on them.

Senior income tax officers organized an outreach program on Monday at ICAI Bhavan and was chaired by Principal Chief Commissioner of income tax (exemption), Delhi, Shri Pramod Kumar Gupta, who has jurisdiction over Trusts, Charitable Institutions and NGOs across India. The programme was attended by the Commissioner of income tax (Exemption), Pune, Sardar Singh Meena and was attended by the Joint Charity commissioner, Aurangabad, Justice Bhosale.

The authorities said that in Aurangabad division alone, during the previous fiscal, the IT department recovered Rs60 crores in income tax from different charitable trusts.

In Maharashtra alone, there are about lakh registered charitable trusts and organizations, of which only a few thousand pay income tax, which is something to worry about, said Gupta, while warning of initiating stringent action against the tax-evading organizations.

The authorities said that due to a series of actions against the charitable trusts evading taxes, during the last one year, 2,500 more charitable trusts have filed their income tax returns.

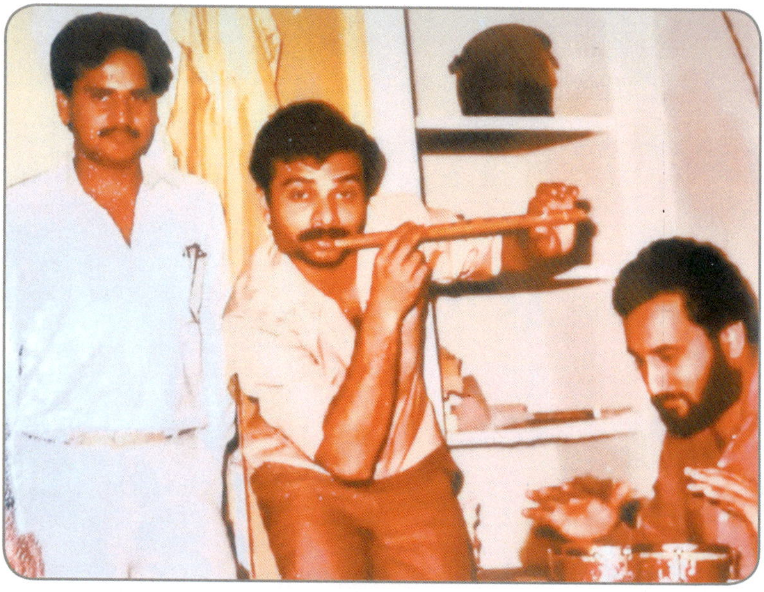

With S.K. Sandhu, IAS (with beards) and A.K. Chauhan, IRS (with flute) in fun moments at the Academy

Outreach Meeting at Deharadun (2017)

Visit to Bajpur, Uttarakhand (2017)

With Swami Chidananda Saraswati of Parmarth Niketan, Rishikesh (2018)

Outreach Meeting at Deharadun (2017)

In the Conference Room at Deharadun (2017)

Outreach Meeting at Kanpur (2019)

At Kanpur (2019)

Outreach Meeting at Barelly (2018)

that. But he was a happy go lucky man and was hardly interested in any academic input to be imparted to me. In fact he asked me to enjoy the next two months and said that it was not a rocket science and that everything could be understood in a matter of days once we were posted after the theoretical inputs at the Academy. I immediately decided to devote the next two months to other issues in life. In fact he also told me not to worry about coming to the office every day and I could go anywhere I wanted. My greatest priority and obsession those days was Mridula. I made a couple of trips to Bhagalpur during that period and met her. We were maturing in our love. In my mind I was planning to get married once I finally came from the Academy towards the end of May 1986. In nutshell the training at Patna was an eventless affair. Even S. D. Jha made frequent trips to his hometown Saharsa in North Bihar.

We came back from Patna to Nagpur. After a few days our Bharat Darshan started. Sometime towards the end of January 1986 we were back to the Academy for the last phase of the training. It was till the end of May. The last phase of the training was slightly more devoted to studies because it was preferable to clear all the departmental examinations before leaving the Academy. Many including me, however, cleared all the departmentals much later. The stressful times started when the time for final postings came closer. However, most got postings of their choice, particularly those who had opted for Metropolitan stations like Mumbai, Delhi, Chennai and Kolkata. Problem was with non-metro stations like Patna. There were 17 officers from Bihar in the batch and 10 wanted to go there. Eight out of ten were in the first twenty itself. I had no issue on this score because I was at No. 1 from Bihar. Stress was caused only when it was rumoured that there was not even one vacancy in Bihar and nobody could be posted there. Finally the orders came and four of us got Bihar posting. We had to report at our places of posting at the end of May.

We said goodbye to the Academy and to our friends. It was a tearful goodbye. The time spent at the Academy was one of the most cherishable times of our life. It is apparently unbelievable that we have superannuated from Service now. Time really travels fast. Times leave a host of issues and experiences to reflect upon. The memories of Nagpur are an inseparable part of our life. Although the Academy itself was self-contained we used to move out to the town sometimes. Nagpur was a cordial place and the market places at Sadar, Sitabuldi and Dharampeth were nice with varieties of shops and restaurants. Nagpur is famous for oranges and we used to get the best varieties at cheap prices. But even the best of times has to come to an end. So was it for our Nagpur times.

I reached Patna on the 31st of May 1986 and applied for leave for a month because I had to make arrangements for my marriage on the 15 June and after that I had a plan to go to Kashmir for a week. Although I hated it, having lost my father I had become fiercely independent in decision making for my personal affairs. There is no greater bliss than the protection of a father and dependence on him. Nobody can be more bothered about your welfare than your parents. They are the greatest well-wishers of yours. It does not matter even if you have to argue with them to drive home your point. I missed my father with a gnawing feeling when the occasion for my marriage came. I did seek my elder brother's approval for marriage with Mridula. He had initial reservations for an intercaste marriage for which he had his arguments. But he relented soon. The rest of the world did not matter. My mother, not in the best of health, and my elder sister had no objection. My younger sister was positively happy. Mridula was an ideal girl in her view. From Mridula's side the family was too modern and liberal in outlook on these issues. One dialogue from Mridula while talking to her mother was enough to settle the issue. The dialogue was 'if you insist I can marry anybody, but if you want to see me happy, I will marry only Pramod.' The preparations for the great day for me, i.e. the 15th June started.

The first saddening, rather shocking, news came from the Central Revenues Building, Patna, most probably on the 17th June. I was posted to a place called Darbhanga. It was a little surprising too because I was under the impression that it was at a very few small towns and cities that there were posts for IRS officers. In fact that was one of the reasons also for me to opt for the IRS in preference to IPS and a few other services. Anyways I acted stoic and decided not to spoil my post marriage upbeat mood. I thought of meeting the Commissioner, Patna after the expiry of my leave. Those days our initial designation was not Assistant Commissioner of Income Tax. It used to be Income Tax Officer, Group A as against Income Tax officers who were Group B officers and became officers on promotion from Inspectors. So I was posted as Income Tax Officer, Group A, Darbhanga.

After the trip of a lifetime covering Srinagar, Pahalgam and Gulmarg I came back to Delhi and stayed there for two days meeting a few close friends. I wanted Mridula to meet them. We came back to Bhagalpur and then to Kahalgaon in about 15 days. My sanctioned leave had expired. I wrote requesting an extension for 15 days. Although we have seen places including foreign countries and travelled extensively during the last 36 years, the memories of the first Kashmir trip with Mridula are the most cherishable. We had started our life together. We were at the best of our youth. I still remember the excitement of Mridula on the flight from Delhi to Srinagar. The breeze everywhere in the valley was intoxicating. The rains at Gulmarg and getting wet by the droplets were unforgettable sources of pleasure. The long Shikara rides in the Dal lake at Srinagar were pleasures you can derive only in Kashmir and at no other place in the world. I have been to Kashmir so many times after 1986. The population explosion has changed it beyond recognition and for the worse.

Mridula went back to Bhagalpur. I came to Patna. I met the commissioner and spoke about my disappointment with the posting. He was hardly sympathetic. He told me that Darbhanga was a good posting and many big cases, particularly of Trusts of the Darbhanga Maharaja family were there for assessment which could be done only by a class I officer. He also told me that once those assessments are over, I will be brought to Patna. I understood he just wanted to avoid me. I have not been able to understand why the senior officers in the bureaucracy cannot be patient and cordial with their junior colleagues. Agreeing or not agreeing to their request is a separate issue altogether. I realised within a few minutes that it was not worth wasting time with him. I was thoroughly dejected.

I left for Darbhanga the next day. I took a bus. On the way was Muzaffarpur where the Additional Commissioner, then called the Inspecting Assistant Commissioner was based and he was the reporting authority for the Income Tax Officer, Darbhanga. I thought it was better to call on him. I broke my journey at Muzaffarpur and went to the Income Tax office. The Inspecting Assistant Commissioner was Mr Jagdish Jha of the 1967 batch. He was known to be a man of high integrity. I sent my slip and he instantly called me. His spacious room was full of officers. He was having tea with them. I was headed for a cultural shock. I greeted him in English to which he said that I should be speaking in Hindi. I love Hindi and I have equal command over Hindi. I found his remarks absolutely unwarranted because, in any case, English was the link language for any All India Service. For the next one hour that I was with him I only spoke in Hindi. He was otherwise very nice and gave me a lot of tips relevant for the job at Darbhanga. He was too courteous to get me dropped at the bus stop in his car. I reached Darbhanga in the next two hours. The local inspectors were there to receive me. They took me to a guesthouse. I went to sleep early to go to the office in the morning for my first day. The office at Darbhanga was in a building of the Maharaja of Darbhanga which was purchased by the Income Tax Department. It had a huge campus. My chamber was fairly big with an attached toilet which had fixtures from London. After all it was a Darbhanga Maharaja property. I may mention that the Maharaja of Darbhanga was not a native state and it was only a Zamindari but its annual revenues were more than that of any native state. The first day at office was spent in meeting the staff members and familiarising myself with the jurisdiction and the workload of the office. There was another Group B Income Tax Officer also posted at Darbhanga. The campus had trees of fruits like Mango and Jackfruit. The night guard of the office used to take care of the plants and trees. I was told that some eminent citizens of the town had sought an appointment to make a courtesy call tomorrow. I asked my office staff to call each one of them.

The next day was spent in meeting eminent citizens of Darbhanga. It was quite an eye opener to listen to the varieties of harassment that people faced. The most potent source of harassment those days used to be issuance of Income Tax refunds and delivering it to the assessee. Refund vouchers signed by the officer used to be lying undelivered in the almirah of the concerned Tax Assistant for months and negotiated for consideration. The only way to minimise the nuisance was to issue refunds chronologically and monitor dispatch by Speed Post every week. I did that. Those were days when there was no limit to the number of cases which could be scrutinised. Unscrupulous assessees, in connivance with the staff, used to ensure that their Returns are never brought to the notice of the officer. These were broadly the major issues that required attention to create a clean image of the Department.

Darbhanga is not a very small town as such. It's a divisional headquarter. It has a famous medical College. The doctors have a flourishing practice there. There are patients from Nepal in large numbers. Naturally some of the doctors are the highest taxpayers and some high earners are big tax evaders too. The Income Tax Department at Darbhanga is supposed to keep a close watch on medical professionals. One doctor Suniti Sinha was the leading gynaecologist those days with huge incomes. She was paying huge taxes too. But somehow she was subjected to a lot of enquiries by my predecessor and she felt unjustly harassed.

In Darbhanga there was a beautiful place called the PTC (Postal Training Centre), Bela. It was located inside the Darbhanga Maharaja main Campus. It had a beautiful garden with a collection of wide varieties of flowers. It was a delight to go there during the daytime in winters. Darbhaga had an airfield too with a senior air force officer stationed. For some time a senior of mine from college was posted there and I visited the place and could not believe that Darbhaga could have such a maintained and beautiful place. In the Darbhanga Maharaja main campus in which the local university known as the Lalit Narayan Mithila University was housed, there was a famous, beautiful and ancient temple of Goddess Kali. The place was serene.

Times flew. Although I had gone to Darbhanga with resentment inside me but it was by and large enjoyable. I enjoyed my time at the office learning the job. I always felt thankful to destiny for the fact that at a young age I was the senior most officer there of a very important wing of the government. It was a good interactive exposure with senior officers of other wings of governance. I of course felt let down by the department because there were no decent infrastructural facilities for the residence of officers and staff. As I was staying alone I had taken a decent flat in a nice residential locality. My mother-in-law had sent a boy to take care of my food etc. I had made the physical life quite comfortable. Going to Bhagalpur every week and Mridula also coming to Darbhanga sometimes made times pass by smoothly. But it was one and a half years now and that was enough of a comparatively small town. I was desperate to move to Patna. Suddenly one fine day I received a call from the Chief Commissioner for Bihar and Jharkhand, a post created recently. He was Mr. S. B. Lall whose style of conversation was quite stylish and impressive. He asked me a few job related questions. I have reasons to believe he got fairly impressed and he asked me to meet him at Patna. Next day I was there where I requested him for my transfer to Patna. He immediately obliged. So after an emotional farewell I was at Patna next week. I have no regrets in retrospect about the Darbhanga posting. After all that small station gave me first exposure towards the actual and practical aspects of assessment making, Income Tax surveys and handling human relations at the workplace.

Mridula now took a transfer to Patna Medical College. She was in the last phases of her house surgeonship. There was a residential facility at Patna but I chose to be closer to Patna Medical College because Mridula used to have night duties. So we took a house on rent at Rajendranagar, Patna. That is a comparatively nicer residential area in Patna. That served another purpose for her. She, besides her duties at the Medical College Hospital, started working for a few hours with Dr Usha Didwania, a senior gynaecologist whose Nursing Home was close to our house. Life had found a nice pattern.

At Patna I was first posted in a Circle (as it is called) where assessments of search cases are done. It was called an Investigation Circle. It is supposed to be a tough posting because it involves perusal of papers seized during a search. The assessee is then to be confronted with these papers and if need be their statements are to be recorded. It is only after proper appraisal of relevant facts emanating from the search in the form of papers and assets found and seized that the assessment of income is finalised and an assessment order passed. In search cases an order is initially required to be passed for retention of the assets seized. A very well-known case that had come before me was that of K. M. Prasad and T. M. Prasad and others who later came to be known as animal husbandry mafias. They were the kingpins of the fodder scam in which the Chief Minister was later convicted. I enjoyed the posting although it involved care, attention and hard work. A very sought after post at our level of seniority used to be that of Assistant Director of Investigation. There were three posts of Assistant Directors at Patna who held concurrent jurisdiction over the entire state of Bihar. The responsibility of the Assistant Directors was to select cases fit for search as per law and process them. The approval for search had to be obtained from the Director of Income Tax (Investigations) who used to be based at Kanpur. In fact the Director at Kanpur used to hold jurisdiction over the entire UP and Bihar which was undivided at that time. There was no Jharkhand.

My posting at the Investigation Circle lasted for a year. One Mr. M. N. Tiwari had taken over as the Chief Commissioner of Income Tax. He was generally known to be a person of high integrity. His command over the English language was extraordinary. Armed with an impeccable language he was rather tough in his dealings with officers. He met each young officer one by one for reasons best known to him. After a few days I was suddenly transferred as the Assistant Director of Income Tax (Investigation). At that stage of career it was something to feel good about. The other two officers posted there were Mr. Vinodanand Jha and Mr. Shishir Sinha. They were a batch senior to me. They were excellent colleagues and in course of time they became best of friends. That continues till date. We had an excellent understanding and we did every sensitive work with mutual consultation and with highest confidentiality. They, as senior colleagues, deserved respect. They commanded it. Our team became very famous in Patna. We were formidable among the tax evaders. We never compromised on personal integrity. Official infrastructure those days was not like it is today, nevertheless we had vehicles in the Investigation Wing. We never misused this. We used to come to the office in our personal Maruti 800 cars. It was very exciting to drive a Maruti Gypsy at that age but we mostly used it for reconnaissance when we needed to go out of Patna. This discipline on our part was appreciated in the Department.

The first experience of mine of a major search operation was that of the coal mafia searches as the press called it. The search was planned from Kolkata but it was an All

India affair because the businesses of the assessees were spread all over the country. It involved the famous (rather notorious) Dhanbad based persons like Surajdeo Singh, Sakaldeo Singh, Naurangdeo Singh and many others. As they were dreaded people we had to take extra measures for the safety of the search teams. Several contingents of the paramilitary forces were requisitioned for the purpose. On the date of search I was deputed to proceed to Sakaldeo Singh's ancestral house in Arhupur village in Chhapra district of Bihar. I had to start very early in the morning to ensure I reached there by 8 a.m. which was the time that was decided to strike for search at every place across the country. I was accompanied by at least 15 civilian officers and officials and two buses full of constabulary drawn mostly from the paramilitary forces. People on the way in the four hours' long journey were looking at our vehicles with a sense of amazement. I was personally feeling like leading a force as military commanders must be doing. At the place of search, however, we did not get anything meaningful. Even Sakaldeo Singh was not there as he was at Dhanbad. After the initial search I was assigned the task of searching all the bank lockers of the Group which were sealed on the day of search. Every week after the initial searches for the next three months I used to visit Dhanbad for the search of the lockers. I used to requisition local inspectors at Dhanbad and go to the bank. The assessees were informed well in advance to be present at the bank on the date fixed. Two interesting encounters come to my memory. In one instance a lot of letters were found in the locker. The person being searched, normally a dreaded mafia, sought my time to talk to him privately for 5 minutes. I graciously granted. It came out that all those letters were from a woman he was having an extra marital affair with. He requested not to seize those letters. I told him not to worry because we were interested only in tax evasion. I had a look at the letters and did not seize. He was visibly grateful. In the case of another locker belonging to another dreaded person of the Group the story was amusing in a different manner. First of all he was supposed to be so dangerous and unpredictable that the Dhanbad Superintendent of Police was personally present for our safety and security. Some Fixed Deposit Receipts were found in the locker for which he had no source to explain. In reply to my telling him that the investment in the FDRs would be treated as unexplained and would be brought to tax. His query in his colloquial Hindi was 'what happens if the tax is not paid'. I explained to him that the Income Tax Department had enormous powers and his assets like his car could be attached. He smiled and said he had no car and the ones he was using belonged to the Bharat Coking Coal Limited, the Dhanbad based subsidiary of Coal India Limited. I next told him that his house could be attached. His carefree reply again was that he had no house and the ones he had were captured from others. He had similar replies on assets. He then enquired whether he could be arrested. I told him we could do that through the court of law. Then he was a little crestfallen. I explained to him the provisions of law and also regarding the disclosure in the course of a search. I told him it was not worthwhile to get into prolonged litigation and it was better to make a disclosure. The FDR was in any case going to be seized till a final adjudication and the payment of due taxes. He was thankful to me for explaining everything so well. He preferred to make a disclosure. I recorded his statement accordingly. Later my seniors congratulated me for this.

The searches processed at Patna were by and large successful but not very high in terms of seizure of assets. I won many admirers including among those searched by me. It was because I always kept in mind that I was primarily a public servant and that I had to exercise the authority vested in me by law with humility. I had this considered feeling that there was black money in traditional businesses but its quantum was not high. It was basically a city of traders and there is a limitation of unaccounted money in trading. Big businesses based on large scale manufacturing did not exist in Patna. At the same time there was black money which could be seen in the city in the form of palatial buildings and the latest models of cars. Basically most of it was amassed through white collared jobs. The corruption in the government was the major source. Once the Director General (Investigation) had visited from Delhi. At that time there used to be only two DGs in the country, one in the North and the other in the South. I had driven him through the city and showed the posh colonies to him. I later told him that most of the imposing buildings belonged to the bureaucrats and the politicians. The Engineers of the state government were also important custodians of ill-gotten and unaccounted money. He apparently appreciated and agreed with all that I said. Next morning I brought before him a case for approval for search. It involved two senior bureaucrats, one politician and a businessman in nexus. He agreed with me in principle but refused to give an authorisation for search. His argument was that I was too young and enthusiastic and that we should avoid controversies. I understood what he wanted to convey. It was a very disappointing experience very early in the service.

A very interesting part of Patna posting was frequent visits to 6, Bailey Road,- the official residence of the Chief Commissioner. One Mr D. B. Lal had come on posting for a very short tenure from Delhi. He was very fond of calling young officers for a game of Badminton followed by nice snacks which he used to carry from Delhi. He invariably offered drinks also. Till the time he was there we used to go to 6, Bailey Road at least thrice a week. We had developed emotional attachment with the place. It was the most sprawling bungalow in Patna and most of the senior IAS officers and even the politicians used to feel envious of the Chief Commissioner of Income Tax on this score.

Patna was a very enjoyable tenure of posting. It has been my city in any case. There were so many friends and acquaintances. Relatives kept visiting. Besides my salary I was also using the rent derived from our house in Bakerganj which was over and above Mridula's stipend. We used to feel rich. Mridula was with me. Both my sons were born while posted at Patna. Mridula, however, went to Bhagalpur to her mother for delivery. In 1992 I became due for transfer having completed more than 5 years in the Charge.

From the month of April, 1992 the stress of a possible transfer started. One day the Chief Commissioner Mr. M. N. Tiwari called me suo motto in this regard. He was too nice in his concern. He suggested that I went to Dhanbad on the post of Assistant Director (Investigation) which was a very important post. He also told me that in his view Dhanbad was the next important place after Mumbai so far as the generation of black money was concerned. To use his expression, 'black money lay by the wayside in Dhanbad and it needed an honest and intelligent officer to tap it'. He also said that he had applied his mind and chosen me. I felt flattered, rather genuinely happy. It was an honour for me. I already had thought of Dhanbad. With coal mining, Coal trading and coal transportation and innumerable dependent business activities the scale of the potential for black money was fathomless there. There was corruption at a very large scale in the Bharat Coking Coal Limited, the Dhanbad based subsidiary of

Coal India Limited. At that time the senior most officer of the Income Tax Department at Dhanbad was the Deputy Commissioner of Income Tax (now re-designated as the Additional Commissioner) and the next in seniority was the Assistant Director of Income tax (Investigation) only. Moreover, the ADIT (Investigation) was the teeth of the Department so far as evasion was concerned. So it was feared more. The post needed a law bound officer with humility in behaviour to reassure people that the honest will never be harassed and the dishonest will not be spared. I found the proposition of going to Dhanbad challenging. But I had to think of Mridula's career also which was always a source of pride for me.

There was some good turn of events. The Coal India Limited had advertised for recruitment of Medical officers which included Bharat Coking Coal Limited also. Mridula appeared for an interview and was selected. She was posted at Dhanbad too. In the meantime my order of transfer to Dhanbad was also passed. I was, however, asked to complete the reports, appraisal report as we used to call it, in respect of a couple of searches carried out by me. Mridula was required to join by a particular date. So she went to Dhanbad before me and joined. I of course went with her. Arrangements for her stay were made at the Jagjivannagar guest house of Bharat Coking Coal Limited. It was a beautiful guesthouse by all standards. An army of inspectors posted with the ADIT was there to take care. I came back to Patna, finished my pending official work and proceeded to Dhanbad to join, I still remember, on the 6th of November 1992.

At Dhanbad the ADIT had a big bungalow for residence allotted by the BCCL. In my absence it was painted as my predecessor had vacated it long back. The bungalow was nice and in the beginning of a career in the IRS one normally didn't get such a big house. It was located in the Jagjivannagar area which was one of the two nice colonies of the BCCL, the other being Koylanagar. The major hospital of BCCL was also located in Jagjivannagar known as the Central Hospital. It was a big hospital with a huge flow of referred patients from other hospitals in the collieries. Mridula was posted initially for a few months in the Kustore Colliery Hospital and then was transferred to the Central Hospital till she was in the BCCL. It was in the vicinity of our house although she was given a vehicle too to commute. Before I start recalling the professional issues at Dhanbad I am reminded of two interesting incidents. The first happened on the day I reached Dhanbad. It so happened that a cooking gas connection was required to be transferred from Patna to Dhanbad. I had requested one of my inspectors to contact the local dealer of Indane and request for that. In any case it should have been done before we shifted to the house, which we planned to do on the day I arrived. Mridula, a few days before I came to Dhanbad finally, had called me to say that she had revived a young boy who had suffered a snakebite. When the boy was brought to the hospital he was in a bad shape and the parents were looking at the doctor with the last hope. Mridula told me that with the assistance of the ward boys and after an hour of work the patient could be resuscitated. The parents were extremely grateful in words and the father introduced himself as the local Indane dealer. Mridula recalled that her gas connection was required to be transferred. She made a request to him without referring to me. He immediately said it would be done the next day. And then he vanished and never showed his face. I had told my inspector that I would like the gas connection to be installed at my house before I came. I reached Dhanbad on the appointed date by train in the morning. My staff members had come to receive me at the station. I reached home with Mridula. I saw that a gentleman also came in some time in his car with a jeep following in which there were gas cylinders. He was the dealer of Indane and otherwise a big businessman with diversified business activities. Mridula came in some time and he was visibly embarrassed seeing her. She reminded him that she had requested for her gas connection which he forgot. He was too apologetic. I just told him that he needed to reflect whether a doctor who, toiling for an hour, saved his son from a likely death was important or an officer who could perhaps trouble his misusing his authority. He was speechless. The incident was a great eye opener about human values and the scant regard people could have for those who served as against those who had a nuisance value, real or imaginary.

Another incident that I recall and which I feel is worth mentioning is the one that relates to the Superintendent of Police, Dhanbad. The SP, Dhanbad was a senior from college and fairly well-known to me. But neither he knew my wife nor my wife knew him. There was a massive road accident near Dhanbad in which a bus had slipped into a river. More than 50 persons had died and the victims were rushed to the Central Hospital by whatever mode of transport possible. A massive crowd had gathered at the hospital. Mridula was on duty and was struggling to save as many as she could. The hospital was receiving phone calls every 10-15 minutes from the SP's office enquiring about the number of victims likely to be saved. The SP wanted to speak to the doctor. Mridula asked the telephone operator to reply that the doctor was too busy with the patients and the SP, if he was keen to get information, should visit the hospital and avoid wasting precious time of the doctor. The life of the victims was more important. For the SP probably this was an unexpected response from a doctor. Next day the SP told me about the bold doctor who did not even bother to talk on the phone. I told him she was my wife and she was only bothered about her work. She never mixed priorities.

Dhanbad was definitely a more sensitive place than Patna. I was the only officer in the investigation. The workload was substantial. The stakes for the tax evaders were high. My reporting officer was the Deputy Director sitting at Ranchi. He was one Mr. Tarkeshwar Singh of the 1976 batch. He was a man of integrity. A man of few words, his job knowledge was of a very high level. Ranchi had three Assistant Directors. The Director was based at Kanpur who held jurisdiction over the entire UP and Bihar. He was one Dr. P. P. Lakkar whose integrity was beyond question. In fact he was an example in all that combined character and professional competence. He had tremendous command over Hindi language.

I was called by Dr. Lakkar to Kanpur one day for some discussion. He had a long discussion with me. I was surprised to find that he had so much information about Dhanbad and even very confidential ones. He reposed tremendous trust in me and told me that he was waiting for me to come to Dhanbad to hand over a file to me. The file was related to one Ramesh Gandhi of Dhanbad. He was fairly well known there. He was alleged to have amassed huge money through illegal coal mining and coal trading in benami names. He was known to be maintaining contacts with the highest authorities to the lowest in the coal industry from Delhi to Kolkata and from Ranchi to Dhanbad. From the Coal Minister to the last peon of the office,- all were on the pay rolls of Mr. Gandhi, it was alleged. The Director told me that he had a reason to feel that discreet enquiries in his case had probably leaked last year and, therefore, he had shelved the matter. Now that enough time had gone by he wanted me to take the enquiries to a logical conclusion and find the extent of truth contained in the allegations and discuss with him in a month's time. He was such a just person that he told me that I should not be carried away by the apparent gravity of the allegations and I should not have any bias. He also advised me that he had allegedly a nexus with the police and, therefore, I should avoid interactions with the Dhanbad Police and never utter his name before them including the SP, Dhanbad and even the IG of Police at Ranchi.

Another issue that he discussed with me was regarding an officer, pretty junior. He had information that he used to assume the role of other officers including that of the ADIT (Investigation) and misused information collected from his office to blackmail the assessees for personal gain. He was very close to the local Deputy Commissioner, the head of the Dhanbad administration and that connection also needed to be seen for the possibility of misuse. He wanted me to talk to him and give a report to him in a month's time. With two responsibilities assigned, I came back to Dhanbad.

About the officer I found substance in the allegations. I called him and spoke to him. Then I gave him a letter requesting for his clarification on certain activities on his part which impinged on the functioning of the ADIT (Investigation). He never responded. About Mr Gandhi I made discreet enquiries at Dhanbad and Kolkata. The enquiries prima facie substantiated the allegations of benami activities in coal trading on a large scale. His nexus with the bigwigs of the coal industry did not need much of enquiry as it was common knowledge. He was a favourite even of the coal minister. Many lower officials of the Coal India Limited treated him like a great benefactor. His prosperity was palpable for a place like Dhanbad as reflected by his house and the number of cars. I wrote a long Note, called the Satisfaction Note, and came to Kanpur for a discussion with the Director. About the officer, I also prepared a report which was not very kind to him. I had also told the officer what I was going to write with which he was apparently unhappy. I did not want to create any problem for him but I had to be truthful. The Director, on the basis of my report, spoke to the Central Board of Direct Taxes and he was transferred to Kolkata. That was not a big punishment as such but he carried a grudge for years against me. He in fact tried to trouble me in different ways. It was a lesson for me in the beginning of my career itself that it was so important to keep your defences in place even for the right things done. Unfortunately though these are unwarranted stresses being a part of the government.

About Mr. Ramesh Gandhi's enquiries, the Director was in complete agreement with me. He suggested that I added one or two paragraphs more in the Satisfaction Note just in case the High Court called for the file in case of a Writ filed by the assessee. I came to know for the first time that our confidential files could become a subject for scrutiny by the High Court also. The Director approved the Note and gave authorisations for search. Five premises were to be searched, some were to be surveyed and if some more searches were required consequential warrants could be obtained from the Deputy Director which the law provided. With all the required briefing and words of caution he said good bye to me. He also mentioned that it could be the most important search carried out by me. It actually turned out to be so later, for mixed reasons.

I came back to Dhanbad and started planning to execute the search. I decided upon the date as February 12, 1993. Officers and officials were requisitioned from the Ranchi Charge. Two Assistant Directors from Ranchi came to assist me. My predecessor at Dhanbad also came from Ranchi who, besides being a batch mate, was a nice personal friend. I strategised and requisitioned the police force from the neighbouring district Bokaro and not from Dhanbad. Adequate number of rooms were reserved in the hotels at Bokaro for the stay of the search teams. It was to ensure that at Dhanbad people should feel that there was no activity by the Income Tax Department there. From Bokaro it is about an hour's drive to Dhanbad. All the search teams were dispatched to Bokaro by the previous evening. They were told the next morning that it was going to be a very long drive and, therefore, they should sleep early. Next morning, i.e. on the 12th February, the search teams were dispatched at 6 a.m. and the strike time was fixed for 7 a.m. They were amused when they found they were moving towards Dhanbad. The teams, however, were told the names and addresses of the persons to be searched only minutes before the destination. At the main residence it was my predecessor who was leading the team duly assisted by an ADIT of Ranchi. The searches were being monitored by the Director at Kanpur. I was moving through different premises. To the best of my memory one factory premises and three offices besides the residence were searched. Mr Ramesh Gandhi was a first generation businessman. I met him for the first time. He was quite shocked that there could be a search at his place. He was, however, very suave and spoke reasonably good English. Lot of documents were found at different places which confirmed tax evasion and also his nexus with politicians, coal India bigwigs and the police. I had informed the SP, Dhanbad also that we were searching a few places and we needed police personnel. He was quite surprised that we had not made any requisition from Dhanbad initially. The searches were very successful, in terms of seizure of documents and by the quantum of disclosure. After midnight I recorded his comprehensive statement and he made a disclosure of one crore rupees. That was the highest disclosure in a search in Bihar at that time.

The search next day was prominently covered in the local newspapers. Generally it had brought a good name to the department. Ramesh Gandhi had developed an image of invincibility vis-à-vis the law enforcement agencies. Seeing the general reactions of the people in office and in Dhanbad generally, I was feeling I had done something good by searching the Group. But in any case I had to be bound by law and act without any bias. The post search investigations and the searches of the lockers sealed and placed under prohibitory orders had to be completed. So after a couple of days for next few days Shri Ramesh Gandhi had to be served with a summon for attending my office. My interrogations and queries on relevant questions used to last for 3-4 hours every day. I soon started getting a feeling that he was not bothered much about the taxes to be paid by him but by the papers seized which contained names of Coal India and Police officials and the politicians. I later discreetly gathered some information that the officials, many of them of a very high level of seniority, were putting pressure on him to get rid of the papers. They were mortally afraid that the Income Tax Department or worse still, the CBI, might start enquiries against them. Getting rid of papers was obviously not possible. I think he could not withstand the pressure on him anymore. Worse still the local SP, CBI was a batch mate and friend who used to visit my office and that was enough to add to apprehensions. In fact he had challenged CBI successfully in some cases at the High Court. This was an additional reason for his apprehensions.

The day which was going to take us by an unimaginable surprise and shock also arrived. In the morning of 6th March 1992 I received a call from the neighbour of our office building that the first floor of the office building was burning. The office of the ADIT (Investigation) was not located in the main Central Revenue Building but in a separate far off building. The first floor had the office of the ADIT. I immediately took my car and collected two of my inspectors on the way and reached the office in next 15 minutes. It must have been 6.30 in the morning. It was an eerie feeling that I got once I reached there. The building in-charge was the Tax Recovery Officer whose office was on the Ground floor. He had no phone at home. I sent somebody to bring him to office. Over phone I informed the Director and the Deputy Director. The Deputy Director came from Ranchi by the evening. The Director also arrived by the next day by Rajdhani Express. I also informed the DC and the SP immediately. I thought it proper to call the SP, CBI also and I did that. The DC and the SP, CBI came in next half an hour. The SP did not come. It was unbelievable that a government office could be burnt with such vengeance. I wanted to tell the SP that among the regular recipients of bribe was listed the Joraphatak Thana also in whose jurisdiction my office was located. After some time somebody came to inform that the SP was requesting me to come to his house to discuss the matter. The DC also asked me to get in touch with the SP. I had little to think till my bosses came.

The Deputy Director and the Director who arrived next morning took a stock of the situation. Then they spoke to me one to one. I was also told that he was advised by the CBDT to satisfy himself whether there was any lapse on my part. The Director was convinced that the whole incident was a brazen act of criminality. Any government official could not have helped it. He told me to not to worry and give him a few hours to suggest future course of action.

During the day he again called me. He had probably spoken to the CBDT in the meantime. He was very sympathetic to me and told me that the CBDT would like to post me to place of my choice in case I was feeling scared after the incident of arson in the office. He asked me to talk to my wife and get back to him. He, however, said that it was a heroic and exemplary search that was carried out and that the CBDT would be happy if I continued at Dhanbad and reconstructed the findings during the searches on the basis of memory. He said the original papers having been destroyed by fire it will require painstaking efforts to reconstruct the case on the basis of memory and then information would have to be collected from the agencies. I told him I would take up the challenge. With such seniors' support and encouragement it was only befitting. An FIR with the Police was to be lodged immediately. It was done in the presence of the SP. My main statement in the FIR lodged in Hindi was "since it is the Gandhi Group whose documents mainly have been destroyed, and the persons of the group are going to be the greatest beneficiaries of the destruction of papers and documents I have reasons to suspect that they only would have set fire to the office". The police could hardly do anything concrete during the next two months and Ramesh Gandhi kept absconding. The Deputy Director and the Director stayed at Dhanbad for two days. They patted me before leaving. It was very supportive and affectionate of them. Before leaving my Director also visited Ranchi to meet the IG of Police. He had met the SP at Dhanbad and he had a rather poor opinion of him. We had a disappointing meeting with the IG too. His repeated question was why we were not taking care of our office security when we were carrying out such sensitive operations. Ultimately I took the Director's permission to reply to this. I told the IG that it was from the same office from which we have been carrying out searches for years and only recently the dreaded coal mafia of Dhanbad was searched. Whether the security of the office was adequate or not was something to be seen by the senior officers of the Department. It was the duty of the police to see how a government office could be set on fire which must have taken hours. What was the police force at the station in the vicinity doing? The IG, although not very happy with what I said, did not have much to say.

I got a summon under section 131 of the Income Tax Act served on Shri Ramesh Gandhi for compliance after 15 days. I was told nobody was found at his residential address. The Summon was, therefore, served by affixture. After 15 days there was no compliance. I got another Summon served by affixture in which I directed that compliance should be made whenever the notice is seen subject to maximum of three months. Lastly he appeared after two months. He was arrested and had got a bail. I explained to him that the destruction of documents could not obliterate the information lying with the coal industry and the banks. I never brought the issue of arson. He suo motto mentioned that he had not got it done. I told him it was in the domain of the police to find out. After a few rounds of discussion he agreed to reiterate the disclosure of Rs 1 crore. As per law the manner of earning the income which was being disclosed was also required to be specified. On these issues, of course, he had done his homework perfectly in consultation with his advisors. His statement was recorded accordingly. For me a battle was won. Subsequently I received monetary reward also for the case. It was by all means an achievement.

In 1993 I had my maiden trip to USA and Europe. My sister-in-law in USA was to deliver in August. So I made a month-long trip. On coming back and till I was there as the ADIT (Investigation) I carried out two more searches at Dhanbad which were quite successful. One of the searches also included a senior functionary of the coal industry as an accomplice who was also searched. The searches at Dhanbad were by and large appreciated by the departmental authorities as well as the media.

Life otherwise also was enjoyable at Dhanbad. Mridula's job was worthwhile with a nice salary-higher than mine with non-practicing allowance included. My elder son had started going to school. There were places around where one could go for a day's relaxation like Maithon and Topchanchi. There was the famous pilgrimage of Jains called Shikharji in neighbouring Giridih. There were many senior officers to interact with at a Dhanbad. But I really enjoyed the company of Sudhir Rakesh, IAS of the 1983 batch who had come there as the joint commissioner, commercial taxes. He was an old senior from Patna College and a man of unimpeachable integrity.

Around the middle of 1994 I was promoted as the Deputy Commissioner of Income Tax, now re-designated as the Joint Commissioner of Income Tax and was posted as the Deputy Commissioner of Income Tax (Appeals) at Dhanbad itself. I had requested the CBDT to retain me at Dhanbad for a year because my wife wished to work with Coal India for a year more. The Board had kindly agreed with the request.

I was in for a shock now. I was suddenly transferred to Patna from Dhanbad by the Chief Commissioner of Income Tax, Delhi. I went to Patna to see him. I confronted him. By now I was growing in confidence to face senior bureaucrats. I was observing the mediocrity and the spinelessness of even the highest functionaries in matters of taking stand and be on the side of what was apparently right.

I asked the Chief Commissioner the reasons for my transfer. He had no convincing reply to make. On my insistence he told me that The Member, CBDT Mr N. Rangachari had asked him do it. Now it became mystery a for me. The only inference that I could draw was that some aggrieved person was egotistical enough and at the same time must be having enough connection to reach the Member. Next morning I reached the CBDT and knocked the door of Mr. Rangachari. It was my first visit to the North Block. Mr. Rangachari called me and asked me funny questions about Dhanbad. I asked him whether he had any occasion to see my work and whether he knew me at all. He had not even remote knowledge of Dhanbad. I told him that the Chief Commissioner, Patna informed me that he wanted me to be transferred out of Dhanbad. He was a little upset at this. He was a little apologetic and told me that he had to get me transferred because the Coal Secretary, a batchmate of his in the IAS told me lot of negative things about me.

My respect for the government functioning was getting eroded gradually by such inane conversations. However, I told the member that he should ask the Coal Secretary whether he even knew me. I was sure within myself that he was in an unholy nexus with the coal mafia at Dhanbad. I informed the member that it was only a week back that I was retained at Dhanbad as a Deputy Commissioner on promotion. With all that happened being absolutely without any basis, my transfer to Patna needed to be cancelled. He had not imagined that I would reach him so fast.

An interesting coincidence took place in the evening. At Janpath while taking a stroll in the afternoon I met

Mr. Anil Sharma, an important person in the Congress party then and an elder brother to me. I told him my purpose of coming to Delhi. He closely knew the Coal Minister and told me that I should postpone my plan to go to Dhanbad for a day and meet the Minister with him. I did that. Next day I met the Union Coal Minister. I explained to him about my problem and the role of the Coal Secretary. He immediately spoke to the Secretary over intercom and asked him whether he knew an officer of my name belonging to the IRS. He replied in the negative and the Minister told him that what he had done was shameful. He directed him to speak to the Member, CBDT immediately. By the time I reached Dhanbad my transfer order was cancelled. The whole experience left a bad taste and it was the beginning of a series of experiences of disillusionment with the government service.

At Dhanbad an important person I met was one Mr. Kedarnath Mittal. He was into the business of hard coke and belonged to a fairly well known business family. He was socially alive and a progressive thinker. Because of his social proclivities he became fairly close and the association with him continues till date. Life as Deputy Commissioner of Appeals was smooth. There were four posts of Deputy Commissioner, Appeals at Patna, Muzaffarnagar, Ranchi and Dhanbad. I was given the Additional Charges of other three stations. I enjoyed touring a lot. I visited Muzaffarpur on a few occasions.

My friend Rajiv Gauba, IAS was the District Magistrate there and I enjoyed staying with him.

In 1995 it was time to leave Dhanbad. I requested the member, CBDT for a posting at Delhi and gave him my reasons. He was gracious and I was transferred to Delhi. I remember I reported at Delhi to join on the May 16, 1995. I had to go to Dhanbad because Mridula was in two minds to leave immediately. Coming to Delhi was also homecoming for me. For a few months initially I stayed in different guest houses. I was looking for my entitled accommodation. It was a very depressing scenario. The general pool entitlement of ours at that level of seniority was that of a Type IV house which was unbelievably small. Although located in central areas the Type IV houses have one bedroom and one bathroom. The departmental pool houses are slightly bigger but located in far-flung areas. After staying in a bungalow at Dhanbad the thought of staying in such houses was indeed a dampener. Mridula came for a few months regularly and she told me that it was so demoralising that after so much of studies and both of us being placed in life reasonably well we had to think of a place to live which was decent. She also decided to resign from Coal India as Coal India did not have a hospital at Delhi. They were still ready to consider transferring her to Delhi on some administrative post. That was, however, not acceptable to Mridula. I still remember her saying "your job is better, so you should do it. My profession is better, so I will do that." It was, however, a difficult decision to leave a lucrative job like Coal India's. We stayed in a rented house at Patparganj for some time. Then in 1996 the Income Tax Department bought two towers at Kaushambi, Ghaziabad for officers posted in Delhi. These are very spacious flats with three bedroomed and four bathrooms. It must be more than 2000 square feet.

So we decided to make Kaushambi our abode. In our view quality of life in terms of living comfort was more important than driving 15 minutes more. I still remember eight of us initially came to Girnar Tower, Kaushambi which included Arvind Kejriwal, the present Chief Minister of Delhi. Mridula started her clinic in a separate tower. Although a different kind of life had commenced she was feeling happy. We were together. It was December 1996.

My first posting at Delhi was as the DCIT, Special Range 19 which involved the assessment of all the professionals like the doctors, lawyers etc. and the non-company contractors. By all means it was an important assignment. It was here that I came in touch with most of the eminent doctors and lawyers of Delhi. Dr. Naresh Trehan personally came twice to explain why as per law certain amounts brought by him from the USA were not taxable but the department was unnecessarily prolonging the litigation despite appellate authorities ruling in his favour. I think he was quite impressed with the attitude of the department because I gave him a patient hearing. He had recently come from the USA at that time. He was relieved when he found that I had agreed with him and put up a proposal before the commissioner for not going in appeal because the law did not warrant that. I also had a fairly long discussion with Mr. Kapil Sibal and Mr. C. S. Agrawal, eminent lawyers of the times. Having come to Delhi there were new experiences on which a behaviour pattern was needed to be evolved. It was after ten years of service in the field that this dilemma had come. It was the crucial question of integrity. Till I was in Patna and Dhanbad nobody ever offered or even brought the possibility of offering cash for any favour. But it seemed in places like a metropolitan city it was an accepted norm. Moreover in the Income Tax Department the tax professionals were an inseparable conduit. Quite a few Chartered Accountants often asked me as to what they should be doing for the cases they were representing. I realised there was no point losing my temper. They were only following a practice which had come to be accepted. It was only in cases of demanding huge amounts that negotiations were involved. The CAs played a nefarious role. I spoke to two of my batch mates who had been here for the last two years. Their reply was that even for the right things done the CAs will collect from the assessee certain amounts and they will be too happy if they didn't have to part with a portion for the officer. Their suggestion was it had to be a personal choice. I am sure in some cases the tax professionals had a gala time in my tenure in assessment. They might have also considered me to be a fool. Nothing could be done about it. It was a sad situation. My next posting was as Dy. Commissioner of Income Tax, Special Range 14 which was yet another important assignment and it involved assessments of Corporate assessees. Everything was smooth till I experienced my first brush with corruption among seniors within the department. I was making an assessment on which I had worked very hard. Suddenly on 30th March the Chief Commissioner called me to his room bypassing my commissioner. He was a wretched person known for his corruption in terms of making money and moral profligacy as well. He was bad at conversation too. It was difficult to make out what he was saying. That was his condition in English as well as Hindi languages. He asked me about the assessment I was making, in fact I had finalised. It had taken me months to marshal facts to prove that a huge income shown as agricultural was actually bogus. He was not prepared to listen to me and ordered verbally that I should change the order. I left his room and came straight to my commissioner who was aware of the case and in fact used to very proudly mention even in meetings with officers that it was an ideal case and brilliantly framed by me. He was otherwise a nice officer and I was his favourite. But to my utter shock, he, rather than speaking to the chief commissioner, started telling me like advice to a child that superiors should not be defied. It was the shock of a lifetime. I came back to my room and thought for a few minutes. I did not make any change and passed the order. It had implications in terms of heavy tax, penalty and prosecution. I was clear in my convictions. I was more disillusioned with the Commissioner than the Chief Commissioner. I was transferred to a non-field post on the 1st of April, something which is unusual. I was clear by now that honesty of conviction had no meaning in government functioning and it was only a matter of personal choice and self-satisfaction. My commissioner was liberal in paying lip service to my unjust transfer. I requested him to grant me leave because I was not going to join soon. Instead of 15 days being asked for he granted me leave for a month. I met the Chairman, CBDT and registered my grievance. He was also very critical of the Chief Commissioner but he did not do anything. I told him I had no problem with the transfer but it should be cancelled for now and I could be transferred in the annual exercise. With nothing forthcoming I tried to meet the Finance Minister. I was advised that I should meet the Personal Secretary of the Minister and explain to him what I wanted to convey. The PS was an officer of the 1988 batch of the IAS and was known to me from Patna. I met him. I did not say much on the Chief Commissioner's personal integrity but I did not mince words about Income Tax administration being protective of the tax evaders under the present Chief Commissioner. In the next 15 days the Chief Commissioner himself was removed. It was some vindication of the genuineness of my protest. The entire episode hardly made me happy. The whole wastage of time and energy was avoidable. But I had learnt my lessons.

The trust in the system was lost. It was very frustrating to think that to survive with peace one had to be a non-performer and there was no way one could defy hierarchy even for the right reasons.

By now I had become an Additional Commissioner of Income and was heading a Range as it is called. Three important corporations that I interacted with were the NTPC, the Nestle and the Oracle. The NTPC was the highest taxpayer of Delhi and the budgetary collection of Delhi largely depended on it. Here again the Chief Commissioner was too interfering and for reasons best known to him he was nasty to the NTPC and made me raise wild and ridiculous issues. I myself felt ashamed and spoke to the CMD of NTPC and assured him that a right assessment as per law would be made. Luckily the Commissioner was a very strong person who was with me and she told me that I should go ahead with the assessment as per law and not to worry about the Chief Commissioner. It was with painstaking effort that the assessment could be framed. Since it was a Public Sector Undertaking and a very important one the CMD also met the Finance Minister. He, however, was very appreciative of me as opposed to the Chief Commissioner. Nestle also had grievances against certain actions by my predecessor. I dealt with them in a lawful and fair manner and they paid a record payment of Advance Tax tax during the year.

It was 2003 now and I was due for my promotion as Commissioner. To my utter shock I came to know that the CBI had made a recommendation for initiation of disciplinary proceedings against me in the 1993 case of Ramesh Gandhi and others of Dhanbad. Their allegation was that being a senior officer I did not take enough care and precaution for the safety and security of the seized papers and the office building. I gathered that the police had closed the case for want of evidence although the allegations in the FIR lodged by me were found to be correct. After that the CBI had taken over the case who made enquiries for eight years and then came out with this conclusion against me. The then SP of the CBI was knowing everything right from the beginning because he was a trusted personal friend besides being a responsible officer of the Government. All these developments were mysterious and intriguing. A case in which I had staked my life, which resulted in record realisation of revenues and for which the department gave me cash reward and for which I was hailed as a hero, the CBI made observations without any understanding of the functioning of the Income Tax department. I knew I could give them a befitting reply but I was scared because of the impending promotion. If an enquiry was initiated and its favourable disposal took time, the promotion could have been denied till the finalisation of the matter. Nevertheless I spoke to the then Deputy Director and the Director. I can never forget them for their conviction and boldness. The then Deputy Director was now a commissioner in Mumbai. He spoke to the Director of Vigilance who advised that he would first seek his comments and then put up the matter before the CBDT. The then Deputy Director gave a very strong report pointing out the mediocrity and lack of application of mind in the CBI's report. He minced no words in highlighting that the empowered committee of officers for grant of reward had examined the relevant points in minute details and found me to be an officer of extraordinary grit and intelligence. The revenues were duly realised. He also wrote that a young officer's extraordinary zeal and commitment deserved special appreciation and CBI's recommendations should be rubbished. The Chairman, CBDT further added to his recommendations and made scathing remarks on the CBI. To their utter frustration they received a cryptic letter saying that an enquiry should still be made. The Chairman further wrote in reply that the CBI should properly go through the report of the then Deputy Director and then arrive at a finding. He alleged that it appeared that the CBI had not gone through the comments offered at all. This time the CBI closed the case. The whole experience left an ugly taste of the functioning of the system. How much precious time and energy is wasted in the government? I was no longer the same man now in the 18th year of service. A cynicism had crept in.

A case of significance I dealt with now as Additional Commissioner was that of NDTV. But at that stage the issues which are there now for which the case has been in the news were not there. One important issue, however, was there, and that was regarding the loan transaction of Rs 4 crore with ABCL Limited. However, on a thorough enquiry into facts and the position of law there was nothing adverse that could be inferred. At that time I met Mr Pranoy Roy who came and explained the position of the Company. He has been in various controversies but he is definitely a very well read man and a glib talker. My promotion as Commissioner of Income Tax came in 2004. It was an occasion to feel nice but my general affinity for being a part of the civil service was gradually dwindling because of the recent experiences. To stay in Delhi after completion of tenure there was a mad race for central deputations. I also explored the possibility. I had a fair chance of getting a deputation to the Ministry of Science and Technology as a Director but I did not find the idea worthwhile. I pulled myself out of the race. I instead met the Chairman, CBDT and requested him to allow me to stay in Delhi for a year more. He was too considerate to grant the request but told me that there was only one post of Director of Income Tax (Research) where I could be posted. I was very happy and not only agreed but also expressed my grateful thanks. It was a newly created post and the scope of the jurisdiction was yet to be defined. I did a couple of studies. The one study on the efficacy of Income Tax searches during the last five years earned the appreciation of the Director General but the CBDT did not act on it in any manner.

In 2003, I got an opportunity to visit Canada because I was made a member of a three officers' team to study and propose a system for computer assisted the selection of cases for scrutiny. The programme was assisted by the CIDA (Canada India Development Agency). I am thankful to my Commissioner Mr. Prashanta Ray for recommending me to the team. It was prestigious and very satisfying in terms of the contents of the responsibilities of the team. The team had to study and recommend the parameters to be considered for a case to be picked up for scrutiny. With no manual intervention the cases were to be picked up for scrutiny by the computer itself. The parameters were to be revised from year to year based on the changing economic scenario. We visited Vancouver, Canada and were attached to their Surrey Tax Centre for a week to study their systems. We learnt so much there. It was great to pick up the salient points in the CCRA (Canada Customs and Revenue Agency) system. We were then sent to Ottawa and met their senior functionaries to discuss relevant issues. It was a very enriching experience. After coming back we worked hard and in the next three months our team headed by Mr. Prashanta Ray handed over our version of the CASS. The CBDT accepted it. A computerised system for selection of cases for scrutiny was introduced in the department. Since then it has been working well with amendments in the system whenever considered necessary. It was a very satisfying experience. We had worked hard on it. The main credit, however, goes to

Mr. Prashanta Ray, the commissioner who was a 1971 batch officer. He was an extraordinarily talented man. He was proficient in computer functioning when computerisation was in nascent stages and not many knew about computer's functioning. He had command over English and Bengali languages. His translation of Gitajali in English found a London based publisher. With a background of Physics from IIT, Kharagpur he had certain patents on scientific subjects to his credit. He was a good singer and an ardent player of mouth organ. Working with him for a year and the trip to Canada with him was a real privilege.

The worst that can happen to a well-meaning civil servant was going to happen to me soon. It could not even be imagined, not even by my enemies, if any. On the February 2, 2005, the CBI came knocking at my door for a search. Initially I thought they had come to a wrong address by mistake but I was told they had a warrant to search my house. I felt humiliated. Nevertheless I was not a person who was going to be intimidated and made to kneel down by adversities of this kind. But I was feeling bad for Mridula whose level of ethics and whose parents' commitment to values was emulated by others. The CBI searched our house, Mridula's clinic and my office at the Drum Shaped building, I. P. Estate, Delhi. They had to draw a blank and they were frustrated. The officials who come for searches of course know nothing about the reasons except the Investigating Officer. Towards late in the evening I spoke to the I.O. who was on the defensive and apologetic too. He showed me the FIR. I was shocked. The FIR was a preposterous document because everything mentioned therein was wrong and imaginary. They had mentioned my salary income for ten years which was less than a class IV official's. They had mentioned Mridula's income which was not even half of what was shown in her Returns of Income. They did not even know that she worked in Coal India earlier at a salary which was more than mine. They had listed properties owned by me which were non-existent. They had not even mentioned the huge loan Mridula had raised for construction of the house in which we are living presently. The FIR was like an imaginary story which somebody had written sitting on his table to make an imaginary case without any clue how to make even a credible fiction. It was wickedness of the highest order and also a sure evidence of India having become a banana republic. I realised that even a senior public servant's integrity had no meaning. It was a fragile existence of a government servant. For the first time I was getting convinced that it was not an advisable proposition to be honest and patriotic and be a public servant at the same time. I had to fight it out in any case.

There were friends and colleagues who expressed sympathy, at least paid lip service. There were genuine reactions of sympathy too. I could see the happiness of jealous colleagues too. All this was indicative of the fact that the so-called watchdog of corruption was a sham. It was in fact a perpetrator of cynicism if not corruption itself. One redeeming fact I could observe was that the seniors with whom I had worked and who themselves were men of principle and integrity spoke to me and said this would pass. They assured me they were always with me. I remember some close friends whose conduct was doubtful, but I had nothing to tell them. Many of those who were themselves officers of known corrupt reputation were scared too. I am thankful to friends who, I think, had genuine appreciation for my honesty, integrity and strength of character. It was not time for me to reflect on these aspects. It was time to strategise a befitting response. And I had to keep Mridula's mental disposition in the right shape.

Once the month of April, 2005 came the stress was compounded because it was time for transfer out of Delhi. My extended tenure in Delhi was also over and transfers on promotion were mandatory. Luckily I got Kolkata which was a place familiar to me. I went to Kolkata on the May 16, 2005. Another disaster was waiting for me. I called on my Chief Commissioner. I have no hesitation in making his name public because nobody would disagree with me if I say that he was one of the most ill reputed officers of the department. He was H. D. Goyal. A debauch of the highest degree his immoral escapades had landed him into trouble so many times. He was known for shamelessly demanding money for everything and from everybody. I had heard that he demanded money for everything including for granting leave. My batch mates posted with him had so many stories to narrate about him. I called on him and I informed him that I was also the General Secretary of the IRS Association. I also narrated the assignments held by me at Delhi. He was hardly interested in all this. Once I told him that I wanted 15 days' leave, he came to the point and told me that leave was not a matter of right and there was a price for that. I lost my temper at this stage. I left his room, came to his office and left a leave application with leave prayed for starting after a week. He sent messages to me during the next two days but I did not respond. He did not sanction the leave. I left an application for three days' casual leave and left Kolkata.

Now I had two issues to deal with. How to deal with the Chief Commissioner at Kolkata was number one. Number two was how to go about the CBI. My elder son was in class XII now. Not that I used to teach him but I wanted to ensure that I was around. I made a decision that I would not go to Kolkata till I was transferred to a different chief commissioner or the one I was posted with retired, which I found out was due on the March 31, 2006. About the CBI also I decided to remain quiet for a year unless they asked something. It was not a pleasant time on the official front. Nevertheless I wanted to remain happy at home. I also assured Mridula that she need not worry at all. I kept receiving letters from Kolkata directing me to join and I kept replying that it was not possible to join because of personal difficulties. After a certain number of days it was the CBDT which could sanction leave and, therefore, I had to reply to the Board after that. The CBI never asked any question during the next one year. Once or twice the I.O. did call asking certain routine and silly questions. The CBI was making itself a laughing stock for me.

The chief commissioner at Kolkata retired on March 31, 2006. I joined there on the 1st of April. Entire Kolkata charge was rejoicing at the retirement of the chief commissioner. His name H. D. Goyal, people used to say, stood for High Demand Goyal. Irony of the system is that the CBDT, CBI or any agency never acts against such anathema to public service. I was in Kolkata till the financial year 2008-09. This was a time I never felt nice being in the government service. Kolkata otherwise was a very congenial station and I was posted to important charges during the three years. But the most important charge that I held for more than a year was Commissioner (Appeals) V. It was the most important appellate charge of Kolkata. The biggest cases of corporate appeals were there. I learnt a lot hearing the CAs and the Advocates and adjudicating complex cases. But the greatest learning came from Mr. D. S. Damle, CA. I would rate him as one of the most knowledgeable CAs I have met in my career. His style of argument was impressive. His citation of case laws was most appropriate. He had a very good command over the English language. He was very good looking and had a very pleasing personality. He had many cases in the charge of CIT(A) V. Practically thrice a week he used to appear before me. I used to enjoy hearing his arguments. Never in my career had I loved Income Tax Law as much as I did there. After my transfer I remained in touch with him. He had become a very good friend. Sometime in 2020 I learnt that he had a cardiac arrest and he expired. He was too young to die. He must have been hardly 60. This was destiny's height of cruelty. I will always miss him in this lifetime. Sometime in 2008 I decided to tackle the CBI. Although the CBI did not bother much, they did visit my hometown Kahalgaon and my younger sister at Gorakhpur. The I.O. had personally gone there. At both the places the I.O. had received polite rebuffs by my elder brother and the younger sister respectively. It was another mindless exercise by the CBI because my financial affairs had to do nothing with my family although I had substantial gains from my HUF. I wonder what and how the CBI investigates and how the bosses there monitor. I am of the considered view that the police should be removed altogether from economic investigations and they should be looking into only cases like pickpocketing, theft, dacoity, murder etc. I myself found that they have no expertise, rather basic skills, to see a Balance Sheet or a Profit and Loss Account or an Income and Expenditure Account. Such cases should be given to officers of the level of Income Tax Officers drawn from the Income Tax Department in large numbers. Alternatively separate recruitment should be made of people with requisite qualification. They should be monitored by an officer of the rank of Commissioner of Income Tax.

It took me a couple of days to think about how to proceed. I had written a few letters to the Director, CBI with copies to the Joint Director and the DIG. Those letters were very critical of the CBI. I had pointed out the basic absurdities and the follies of the CBI, duly supported by facts. For example, my basic question was that the SP of the CBI, the signatory of the FIR, knew my rank but the salary income of mine that they mentioned was that of a class IV employee of the government. Similarly, does the CBI not know the basic document which could show the declared income of a doctor? Should the CBI not refer to the Returns of Income? Should the CBI outrage the integrity of a highly qualified doctor wife just because the husband is a public servant? Should the CBI not try to know whether a property alleged to be owned even exists? Should the author of an erroneous FIR not be punished along with his supervisors? All these letters were un-responded. In fact I called up the I.O. to enquire. He was aware of all the letters. His bosses must have discussed it with him and he chose to remain silent. He told me that nobody ever wrote such strong letters to the CBI. He also said that his superiors had instructed to be very meticulous in collecting information and efforts should be made to find disproportionate assets to income the figures of which should have no errors. By their own story on the basis of what was written and what they found, there was actually a surplus of income of more than double the amount alleged to be disproportionate. I asked him to expedite his fact finding and reach a conclusion. I also told him that I was thinking of meeting the Joint Director. He requested that it would be nice if I avoided that.

Before I could decide how to deal with the CBI, I thought of taking a chance with the courts for a relief. I filed a quashing petition before the Hon'ble High Court of Delhi praying for the annulment of the action of the CBI because the FIR itself was erroneous and absurd. The CBI themselves told the court that soon they would close the case. The judge then ordered that in view of the submission of the CBI he was not quashing the FIR but gave me the liberty to seek suitable remedies on the conclusion of the case. The judge did not go into the merits of my arguments. In fact he told my lawyer Mr. Ajit Sinha that arguments were not required as he was giving the petitioner the right to suitable remedies. I had a mixed reaction to the ruling by the judiciary. I would have been happier and more respectful of the judiciary if a finding would have come on the substantive points raised in the petition.

I thought of meeting the Director, CBI. I sought an appointment for which I wrote a letter. For some time no response came. I then sought the help of an IAS officer Mr. Pradeep Kumar who was the Coal Secretary then. I knew him through a friend R. D. Gupta. He was known to be an officer of high integrity. I requested R. D. Gupta to accompany me to him. We went to his office and I explained to him that I was not seeking any favour and the Director should only hear me for a few minutes. He immediately spoke to the Director over the phone. Within a couple of days my office at Kolkata received a fax by which I was informed that the Director had called me to his office on a particular date and time. I geared myself up, ensured that I didn't get emotional and framed my points in my mind to be brought before the Director in my meeting with him. On the appointed date I was there at the Director's office. The Director was one Mr. Vjay Shankar sporting a big moustache. Our conversation started. He made an objectionable statement when he said that everybody was an offender once a case was registered. It was the offender's onus to prove that he was not an offender. I politely told him that by such logic any empowered government authority could make a fiction of offence and declare anybody an offender. It is like any tax authority declaring anybody a tax evader by writing a fiction of anybody's income. There has to be some semblance of sanity and credibility in making an allegation. Prima facie perverse allegations are shunned by law. He then asked me why I thought allegations against me were perverse. I told him that I had come just to show that. I requested him to give me half an hour to speak uninterrupted and by the 31st minute I was sure he would not have anything to ask further. He was visibly intrigued at my confidence. It was the confidence of my integrity and my courage of conviction. I then explained the whole case and the anomalies in the FIR. I pointed out that it was unbelievable that the SP of the CBI who wrote the FIR would not know the salary of a Commissioner of Income Tax who was an officer of the level of Joint Secretary to the government of India. It was equally unbelievable that the fact of my wife having earned a handsome salary from the Coal India Limited was unknown to him. For these two reasons he should be dismissed from the service. He also needs to explain where the property mentioned existed. In any case should the CBI be entitled to interfere with the educational dignity of a highly educated woman who may be a public servant's wife. On the face of it my wife was more qualified than me. My general reputation in the department was of an officer with a high level of ethics and integrity. What enquiries did the SP make about me? I think I must have spoken for more than 20 minutes. In the end I added that the country was already going through difficult times and the government was becoming a laughing stock. It has the unenviable reputation of being inefficient and corrupt. The CBI was no exception. Such actions only reinforce the negative reputation. After hearing me, which he patiently did and for which I am appreciative and thankful, he told me that enquiries needed to be completed because the CBI could not close the case otherwise. I satirically but with humility told him that no sanity was required on the part of the government to start an inquiry but it was needed to conclude it. He asked me how fast I could answer the questions raised by the I.O. I told him I was a taxman and I was trained to look into accounts running into hundreds of pages. This was too small a matter and it was my personal affair. I won't even be required to refer to any paper and I could answer any question right now. He told me that he was going to direct his officers to expedite all enquiries and reach a conclusion fast. On that note I left his room. As soon as I reached my car, I received a call on my cell phone from the Joint Director asking me whether I could see him right then. I said yes and reached his room. He was Mr. V. Raju who later became Director, NIA. I must say he was the best IPS officer I ever met. He was suave, humble and straightforward. For the first time I saw an officer of his seniority taking notes in his hand on a piece of paper. He asked me relevant questions. It seemed the Director had briefed him. I explained to him all that I had said to the Director. He was seemingly upset about the anomalies in the FIR. He noted down everything that I told and assured me that the case would be concluded fast. I thanked him and left his room. It turned out to be a fruitful visit to the CBI. I only hoped the Joint Director honoured his words.

As soon as I reached home I received a call from the I.O. who sounded a little upset and asked me as to why I was angry and what was the necessity of meeting the Director and the Joint Director. I told him he should not worry because I had not made any complaints against him. I also told him that I did point out the anomalies and the absurdities in the FIR. He asked me about my convenience to appear before him. I told him that I was still in Delhi and I could extend my leave for a few days. He wanted to come to my house and record my statement. He asked me whether he could come tomorrow. I also told him that I could come to his office. But he was insistent that there could be unnecessary disturbances in the office and my house would be better. He also sought my permission to bring his stenographer and use my computer. I informed him that ideally he should record a statement of my wife also for her clarification on her affairs. He replied that the Joint Director had instructed him not to bother my wife at all because she was a busy professional and whatever clarification was required should be sought from me. I understood the Joint Director had given clear instructions. That made me happy. At least some people in the otherwise defunct system had sanity.

Next morning the I.O. who was of the rank of an ASP arrived with his stenographer. He told me that he wanted to record my statement on all relevant points. I first asked him what in his view were relevant issues. He rattled out a few issues. I added at least ten more. Then he started raising his questions. My answers were always clearer than his questions. I told him many a times that he should not leave certain questions on which my clarification would make my statement complete and his bosses would appreciate it. I requested him that he should record a statement of my wife also and he need not hesitate. She was at home only and I was present too. I insisted and my wife's statement too was recorded. Basically through these statements I corrected everything wrong in the FIR. During the searches of course they had found nothing incriminating. So they hardly had anything sensational to ask. The whole process took the whole day. I thanked him and he went. I appreciated when he said none of the senior officers in his organisation ever offered so much learning. He was a sincere fellow and appeared to be honest. To me in any case he was extra nice in his behaviour. Within the next few days he asked me for some information on sundry points over phone.

In the meantime I received a big questionnaire from our departmental vigilance for my reply. I gathered from our departmental officer that the CBI had referred that. I replied the next day. I also added that the department needed to seek an explanation from the CBI for the erroneous FIR and the harassment of an honest officer. It was 2009 now and soon the CBI filed a closure report in which they held that my incomes were actually more than my expenditure and investments. The court took a few months and eventually closed the case. The I.O. told me that in his more than 30 years of service he had not seen such an honourable closure of a case. For me it was a relieving moment. It made me happy. But what an unwarranted struggle it was. I had lost trust in the system.

The enthusiasm had died but not the spirit to be a good public servant.

It was four years in Kolkata now out of which I remained on leave for a year initially. To regularise the leave was also a battle with the CBDT. With a corrupt Deputy Secretary and a Director it was a tough time arguing with the Board because the Members and the Chairman of the CBDT would follow the lower functionaries and would not apply their mind. Eventually my strong letters from time to time against the rogue chief commissioner prevailed and a chapter ended. I enjoyed my Kolkata stay generally although staying alone was very depressing. I was frequently commuting between Kolkata and Delhi which itself was taxing. I had a nice house with a maid who was a good cook. Most of the evenings were spent listening to ghazals. I would have heard all my favourite songs so many times. Sometimes I spent the evenings at Kolkata club, The Bengal club or the Tollygunge club with friends. I met the member, CBDT requesting for a transfer to Delhi. But he would not listen. I requested for Meerut but he did not agree even with that. I then found a connection to meet the Finance Minister. He was convinced by my reasons and I got a transfer to Meerut which made me more than happy. It was time to say goodbye to Kolkata, a city I really loved.

I joined Meerut as Commissioner of Appeals. There was another commissioner who was a senior colleague and an administrative commissioner. I had enough experience of appellate functioning by now having worked at Kolkata for two years in the appellate charges. The profile of cases at Meerut was varied. Interestingly all the cases of search of the Ghaziabad charge had their appellate jurisdiction with the Commissioner (Appeals), Meerut. These used to be difficult and challenging cases. I remained posted at Meerut for more than three years. I enjoyed being there. I had become more disciplined in my daily routine. I never stayed there and used to commute every day from my home at Ghaziabad. It used to take an hour normally except when there was unusual traffic on the way. I always used to be on time to reach the office. The boss being the Chief Commissioner (West UP) stationed at Kanpur knew me because he had come from Kolkata. He used to talk to me at least twice a week and compliment me for my punctuality and discipline. A dear friend O. P. Singh. IPS was also posted at Meerut as an IG of the Police Training Centre. Sometimes I used to go his house in the evening and go back home after dinner. I used to be participative in the cultural activities at Meerut and had developed a good equation with people of literary taste. Kavi Sammelans used to be frequently happening there in which I was mostly called as the Chief Guest. All these made Meerut a very enjoyable posting. I had become fairly popular socially. The local Chief Medical officer was an accomplished poet. I used to enjoy listening to him. I made a record disposal of Appeals at Meerut which was admired by my seniors. In nutshell Meerut posting gave the pleasure of both home and work. Times passed by rather fast. Three years passed by at an unbelievably fast pace. It was time to say goodbye to Meerut after March 2012.

I desperately wanted to come to Delhi now. I again visited the CBDT and met the member and the Chairman. It yielded no results. Their standard reply used to be that there was no vacancy at Delhi. But wheeler dealers were able to manage a Delhi posting. I was too senior by now to see and understand everything. It was frustrating. In May 2012 the Annual General Transfer orders came. To my shock I was transferred to Bareilly as a Commissioner (Appeals) while I was expecting Delhi. The Member in fact had indicated it. Now transfer is a matter of administrative exigency as the transferring authority would argue. But these arguments are only for verbal consumption. Nevertheless I went to the CBDT once to meet the Chairperson and the member. Both of them had to routinely tell me that Bareilly was the nearest place to Delhi and needed an efficient Commissioner (Appeals) to liquidate the huge pendency there. There were other violations of rules and norms in the Transfer Order but there was no point of talking about those. When the authorities up to the Finance Minister had no commitment to governance and they were only there to sign on the dotted lines nothing could be done to improve things. It was only a miniscule of people in the government who were performing for self-satisfaction. I could and the whole department could see that some of the most ill reputed officers were transferred to Mumbai and Delhi on perceived lucrative assignments in the same Transfer Order. It was the same Chairman and the member who, till yesterday, used to talk about falling standards in governance. It was disgusting. For me a small comfort was that I was given the additional charge of Moradabad too which was two hours' drive from home.

I went to Bareilly. Luckily another Commissioner there was a good friend. He had stayed in Bareilly for several years. So my comfort level there was good. There was a fairly good guesthouse to stay in. Bareilly was not a small place. Its territorial jurisdiction was quite large. As a city also I would rate it as one of the best five in UP. I discovered Bareilly only after going there. The Bareilly club is an old, nice and comfortable club. The office building known as the Aayakar Bhawan is imposing. There is a post of Chief Commissioner also at Bareilly. The one posted there is not worth mentioning. There was a celebration among the staff when he retired. For me there was a huge pendency of work. It was clear that my predecessor had hardly disposed of any matter in 3 years. The cases were simple in terms of complexity. In next two years I brought the pendency to nil for which the CBDT gave me a letter of appreciation rating me as the best functioning Commissioner (Appeals) of the country. By now I had understood that such letters of appreciation were not even worth the piece of paper these were written on. I often visited Moradabad and did equal justice to the work there. Moradabad, however, was not a congenial place to work at. The tax professionals were mostly mediocres and wheeler dealers. In the last phase at Bareilly a new Chief Commissioner had come who, intellectually, was a good company. It took me more than two years to come to Delhi on transfer from Bareilly. I had gone there towards the end of 2012 and was transferred to Delhi in April 2015.

I joined Delhi in April 2015. It has been exactly ten years since I left Delhi after a stint of ten years. It was homecoming. I was feeling nostalgic of the earlier memories. The same Central Revenue Building was looking like my own home from where I had gone away. The department had also undergone a restructuring of the cadre by now. The Commissioners of a particular seniority in terms of scale of pay were re-designated as the Principal Commissioners. This was a post equivalent to a senior Joint Secretary to the Government of India. They were to be posted as the administrative commissioners. The junior ones were to be posted as the appellate commissioners. I was posted as the Principal Commissioner of Income Tax VII. There were 9 Principal Commissioners of corporate charges in Delhi whose jurisdiction was alphabetical. My jurisdiction was over companies whose names started with N and O alphabets. The jurisdiction was almost the same as I held as Additional Commissioner ten years ago. So in this respect also it was homecoming. I was going to meet the new generation of some high profile assessees professionally in the days to come with whom I had interacted earlier. Besides I also held the charge of Principal Commissioner

II. It had jurisdiction over companies like Airtel, BSNL etc. The Principal Commissioner VII had jurisdiction over Nestle, NTPC, P. C. Jewellers etc. NDTV also was in my jurisdiction but it was later transferred to Principal Commissioner VI, my batchmate and dear friend Sanjay Mishra, now the ED, for coordinated investigation in other cases which were already there. Next two years were very satisfying professionally. The post of the Principal Commissioner is a very important post with a crucial role of supervision. With two charges the workload used to be heavy but with my style of time management it was not a big deal. A great advantage of being in a metropolitan city is the presence of so many colleagues. It becomes easier to handle complex legal issues in consultation with worthy colleagues. I had the advantage of having Mr. Arbind Modi of the 1981 batch who was a Chief Commissioner. He was a person with whom I could discuss anything any time. Sanjay Mishra was there with whom I used to have lunch every day. Lunch time used to be so fruitful. I have always been close to him but these two years brought us closer. My charges made record collection of taxes during the two years. The Principal Chief Commissioner of Income Tax, Delhi was Mr. A. K. Sinha of the 1979 batch. He had been my predecessor at Patna in 1988 as the Asst. Director of Income Tax (Investigation). He was always very nice to me and trusted me with responsibilities. Once there was an agitation by the Staff Union for the delay in their promotions. He made me the chairman of the

Departmental Promotion Committee to expedite things. I completed the task in two weeks. The Union thanked him and me and he thanked and patted me.

One important responsibility that came my way was my appointment as Rajbhasha Adhikari (Officer for the Official Language) for Delhi. I loved it although I had to devote a few hours to this every week. The Department of Official Languages comes under the Ministry of Home. The Principal Chief Commissioner is the head of the Implementation Committee of Rajbhasha. His powers are delegated to a Principal Commissioner appointed for the purpose. Delhi falls under Region A for the purpose of Rajbhasha. On September 14, 1949 the Constituent Assembly resolved that Hindi would be the official language of the Central Government and it was made the Rajbhasha. It was so resolved in view of the fact that Hindi is spoken in several states. September 14, therefore, is observed and celebrated as Hindi Diwas. In the year 2022 World Hindi Day has been celebrated. The theme of the World Hindi Day has been to promote Hindi in the Indian subcontinent so that everybody understands Hindi and efforts are to be made to propagate Hindi in the entire world. The celebration of the Hindi Diwas is followed by Hindi fortnight. The Union Government has framed rules for implementation of the Rajbhasha Adhiniyam. These rules are required to be followed scrupulously. There are Regions in which the whole country is divided for the implementation of the Rajbhasha Adhiniyam. These are

Regions A, B and C. Rules and instructions are framed to ensure the prescribed percentage of work to be done in Hindi in different Regions. It is also prescribed how the correspondence is to be handled. During the entire year the Implementation committee oversees whether the rules are being followed in different offices. There is a Section with each Principal Chief Commissioner where officers like Assistant Director onwards and staff are posted for the purpose. Their job is also to help any office, if required, in translation, etc. Delhi being a big charge has a fairly large Rajbhasha Section (Anubhag). Many of them are shirkers and here comes the responsibility of the Rajbhasha Adhikari. I tried to keep them geared up during my tenure. At the same time issues relating to their service matters and conditions also need to be addressed. They have a feeling that they receive a step motherly treatment in the Department. I took up their promotion issue with the CBDT through the Principal Chief Commissioner. Despite the extra effort that I made, the CBDT's response was not forthcoming. They treated it as a 'no priority' matter. This attitude needs to change. If the Rajbhasha Adhiniyam has to be implemented in letter and spirit we need a motivated workforce.

In Delhi a huge function is organised on the Hindi Diwas. For two years consecutively I enjoyed organising the function. Both the years it was organised in the grand auditorium at the Civic Centre. The function is organised in the name of the Principal Chief Commissioner with other Chief Commissioners attending. Chairman and the Members from the CBDT are also invited and quite a few of them attend. The Rajbhasha Adhikari is supposed to apprise on the progress made towards the implementation of the Rajbhasha Adhiniyam. I enjoyed speaking in Hindi on the occasion, something that I always miss. The participants of different events like essay competition, debates, etc., organised in advance are awarded on the occasion. The whole function is followed by a cultural programme with artists brought from outside and some in-house talent as well. I will always remember having functioned as the Rajbhasha Adhikari. It was an honour for me and pleasure as well.

For two years it was an extremely enjoyable time in Delhi. Two years passed like two days. I can never forget the supportive seniors like Mr. A. K. Sinha and Mr. Arbind Modi who reposed so much trust in me. I will never forget the two years spent with Sanjay Mishra. He has a very good command over Law and Accounts and his inputs on many issues were very helpful at times. I feel the one appointment made by the government on which no questions can be raised is his appointment to the post of Enforcement Director. His investigative skills are difficult to match. One more officer I will always remember was a very junior officer. He was S. N. Pandey who was a Deputy Commissioner in the Principal CIT VII Charge. His job knowledge was extraordinary. His human handling was skilful. His willingness to take extra and even thankless responsibilities was exemplary. And he was a promoted officer and not a direct recruit IRS officer. During those two years at Delhi I did not find any direct officer who could match him. His drafting skills were also very good.

There are interesting memories of the interface with the CBDT and the Finance Minister too. In the case of Oracle Software India which was a subsidiary of the Oracle, USA the department had been ordering Special Audit from year to year for the last three years. The assessee had gone even for a writ which they had lost. When the matter came before me, I examined the case in depth. I was also of the considered view that it was a fit case for getting a Special Audit done. The reasons were not far to seek. The complexity of the accounts was one. More important than that was the voluminousness of the accounts. There were other issues like the reasonableness of the royalties paid. Moreover, there were thousands of Agreements signed with parties across the globe for execution of work. For the assessing officer of the department with a skeleton staff it was impossible to examine all these and arrive at a correct total income as the law stipulates. I, therefore, again made a reference for a special Audit after recording my reasons. The assessee was aggrieved. They wrote a letter of protest. They hardly referred to the reasons record by me. A letter of protest had no meaning under the law. I ignored it. After a couple of days the Chief Commissioner and I were called by the Revenue Secretary Mr Adhia. I later learnt that the

CEO of Oracle, USA had spoken to the Prime Minister during his visit to the USA. He had alleged harassment by the Indian tax authorities because they had been referring their case for special audit every year without any application of mind. The CEO was meeting the Revenue Secretary in Delhi soon when he had a business visit. We were called on a particular date and time. The Revenue Secretary had called the CEO at the same time. We reached the RS at the appointed time. The CEO had nothing to say except alleging harassment because of repeated reference for a special audit. He also added that it was adversely affecting their international reputation. Then Mr. Adhia wanted me to explain our position. Besides referring to voluminous accounts, complexity of accounts and the need to get the thousands of Agreements examined I also added that it was difficult to understand how we were harassing. The special auditor was only doing it for a proper understanding for the assessee as well as the department. The objective after all was to arrive at the correct total income and not a pie more and not a pie less. Moreover, it was the department which was paying the fees for the special audit. There was no burden on the assessee. It was also not understood how the global reputation was affected. Special audit was a routine scrutiny of accounts except that the assessing officer was taking the help of an auditor from outside. The assessing officer himself had only an Inspector and a Tax Assistant to run his office. It was surprising how anybody abroad would even know that there was anything called a special audit by an assessing officer in India. I think Mr. Adhia was more than clear after hearing me. He got up abruptly and told the CEO of Oracle, USA that they had no case. We had aborted the unwarranted attempt made by Oracle to scuttle a proper assessment.

Suddenly our promotion as Chief Commissioner started getting processed. The promotion had fallen due. The Chief Commissioner is of the rank of Additional Secretary to the Government of India. It was something to feel good about but it was a cause for stress too because the promotion necessarily involved transfer. With the expansion and increase in the number of posts at all levels the number of Chief Commissioner's post had also increased and the possibility of landing up at an undesired station was also there. I again met the chairman to request him that I should be posted at Delhi on promotion because I had come to Delhi only two years ago after staying away for 10 years. The Chairman Mr. Sushil Chandra knew me well and he had a fondness for me. He did not tell me that he would surely accommodate me at Delhi but he did assure me that he would give me a befitting posting. The promotion order came around the end of July. I was posted as Chief Commissioner, Uttarakhand headquartered at Dehradun. I was happy at the promotion but not so happy with a posting away from Delhi. But I had to go. I joined Dehradun in the first week of August 2017. The Chairman was too nice to call me over the phone and told me that Dehradun was an excellent place and I was going to enjoy the posting. He also assured me that he would soon call me to Delhi. This was enough. I felt nice at the Chairman's concern even if it could have been just lip service. I said goodbye to Delhi.

I joined Dehradun in the first week of August 2017. The officers were there in the guesthouse of the department in the campus of the office itself. It was lunch time. It was a nice feeling entering the city of Dehradun and nicer still when I reached the office. The vibes that one gets when one enters a new place are very important to set the tone for the days to come. I must say I got very positive vibes. The officers were all, by and large, very nice, smart and impressive. Some of them were known to me from earlier times. Two officers impressed me during the next few minutes. One was Nikhil Chaudhary, the Commissioner (Appeals), Dehradun and another was Nidhi Singh, the Additional Commissioner (Headquarters). She was going to handle my office. A senior officer like the Chief Commissioner is greatly relieved when a sincere, honest and intelligent officer is posted in the headquarters. Dehradun is a big charge for a chief commissioner in terms of territorial size. In terms of revenues also it becomes fairly big, but that is mainly because of ONGC. They pay more than Rs 10,000 crore towards taxes during the year. Dehradun basically is a ONGC city in many respects. They have created substantial infrastructure in the city. Uttarakhand is divided into Kumaon and Garhwal regions. Kumaon consists of six districts with

Nainital as Zonal headquarters. Garhwal consists of seven with Pauri Garhwal as headquarters. Dehradun, the capital, is part of Garhwal. From a physiographic point of view the mountains and the valleys that form the system of rivers that become Ganga are classified under Garhwal, whereas the landmass that forges the Sharayu river forms Kumaon. After India became independent in 1947, United Provinces were converted into the newly formed Indian state of Uttar Pradesh. The princely state of Tehri Garhwal joined the Indian Union in 1949, and became a district under the Kumaon division. Initially the administration was entrusted to the commissioner of the Kumaon and Garhwal with his headquarters at Nainital, but later Garhwal was separated and formed into a separate district in 1840 AD. To be simpler Garhwal and Kumaon are the two administrative divisions of the Indian state of Uttarakhand. Lying in the Himalayas, Garhwal is bounded on the North by Tibet, on the east by Kumaon, on the south by Uttar Pradesh state, and on the northwest by Himachal Pradesh state. The Income Tax department has two administrative commissioners in the state of Uttarakhand, one at Dehradun and another at Haldwani. Similarly there are two appellate commissioners at the two stations. In Uttarakhand one can combine work with visiting beautiful places because there is a surfeit of that. Mussoorie of course is well known to the world which is in the vicinity of Dehradun. One can see Mussoorie from Dehradun. For the civil service entrants Mussoorie becomes a part of life because of the Lal Bahadur Shastri National Academy of Administration being there. Every class I civil service entrant goes there for the Foundation Course as it is called. With too many visitors Mussoorie has become crowded. There are so many famous boarding schools there. But Mussoorie holds an irresistible charm for the scenic beauty around and for official and historical reasons. Mussoorie is 1987.59 metres or 6520.97 feet in terms of elevation.

Another beautiful place in Uttarakhand is Lansdowne. Its elevation is 1703.55 metres or 5589.09 feet. Difference between the elevations of Mussoorie and Lansdowne is 284.04 metres or 931.88 feet. Weather of Mussoorie is extremely pleasant from March to November. Lansdowne is a paradise surrounded by beautiful valleys. Nature can be seen here in untouched form as compared to other hill stations. I would rate it as one of the most beautiful hill stations in the country,-a paradise in fact. Incidentally Lansdowne was a major place of the activities of the freedom fighters from British Garhwal during the British period. Nowadays, the famous Garhwal Rifles of the Indian Army has its regimental center here. One of the quietest hill stations in India, it is popular since the British came to India. Another beautiful place in Uttarakhand is Kausani. It is situated in Bageshwar district in Uttarakhand. It is a hill station. It is famous for its scenic splendour and its 300 km wide panoramic view of Himalayan peaks like Trisul, Nanda Devi and Panchchuli. Mahatma Gandhi called this place the Switzerland of India, due to similarity in landscapes. Another beautiful place in Uttarakhand is Jim Corbett named after Edward James Corbett who was a British hunter, tracker, naturalist, and author who hunted a number of man-eating tigers and leopards in the Indian subcontinent. He held the rank of colonel in the British Indian Army and was frequently called upon by the Government of the United Provinces of Agra and Oudh, now the Indian states of Uttar Pradesh and Uttarakhand, to kill man-eating tigers and leopards that were preying on people in the nearby villages of Kumaon-Garhwal regions. He authored Man-eaters of Kumaon, Jungle Love, and other books recounting his hunts and experiences, which enjoyed critical acclaim and commercial success. He became an avid photographer and spoke out for the need to protect India's wildlife from extermination. Jim Corbett National Park is located in the Nainital district of Uttarakhand. The first National Park in India, it was established in 1936 during the British Raj and named Hailey National Park after William Maloolm Hailey, a governor of the United Provinces in which it was then located. In 1956, nearly a decade after India's independence, it was renamed Corbett National Park after Jim Corbett, who had played a leading role in its establishment and had died the year before. The park was the first to come under the Project Tiger initiative. An eco-tourism destination, the park contains 488 different species of plants and a diverse variety of fauna. The increase in tourist activities, however, continues to present a serious challenge to the park's ecological balance.

Uttarakhand is incomplete without Nainital. Every Indian must have heard about its beauty. The headquarters of Nainital district of Kumaon division, it is the judicial capital also of Uttarakhand, the High Court of the state being located there and is the headquarters of an eponymous district. It also houses the Governor of Uttarakhand who resides in the Raj Bhawan. Nainital was the summer capital of the United Provinces. Nainital is located in the Kumaon foothills of the Jagbeer Himalayas at a distance of 285 kilometres from Dehradun. Situated at an altitude of 6,358 feet above sea level, the city is set in a valley containing an eye-shaped lake, approximately two miles in circumference, and surrounded by mountains, of which the highest are Naina Peak on the north, Deopatha on the west and Ayarpatha on the south. From the tops of the higher peaks, magnificent views can be obtained of the vast plain to the south, or the mass of tangled ridges lying north, bound by the great snowy range which forms the central axis of the Himalayas. Nainital has got a beautiful club on the lake. I had the privilege of being their guest once. Besides delectable food the President of the club gave me life membership of the club. The Golf Club is another scenic place to visit. There are other beautiful places nearby. There is Naukuchiatal which literally means a lake with nine corners. It is situated in Bhimtal. It is considered as one of the deepest lakes in Nainital, having a length of 983 metres, breadth 693 metres and depth about 40.3 metres. The lake is surrounded by enchanting flora and fauna, making it a pleasant sight to savour.

After a long lunch with the officers I reached my office chamber. I was amazed at the beautiful decor of the chamber. It was done up in precise details. The upholstery in the room which was fairly big was of a very high quality. I am sure some predecessors of mine must have had very high aesthetic sense for these things. It was by far the best office chamber I had in my entire service. Adjoining was an impressive conference room with a seating capacity of more than fifty. The guesthouse was also within the office campus. It was a nice and comfortable guesthouse with one floor earmarked for the chief commissioner. I had to stay here only on all the days that I was in Dehradun. I had decided I was not going to be deskbound and tour extensively. That in fact is expected from a Chief Commissioner. Sensitising officers and staff on expectations from them of the people and the government was in any case the main job of the Chief Commissioner. He had to be a meaningful commander of people whom had to motivate and inspire. I toured extensively during the next one year till I came to Delhi. It had a tremendous effect. I could see that and the bosses in the CBDT acknowledged it with admiration. That was satisfying.

At Dehradun I always took out time to visit places and meet people either officially or on personal visits. I have wonderful memories of a few places where I went in my personal capacity. One was hotel Savoy in Mussoorie. Although there are so many hotels in Mussoorie, Savoy is a class apart. Its grandeur has an old world charm. The undulating levels make the place so different. Its restaurant, its bar, the reading place, all are different from a normal place. It has an area for reading where autographed photos of famous writers from the world who visited the hotel during the last more than 100 years are hanging. It also boasts of a beautiful ballroom. I visited the place and stayed there twice with Mridula coming from Delhi. It was a sheer pleasure to meet Mr Ruskin Bond at his place at Mussoorie. I visited his place and met him about 15 years ago. Going again was reliving the past. He is an epitome of simplicity. I had lunch with him. Another fascinating place is the club known as WIC. The World Integrity Centre, India (WIC) located at Dehradun is the hub of social, intellectual and cultural entertainment. It has a dining facility serving Indian and continental cuisine and a bar too. At Rishikesh there is Parmarth Niketan which is a place devoted to the pursuit of Yoga and the ways of the spirit. Swami Chidananda Saraswati is the chairman of the Ahrama. He is also the spiritual Guru there. I had the privilege of spending a couple of hours with him. He is a very learned man and his canvas of knowledge is very wide. Subsequently when I was the Principal Chief Commissioner of Exemptions at Delhi he had spoken to me in connection with some Income

Tax matters concerning the Ashram. He was very happy for my prompt and reasoned advice.

The chief commissioner does not have much original work as such. It is basically monitoring and overseeing the work of the subordinates. The ONGC of course had many issues under litigation. They used to be in touch. For us ONGC was a very important assessee because of the huge amount of taxes they were paying. Their Director (Finance) Mr. Subhash Kumar who later became Chairman of the ONGC was a thorough professional. All the legal issues used to be on his tips. I always ensured expeditious disposal of their issues which was just and according to law, whether it meant advising the Commissioner or the Commissioner (Appeals). Dehradun is known for boarding schools. Some of the schools like the Doon School and the Welham for girls have a big name at a national level. Some schools are doing well and upcoming. One such school is Kasiga School. The head of the school is one Mr. Ramesh Batta. The school had some issues with the Income Tax Department. Mr. Batta met me in that connection. I got the issues resolved to the extent the law permitted. Another famous school in Uttarakhand is Sherwood School at Nainital. I once visited the school and met the children there. I once visited a small place called Bajpur which is in the Udham Singh Nagar district under Kumaon Division. I had gone there to inaugurate a new office of the Income Tax Officer. It was nice to interact with the taxpayers there.

Some social activists of Dehradun met me once to raise a complaint against an organisation of the name of The Civil Services Institute. Their complaint was that they ran a club with all modern facilities. They, as alleged, had grabbed the most coveted property in terms of land. A handful of IAS officers who were very powerful were using the place for their personal pleasures. There was no transparent system of granting membership to the club. It was also alleged that ill-gotten money was used by certain members to purchase furniture, fixtures and equipment. The status of the organisation was needed to be seen by the Income Tax Department. I assured them that necessary enquiries would be made. I discussed the case with the assessing officer and advised him that enquiries should be made. I also advised him about the direction of enquiry. Enquiries revealed that the Civil Services Institute was a Society under the Societies Registration Act. It was located close to the old Mussoorie Road on a mountain spur, surrounded by lush green forests, wildlife and picturesque landscape. It was no less than a five star resort. Apart from providing Catering Services and housing a Residential Complex it had within it the indoor Sports Facilities and a multipurpose auditorium. It had a 25 metres swimming pool and facilities for steam baths. The sources of funds for this kind of infrastructure were far from credible. There was no defined system of appointment of office bearers and a few officers of the government were in the thick of things for innumerable years. There was no transparent system of induction of new members. On these facts an assessment was made which resulted in huge demand for tax. Naturally it became a very talked about case. Some powerful people met me too. They were politely told that it was only the appellate commissioner who could now look into the matter. The Commissioner (Appeals) also was a very thorough officer who analysed the relevant points threadbare. He passed a very speaking order and in fact strengthened the order of the assessing officer. The tax demand was confirmed.

One very interesting thing was monthly meetings with all other agencies under the chairmanship of the Chief Commissioner of Income Tax. These meetings were basically to share information. Officers from other agencies like the CBI, ED, Sales Tax, Banks, etc. used to attend. I tried to enthuse the other agencies so that these coordination meetings could be efficacious. During my tenure valuable information was shared. In some cases action was also taken. The local SP and the DIG of the CBI were very meticulous officers. On certain information gathered from the Income Tax Department they could develop good cases of disproportionate assets.

I had started enjoying the Dehradun posting. The feeling of being away from home was also minimised because I was touring most of the time. The CCIT, Ghaziabad and the CCIT, Dehradun,- both came under the Principal CCIT, Kanpur (West UP). There used to be meetings often at Ghaziabad. So I was at home. The

CCIT, Ghaziabad often used to be on leave. I used to hold the Charge in his absence. Moreover, Dehradun was a very congenial place and had a large jurisdiction. In retrospect I felt that it was much better to be at Dehradun as a CCIT than to be at Delhi where the identity of a CCIT was not noticeable because there were too many. As a CCIT there was enough time at the office because it needed a few hours in a week only. There used to be some judicial work in a month where reading a file was involved. Rest all were advisory and involved directions for desirable functioning. These could be done over the phone as well. So I decided to take a call on the best utilisation of time going with the desired role of a Chief Commissioner. Besides routine administration the desired role constituted motivating, making it clear that there was zero tolerance for conscious wrongdoing and that good work always would be noticed and acknowledged. In the monthly video conferences with the Chief Commissioners, the Chairman, CBDT also used to say that the Chief Commissioners had enough time at their disposal which should be utilised towards the larger goal of engaging with the departmental personnel and the citizens who were stakeholders. The Chairman now was Mr. Sushil Chandra who was street smart and had personal knowledge of what was going on at places and officers. He was a great survivor and there must have been some strength in him. He knew the system well. To me personally he was very nice. That was enough. It was not the stage in my career to make an analysis of things. One had understood everything. One had to be clear that self-satisfaction was the guiding spirit. Nobody punishes in the system for wrongdoing unless you are crossing limits in the public domain or somebody is after you personally. And good work is seldom evaluated by the system or the government, leave aside getting rewarded.

It was at this time that I came across a news item in an insignificant corner of a newspaper that the Hon'ble Prime Minister had said that the senior civil servants should not remain glued to their desks and they should take time to reach out to people and different sections of society and interact with them to take a feedback about their expectations from the government and also inform them about what the government was actually doing for them. He had also got a Circular issued to this effect from the PMO (Prime Minister's Office). I found this to be a great idea and I was convinced that this was the job senior officers in the government, especially those whose actions impinged on the lives of the people. The IRS officers were definitely the people whose actions concerned everybody. The officers of the Indian Police Service also mattered a lot for everybody. And the next will be the Indian Administrative Service which has a crucial role of advising the government in policy making on various issues. I, therefore, resolved that I would engage with stakeholders as also the citizens irrespective of whether they had to do anything about taxes. After all, I was a senior representative of the government besides being a taxman. Next ten months were devoted towards talking to students at schools and colleges with whom I engaged on qualities of good citizenship. I spoke to Chartered Accountants, lawyers, tax paying individuals, trade bodies, chambers of commerce etc. about their responsibilities as citizens, their duty of paying their taxes honestly and the consequences of not doing so. I had my meetings at Dehradun, Nainital, Meerut, Haldwani, Rishikesh, Mussoorie etc. We used to call these "outreach meetings" which meant reaching out to people. The meetings received tremendous response. In the halls or auditoria a large number of people assembled and eminent citizens invariably thanked me for the initiative.

Chartered Accountants and lawyers, eminent citizens and taxpayers in packed auditoriums or halls were always a difficult task, more so because I always made it an open house for an hour or so after my 30 to 45 minutes long speech. To answer their concerns was daunting. I, therefore, always told them that I was a little intimidated speaking to them because they were experts and master players of the game of law and accounts which we were administering. The task of making a meaningful and efficacious dialogue for me was a little challenging. But I reminded them that they were not just stakeholders but equal partners in the endeavours of the government to usher in a healthy tax regime. I also told them the right caption of our meetings should have been 'meeting partners at work to devise a strategy to achieve common goals' instead of 'outreach'. Having said that, I used to outline what was expected of them and what was expected of us. I never minced words in telling them that their pens were actually more powerful than that of the Prime Minister. The Prime Minister had himself said it in his meeting with the Chartered Accountants. It was because they certified the correct incomes of a taxable entity. We only verified what they had certified. We didn't possess any superior wisdom. In fact we learnt a lot from them when we entered into a discussion on legal issues. They actually were our educators. In fact they were like our amicus curiae in all the proceedings. In the light of this scenario they had to understand our mutual responsibilities.

I used to spell out their responsibilities as follows:

(1) You need to exercise due intelligence when you certify the accounts of an assessee. That is your job and that is why you have to maintain the highest level professional competence and ethics while doing so.

(2) You as tax professionals are always in touch with people who come to you for advice about your tax obligations. You must give them the right advice. Please always remember the thin difference between tax avoidance and tax evasion, which, more often than not, is thinner than what we think and try to prove.

(3) As tax professionals you have to spread the message that not paying taxes does not help and paying taxes and filing returns help you grow in life inasmuch as no lender will ever come forward to you if you don't have a credible balance sheet. Money stashed in cash has no value beyond which can be consumed as what we call 'conspicuous consumption'. You command respect only if you pay your taxes.

(4) There are countless marginal earners who should be paying taxes. We Indians look like fools to outsiders when we look at the statistics of how few people show incomes of more than Rs 1 crore and even Rs 10 lakh. We see so much prosperity by the wayside. You have to spread the message as professionals that not paying taxes if one is beyond the threshold limit of exemption is unpatriotic and may be counterproductive. Filing returns helps the government widen the tax base. It is surprising why in a country of more than 130 crore people there should not be even 13 crore of filers of returns. The people need to be told that the Income Tax Department was sitting on a huge data bank of various kinds of not only high value transactions but of all transactions which could palpably make somebody a taxpayer. The department could act on the information any day.

(5) As tax professionals you should treat people in the department as your partners towards the same goal. You need to be competent and transparent and quintessential professionals. Maintain the thin difference between professional friendliness and professional ethics. Don't do anything, which, by any definition, could be called corruption abetted.

(6) We as taxmen make enquiries, conduct surveys and searches and make assessments. We necessarily end up in any of the four situations,

  (i) Innocent proven innocent—It is a situation which should not be there in an ideal state. Why should there be any inquiry in the case of an innocent? Probably it would be utopian to think of this situation at this stage of development. We expect you to enable us to prove an innocent to be an innocent. Your knowledge and expertise must be at its best, because as it is said in jurisprudence,- thousand criminals may go scot free, but not one innocent should be punished.

  (ii) Guilty proven guilty—That's our job. We expect that you don't misuse your knowledge and expertise, fabricate evidence and knowingly misinterpret.

  (iii) Innocent proven guilty—It would be our cardinal and unpardonable mutual failure.

(iv) Guilty proven innocent—This will be heinous. We expect an ideal professional conduct by you.

Being equal partners in creating a healthy tax regime the department can assure you that you won't find the officers lacking in anything, at least for things which needed to be done as per law and are not getting done. At least you can depend on the Chief Commissioner who will be at your disposal always. As taxmen we had no business to be pro-assessee or pro-revenue. These are stupid and redundant phrases. We are there to implement the Income Tax Act in letter and spirit. We are there to collect not a pie more and not a pie less.

We are committed to the government's avowed objective of ushering in a non-adversarial tax regime. Besides being the authorities under the law, we were primarily public servants and we were committed to discharge our responsibilities in the quintessential spirit of public service in which arrogance and highhandedness had no place. There are certain cardinal principles that I always prescribed. What was doable and ought to have been done in the normal course must be done expeditiously and with grace. What was not doable and could not be done as per law should not be done at any cost or under any circumstances. But in that situation also we would explain in the spirit of public service why it was not doable.

I never missed to mention that times had changed. We were no longer seen as mere tax collectors. We were perceived as agents of social change by cleansing the system of not only rampant tax evasion but also creating a value system by our conduct and actions in which tax evaders and hoarders of dirty money were frowned upon and isolated and the honest and the well-meaning respected. It was time for us to come together and work together toward the goals of revenue, towards strengthening the sinews of the nation and towards rendering justice to the honest tax paying citizens of India.

My outreach meetings became a hit and a great success. In the monthly video conferences with the Chairman, CBDT, he mentioned more than twice about the role of the Chief Commissioner and cited my meetings as examples of ideal conduct of a public servant. He called me to his chamber at the North Block and admired me for my courage of conviction which, as he himself believed, was not possible without a high level of personal integrity and command over verbal skills. That was satisfying although it mattered little because I had no trust in the system. I believed in self-satisfaction only.

In July, 2018 I got transferred to Delhi as Chief Commissioner of Exemptions. This is a post with an All India jurisdiction. There are 14 Commissioners of Exemption all over the country reporting to the chief commissioner. The Dehradun posting was memorable. I really enjoyed and felt nice to be able to do my job with positive autonomy. Interacting with school students of famous boarding schools at Dehradun and Nainital and talking to the future citizens who had to take charge of the country was an enriching experience. They were aware of the anomalies in the system. Issues like corruption and poverty bothered them. I had to be very practical in answering their concerns. I wanted them to keep their hopes for better India alive. I also had occasions to speak to renowned artisans and craftsmen at Dehradun. It was a different experience altogether. Once I had an occasion to watch a play 'Macbeth' at Dehradun by artists from Arunachal Pradesh. In my speech at the end I not only complimented them but also recited the famous lines 'tomorrow and tomorrow and tomorrow creeps on this petty pace from day to day to the last syllable of recorded time'. The audience was spellbound. I had created enough cherishable memories in a year. The officers and staff gave me an overwhelming farewell. Mridula also came for that. I said goodbye to Dehradun and joined Delhi in the first week of August, 2018.

Chief Commissioner (Exemptions) is a very sensitive post. It is involved in various kinds of approvals relating to exemptions in the Income tax Act, 1961. Further, the Chief Commissioner (Exemption) is responsible for administration of Tax Returns of exempted entities and implementation of various provisions relating to exemptions in the Income Tax Act, 1961. It also holds jurisdiction over political parties. It has administrative control of the 14 Commissioners of Exemption posted across the country. This is the only post at the level of Chief Commissioner with an All India jurisdiction.

The office of the Chief Commissioner (Exemptions) is located in the Civic Centre in Delhi. It is on the 23rd floor of a massive building. The size and the decor of the office are impressive. The best part is the view of Delhi that it provides from the 23rd floor. From the room the entire city can be overseen. Five minutes in the morning itself makes the day. Work becomes a pleasure.

Basically incomes derived from property held under Trust wholly for charitable or religious purposes to the extent to which such income is applied to such purposes in India come within the purview of Exemptions. Similarly a Section 8 company comes under the jurisdiction of Exemptions. A company when registered as a Non-Profit Organisation (NPO), i.e. when it has the motive of promoting arts, commerce, education, charity, protecting the environment, sports, science, research, social welfare, religion and intends to use its profits (if any) or other income for promoting these objectives is known as a Section 8 company. Whether the incomes earned are exempt or not in view of the conditions laid down under the law is a vexatious issue. Too much litigation has been there on these issues. In fact substantial time of the Chief Commissioner (Exemptions) goes towards judicial matters on a day to day basis. In totality the work as Chief Commissioner (Exemptions) is very challenging and substantial in volume.

Seeing the importance of Exemptions, the quantum of revenues involved and the volume of work I proposed to the CBDT for the desirability of upgradation of the post of Chief Commissioner, Exemptions to that of Principal Chief Commissioner. The CBDT found substance in my logic and arguments and the post was upgraded. The Principal Chief Commissioner is a post of the Apex scale of the Government of India. In other words this is the highest level one can reach under the government. The whole country is divided into 18 Principal Chief Commissioners administratively. There are a few heading the Directorates at Delhi and now a new Principal Chief Commissioner of Exemptions came into existence.

With an All India jurisdiction my travelling continued and so did my outreach meetings at various places across the country. I sensitised people on the provisions of exemptions everywhere I went. It was surprising for me to see the response of the eminent people and tax professionals attending in large numbers at Hyderabad, Pune and Aurangabad. At Hyderabad the heads of organisations like Apollo also attended. So did Mr. F. Gopichand, the badminton star. At Pune they had too many queries but it was a pleasure clarifying issues. At Aurangabad representatives of several political parties attended.

An important development that took place around September 2018 was the election to the IRS Association (All India Body). I was hardly interested but officers approached me to take over as the President. I was the General Secretary in the year 2004-05. I accepted and hoped that in the next one year I would be able to do something for the IRS community. We took up many issues. However, we could achieve little with finality.

Around the month of April 2019 my turn for getting promoted as Principal Chief Commissioner came. Delhi has only one field post at this level. I was posted as Principal Chief Commissioner (West UP) Headquartered at Kanpur. However, the Principal CCIT (Exemption) remained with me as an additional Charge. So the next few months were spent shuttling between Kanpur and Delhi. I did justice to both to the best of my abilities. My outreach programmes continued as Principal Chief Commissioner, Kanpur. The meetings at Kanpur, Noida and Agra drew huge crowds of taxpayers and eminent citizens. Memorable has been the meeting at Agra. The incessant garlanding in my welcome had to be stopped politely. I addressed and redressed several grievances on the spot. The grievances relating to exemptions were resolved there itself through the Assistant Commissioner present there and the Commissioner, exemptions, Lucknow connected on phone. The stakeholders were apparently overwhelmed by this method of handling grievances.

Around August 2019 the Finance Minister Mrs. Nirmala Sitharaman visited Varanasi as part of her outreach programme. Varanasi came within the jurisdiction of the Principal Chief Commissioner of Income Tax, Lucknow and not Kanpur. Yet I was asked by the Chairman,

> **"The hardest thing in the world to understand is the income tax."**
> ***–Albert Einstein***

CBDT to be there and do the summing up speech and present a Vote of Thanks. I felt nice about it. Even the Finance Minister liked what I said in my speech and she complimented me. She also gave me a one to one audience for 15 minutes after the meeting.

I superannuated on the October 31, 2019. Valedictory functions at Kanpur, Noida and Delhi were overwhelming with an emotional overtone. A phase of 35 years had come to an end.

It is very difficult to evaluate the 35 years in the Indian Revenue Service in any manner. The fact remains that the prime of life was spent. As a source of livelihood it was good and dignified. The total earnings by way of salaries with the accompanying perquisites by all means were more than enough. There was of course a different perception of the things to unfold when one joined the service as a choice exercised. One realised that an efficient and honest functioning could mean a lot for the people whose affairs came within your purview at any given point of time. But to think that you could do anything meaningful and novel for the system was exclusively in the domain of the political executive. I think personally that it was absolutely fine. At the same time it is desirable that political bosses were more alive to the need for the desired level of honesty and integrity in their personal capacities and on the part of the bureaucratic manpower. Intelligence is often cited as a requirement for the civil servant. That is desirable. In my view more important is integrity in carrying out the responsibilities assigned. High level of honesty and integrity is more required than academic brilliance. There needs to be a sounder mechanism of evaluation of merit. What exists is subjective. That demotivates a sincere worker. There needs to be an efficient and objective mechanism to reward the honest and sincere and punish the erring. I had rough patches in my career which were absolutely unwarranted. But the system is much bigger than an individual. One can be happier if self-satisfaction is the guiding spirit and not meaningless self-importance.

I never tried a government assignment after superannuation because nothing came without extraneous efforts. I thank the government because it gave me a satisfying identity. There was still more to explore till one was alive. After a short break I was offered the position of CEO of the Confederation of Real Estate Developers Association of India. I joined in April 2020. I had to leave it once the Stroke hit on the April 9, 2021.

7

UPSC, IAS & Other Civil Services

I have already devoted a chapter to the Indian Revenue Service. That's because I have been a part of the Service for almost 35 years. There are, however, 24 Services the recruitment to which takes place through the Civil Services Examination. Presently the Preliminary Examination consists of two papers called General Studies I and General Studies II. These papers carry 400 marks and have negative marking too. Both the papers comprise objective type questions with multiple choices of answers. This Examination is a qualifying stage to filter candidates for the Mains Examination. The marks secured at this stage are not counted towards the final merit list although securing 33% in General Studies II is mandatory. The Mains Examination consists of 9 papers. All the papers consist of descriptive answer type questions. The marks for the Mains phase act as a key factor in merit declaration. The papers for the Mains

Examination are Papers I & II which are Compulsory Indian Language and English. Papers I to VII are Essay, General Studies I to IV and Optional I & II. The papers on Indian Language and English contain 300 marks each. These two papers are of qualifying nature and candidates have to secure at least 25% in each. The Indian Language Paper covers any of the languages included in the 8th Schedule of the Constitution. The General Studies Papers cover a variety of subjects like Indian Heritage and Culture, History and Geography of the World, Society etc. The Optional subjects for Paper VI & VII include a wide range of subjects like Agriculture, Civil Engineering, Geology, Mechanical Engineering, Psychology, Literature, etc. Then there is an Interview or the Personality Test which consists of 275 marks. Thus the total marks for the UPSC Mains and Interview for the merit list is 2025. There have been changes in the syllabus and the papers over the years but by and large the structure has remained the same during the last 40 years. By my personal experience I have found the subjectivity in the marking of 7 descriptive papers. In a total of 1750 marks the difference of 100 to 200 marks is not unlikely between two different sets of examiners. In the opted optional subjects consisting of 500 marks the difference of more than 100 marks is not unlikely depending on the subjects like Mathematics on the one hand and, say, Sociology on the other. For the same subject like History or Political Science or any subject of Humanities the subjectivity between two examiners or even the same examiner creating a difference of 100 marks can't be ruled out. The difference is enough to ensure that you are in the list of successful candidates or out of it. Worse still the interview of 275 marks can fetch you 45 or even 250. That difference can place you at rank 1 or out of the list. From 1983 onwards I often used to hear of rationalisation in marking. But it has never been in the public domain. Only the UPSC knows how that rationalisation has been done.

A myth about the best and the brightest entering the Civil Services needs to be looked at. The age of 15 to 19 when one is in class X & XII is the stage when intelligence as reflected by application of mental faculties to the knowledge imparted, the willingness to do it in a sustained manner and the number of hours put in for this get a shape. All these by and large determine how well one scores at the examination. I would call it raw brilliance because the mind is also comparatively free from distractions at this stage because the elders around, mostly parents, take care of other worldly needs. At this stage one takes a call for the career to choose and the child enters Engineering, Medicine, Science, Humanities or law. After 1990 there has been an expansion in the areas of study to choose from. From the early 20s the maturity levels start getting crystallised. The Civil Services come as an option at this stage. And this option continues to be there till the age of 32 and six attempts currently (for General category candidate). In our times it used to be 28 years of age and three attempts. Can passing an examination at this stage and with so many attempts be considered innate brilliance in all cases? I, along with a friend who was in the IAS, in 1985, had made a study of the academic profiles of successful candidates of the Civil Services Examination of 1982, 1983 and 1984 out of curiosity. Going through the academic status of successful candidates, it was a startling revelation. We had the entire academic profile from class X of more than 200 candidates. We found that almost 40% of the candidates were high rank holders in class X & XII. Incidentally most of them had cleared the UPSC Civil Services by the age of 26 and in their first attempt. Thirty per cent were above average in terms of their academic performance at school and college levels. Thirty per cent were below average at their class X and XII and degree level results. Many of those in these two categories had cleared the examination in their last attempt. All that it showed was that the success at the Civil Services Examination was necessarily not a sign of academic brilliance. It was in large measure a combination of several factors—maturity through age, choice of subjects, a fair amount of luck in terms of examiners, choice of subjects, etc. And for a difference of few marks in an examination of 2025 of maximum marks, somebody got allotted the Indian Foreign Service and somebody got the Armed Forces Headquarters Civil Service which is a Group 'B' Civil Service. The situation of final results of the examination by and large remains the same even today. Moreover, like Medicine and Engineering the Civil Services is not the first preference all over the country. Few states only contribute an overwhelming number. These are Delhi, Uttar Pradesh, Bihar, Rajasthan, Tamilnadu, Karnataka, Andhra Pradesh, Punjab, Haryana, Uttarakhand, Jharkhand, Madhya Pradesh and West Bengal. Among the institutions the largest contributors to Civil Services are the IITs, the Delhi University and the Jawaharlal University. Obviously the preference for Civil Services is not an All India phenomenon. It is limited to parts of the country. So the arrogance on the part of the Civil Servants, some if not all, that they are the brightest is more than unjustified. It is something else that the civil servants need not be the brightest. They should be a workforce with a high level of commitment and integrity.

The crucial question is whether the civil services, particularly the IAS has delivered the results it has been expected to during the last 75 years. Should efficient and the honest in the other more than two dozen services through the same examination not be associated with the core governance which is the prerogative of the IAS? There is an erroneous situation that prevails. And that is the knowledge that once recruited, civil servants are not obliged to prove their competence ever again. It kills performance and in case of the IAS it becomes a loss to the nation, the development process and public welfare because they are the ones assigned with the responsibility.

This situation of thriving, in fact flourishing, without achieving any concrete result has been a potent disincentive to performance. In drawing room discussions our IAS colleagues often talk about political interference. That may be there. But my questions are very simple. If every District Magistrate, even if his tenure in the district lasted for just a year, had ensured that 10 kilometres of road in the district had been made durable since 1947, the scenario of development would have been different from what we have witnessed.

Mr. N. C. Asthana, a retired IPS officer, an erudite scholar and a great thinker wrote a very nice Article which I came across on the internet (it was in the Wire). In the paragraphs below I am borrowing facts and references from that. It puts the issue in perspective.

"It is widely believed that the patience of our well-meaning Prime Minister with the IAS is wearing thin. One of the reasons for this is that the efforts of the government do not seem to percolate down towards its intended recipients. It is being widely believed that the government is seriously thinking of taking more and more senior officers through the lateral induction process from the private sector. Whatever may be the government's reason, it is a welcome step as the IAS has miserably failed to deliver. The IAS and the graduates of the IIT graduates have an aura of mystery around them. Many think that those who manage to crack these exams are the creme de la creme of the country and their inherent superiority will take India to great heights. Fact is that neither the IAS nor the IITs have done any wonders for India. Indian Space Research Organisation (ISRO) has been a great success story for the country. The ISRO has just 2% of its engineers from the IITs and the NITs. The rest 98% are from small engineering colleges. Similarly, the IAS must be judged on what it has delivered over the decades in terms of introducing better administrative practices, policies or imparting superior domain knowledge. The crucial question is what the IAS, based on a competitive examination based selection, by and large the highest rankers, has delivered in 75 years, which could arguably be delivered only by them and not by others. The academicians and the common citizens often ask this question. The sad reality is that the Indian administration still functions the same way it functioned before independence. Resources have changed, objectives in an independent nation have changed, but the mind and spirit of the IAS have not. The state of the country in terms of the economy, public healthcare and education even after 75 years of independence leaves much to be desired. The seniors in the IAS claim a hand in formulating national policies too. By that logic the blame for the many failed policies of the past 75 years must fall on the IAS.

Apologists of the IAS argue that it is a multi-functional service for senior positions in the government that require a broad understanding of the various subjects that go into the making of overall policy. Question is what is the criteria for determining this so-called 'broad understanding' and who is competent to determine it? Moreover, there is no objective test for determining someone's level of broad understanding. This is actually a euphemistic way of admitting that they do not know more than an ordinary man. IAS, in fact all the civil services, are the only jobs in the world where one is paid for the entire career for having obtained the job. No single exam, however tough, can guarantee lifelong delivery, particularly because there is no system of rigorous in-service examinations to check one's competence to continue.

All over the world, people are recruited at the bottom of the ladder and from there they earn their promotions depending on their merit, proved through departmental examinations. Dermont F. Shea was the New York City Police Department Commissioner who had joined the police as a patrolman (that is, at the bottom of the ladder) in 1991. He became a sergeant in 1995, a lieutenant in 1999, a captain 2003, a deputy inspector in 2008, an inspector in 2010, a deputy chief in 2013, the deputy commissioner of operations in 2014, the designated chief of crime control strategies in 2017, the chief of detectives in 2018 and the New York City Police Commissioner in December, 2019. Even by American standards, he gets a very high pay of 2,38,000 dollars per annum which is higher than the average pay 1,86,622 dollars per annum of a Lieutenant General of the US Army. If a patrolman can head the New

York City Police, why do we also not devise a proper system of promotions through examinations?

IAS is referred to as the 'steel frame'. It is forgotten that when Lloyd George had spoken of the 'steel frame', he meant it as an instrument of perpetuating the British Empire. He had no concern for India or Indians. Speaking in the House of Lords on February 26, 1924, Marquess Curzon of Kedleston had clearly said, "The British Raj in India will fade away and disappear unless you have a sound Civil Service to support it". In the same debate, Lord Olivier, the Secretary of State for India, also said that it was impossible to associate the idea of maintenance and perpetuity of the British Civil Service in India with the ultimate idea of Indian nationalism and responsible government. While the fealty of the civil servants to the Empire was never in doubt, their real contribution is grossly overestimated. ICS officers could go about their careers because it was so ridiculously easy to go about it. Eric Hobsbawm, noted historian and Fellow of King's College, Cambridge, has pointed out that the Raj was 'so easily won, so narrowly based, so absurdly easily ruled, thanks to the devotion of a few and the passivity of the many'. After 30 years in the ICS, H. Fielding Hall wrote in 1895, "The whole attitude of government to the people it governs is vitiated. There is a want of knowledge and understanding. In place of it, are fixed opinions based usually on prejudice or on faulty observation, or on circumstances which have changed, and they are never corrected. Young secretaries read up back circulars, and repeat their errors indefinitely … 'following precedent'. Liberal statesman John Bright described the Empire as a 'gigantic system of outdoor relief for the aristocracy of Great Britain'.

Ideally the nation should have disbanded the ICS immediately after independence to make way for a truly nationalist cadre of officers. However, rattled by the traumatic experience of the centrifugal tendencies in some princely states, Sadar Patel pitched for continuity of the civil service. In October, 1949, he told the Constituent Assembly, 'You will not have a united India if you do not have a good All-India Service which has independence to speak out its mind', even as many chief Ministers had vehemently opposed it and wanted state Civil Services as they felt that the idea of All-India Service opposed the federal principle. The civil service has belied Sardar's expectations and disproved his wishful thinking on both counts. First, there has been any instance in 75 years when they spoke their mind. On the contrary, there are a million examples to prove that they have been yes-men par excellence—the quintessential courtiers reciting 'huzoor behtar jaante hain' (the master knows better). Moreover, there is no evidence at all that the civil service has promoted the unity and integrity of the country, whereas the state services could not have done the same thing or better. In fact, until December 2018, as many as 1,669 Kashmiri

"My dilemma is that of the civil servant. If a civil servant takes an initiative and things go right with it, he cannot, in the nature of his employment, look for much in the way of reward; whereas if his initiative goes wrong, he can expect all kinds of trouble, everything from reprimand to blocked promotion, and a permanent black mark against his name in the files. It is accepted, therefore, that the way to advance in the civil service, or in any field where civil service conditions prevail, is never take an initiative and never to support anyone else's. It is inevitable that this should be so."

–*Robert Aickman*, The Unsettled Dust

subordinate police officers have sacrificed their lives in fighting terrorism.

Britain had produced a veritable battery of outstanding scholars in the 19th and 20th centuries in various fields. But not one of them joined the ICS. The reason was simple. The Empire did not want the risk of 'independent thinkers' questioning the immoral ways of the Empire and its servants, whom Edmunde Burke had described as 'birds of prey and passage'. The Empire wanted

"Every reformer is a public servant, but not every public servant is a reformer."

***–Abhijit Naskar,* Mücadele Muhabbet: Gospel of An Unarmed Soldier**

submissive, impressionable boys for whom working in the colonies was a thrilling adventure with good money to boot, and who would do their bidding happily. Thus, a culture was born in which the primary requirement from civil servants was meekness. Meekness dovetails with sycophancy and everything associated with it.

V. S. Naipaul says that the attitudes of the ICS men brought to bear on their work in India had greatly deteriorated by the end of 19th century from curiosity and concern to complacency. Gopalkrishna Gandhi calls the ICS a set of small-minded, small-sighted, small-feeling men. They had only to act pompous and pass their time in splendid isolation. The civil service, in its new avatar of IAS, took its 'fortuitous' continuation after independence as the license to exacerbate its feudal traits. The revolutionary poet Josh Maleehabadi expressed his anguish over this eloquently in his poem 'Maatame-e-Azaadi'; "Shaitan ek raat mein insaan ban gaye (devils turned into humans overnight)". A retired civil servant has noted that most IAS officers have very high levels of 'schadenfreude' (pleasure derived by someone from another person's misfortune), and love nothing better than to see the proletariat squirm. You would never find a citizen who could claim that civil servants were kind to him or made his life better in such-and-such manner without any recommendation, pressure or outright bribe. No wonder, in spite of all the progress that the country has made, India ranks 140 in terms of happiness in the list of 156 countries (World Happiness Report, 2019) with even Pakistan ahead of us at 67.

As James Bond quipped in Goldeneye, "Hope springs eternal". In spite of suffering at the hands of the civil servants and knowing well that the Civil Services have failed to deliver, many young people hope to join the elite group someday, to enjoy the powers and privileges, not to speak of the hundreds of crores they could make if they chose to be corrupt. That hope is the reason that few people oppose the illogical system. Not long ago, we had proper feudal lords who got their positions and titles through birth or sheer force of arms; the Civil Services have replaced them with 'feudalism through exam'. The earlier we do away with this, the better."

In the preceding few paragraphs Mr. N. C. Saxena has brilliantly analysed and described the historical background explaining the attitudinal issues and the fact that we did not shake off the mind-set even after independence. But the issue which is of prime concern is corruption that has permeated the IAS, and in fact the entire Civil Services. It is something that is common to other walks of national life also. Here I am concerned only with the Civil Services.

One point noteworthy, however, is that the credibility of the government suffers more when those in senior positions in the government who are always in the public gaze are found to be corrupt. IAS comes at the top in this respect because these officers are more concerned with activities relating to public welfare. The areas of activity coming within their purview are far too many. This is not to discount the corruption prevalent in the IRS, the IPS and the Customs and Central Excise etc.

What is corruption after all? Put simply it is abuse of power by those in positions of authority. Absence of transparency and accountability leads to prevalence of corruption in civil services. Corruption as a practice would include bribery, patronage, nepotism, embezzlement, influence peddling, use of one's public position for self-enrichment, partiality, absenteeism, abuse of public property, abuse of information and the like. Obstruction of justice would be also one prominent for civil servants. In the Corruption Perception Index India ranks pretty high, at around 80 among 185 countries. Bribery is the act of promising, offering, or providing a benefit in such a way as to improperly influence a public servant's acts or decisions. Bribery is frequently seen as the most prevalent kind of corruption. Bribes can influence the allocation of monetary benefits such as credit subsidies and can speed up the granting of permission, licenses, and permits to carry out activities that are perfectly legal. This is the so-called grease-money. Extortion entails pressuring a person or group to give something to a public servant in exchange for acting or not acting in a specified way. The difference between it and bribery is the use of violence or the threat of violence to extract money. When the public servant who has been given the authority and responsibility over public resources, whether they are financial or not, misappropriates, it is called embezzlement. Fraud is a public servant's action or behaviour that misleads other people or organisations, such as the government, NGOs, or private enterprises into giving the public servant a benefit that they would otherwise not receive. Abuse of power occurs when a public servant uses his position of trust to improperly benefit an individual or group. Using discretion improperly for personal gain without outside coercion or extortion implies abuse of power. Cases involving conflicts of interest include circumstances in which a public servant acts or fails to act on an issue in which the public servant's personal interest or the interest of people or entities connected to the concerned official is directly or indirectly affected. Abuse of privilege or insider trading refers to the use of confidential information or knowledge that a public servant has access to as a result of holding a public office in order to further his own interests or the interests of entities or people close to him. Favouritism is the practice of granting preferential treatment or favours by a person in a position of trust based on preconceived notions such as friendship, racial or ethnic prejudice, or even family relations. When the natural course of justice or fairness is obstructed for the benefit of a select group of affluent, influential, and well-connected people and groups at the detriment of the general public, this is known as obstruction of justice. Selective application of regulation would be a good example of this. Influence peddling, often referred to as trading in influence, is the practice of using one's power to improperly influence a person, organisation, or government in exchange for money, loyalty, or any other tangible or intangible unfair advantage.

The causes of corruption are quite a few. Absence of efficient enforcement agencies, properly established regulations, rules, or codes of behaviour that apply to public officials are important causes. The watch-dog agencies are there but their credibility itself is not high. Complex, ill-defined and inadequate laws and regulations also provide opportunities to the unscrupulous. Some even cite inadequate wages as one of the causes. In my view this is misplaced because after the 6th and the 7th Pay Commissions the salaries along with other facilities and perquisites of civil servants are good enough. I feel a highly politicised civil service is a very important cause. It applies to the largest extent for the IAS. The unethical among them are willing to forgo the interests of the public in order to appease the political masters. This is mostly done to get the so-called lucrative postings and post-retirement assignments. Corruption is principally a governance issue—a failure of institutions and a lack of capacity to manage society by means of a framework of social, judicial, political, and economic checks and balances. Implementing and enforcing laws and regulations that guarantee accountability and transparency becomes more challenging when these formal and informal systems fail. I think strengthening the rewards and penalties system would be essential. Integrity must be rewarded at any cost and corrupt behaviour must be punished. That can be the simplest strategy for fighting corruption.

While the rampant corruption in Civil Services is a matter of great concern we need not lament over it in isolation. After all, corruption is a phenomenon that is pervasive across all walks of life. The civil servants are a part of the society. The social influences are difficult to withstand. Moreover, the confidence that one can go scot free even after demanding a bribe for something which was a matter of right for the person who was forced to pay bribe perpetuates it. Indeed I know of friends who are in the IAS now who had to pay a bribe for some certificate to be obtained from the office of the Sub Divisional Magistrate and the Collector. The Collector or the SDM might not have been a beneficiary of the bribe, but he had no control over the person who demanded it. I also know of a friend in the IPS who could not ensure that his cousin's police verification report for issuance of a passport went without paying a bribe. I also know a friend in the Railways who himself had to pay a bribe to the TTE for travelling with a reserved berth for his civil services

Interview. Similarly I could not ensure a quick refund of taxes to a colleague by the office of an Income Tax Officer in Kerala. These are ironic situations. But these are surely indicative of a society in crisis. The pressure of a massive and unwieldy population on resources, the absence of fear for wrongdoing, the insensitivity generated by bitter experiences causing situations of helplessness, all these perpetuate corruption and speed money for routine but vital jobs for a living. This is all about corruption on a day to day basis and would come in the category of petty corruption which vitiates national life. The matters of corruption at higher levels which thwart development are far too many. Politicians across political affiliations and civil servants at senior positions are to be blamed for that. Every day the newspaper reads like the fever chart of a sick society. News of some politician or a civil servant has become a routine affair. In many cases the news may be biased. In many the whole allegation may be engineered to malign. In many instances the cases instituted and investigations carried out, the actions like a raid may all be a face wash. But the redressal of the grievances may not be forthcoming quickly even from the Judiciary. The judiciary itself may be embroiled and beset with a host of issues. So the civil service need not be blamed in isolation. An honest commitment to a better India on the part of each citizen is a sine qua non.

No country is immune to corruption. The abuse of public office for political gain erodes people's trust in government and institutions, makes public policy less effective and fair, and siphons taxpayers' money away from schools, roads, and hospitals. While the wasted money is important, the cost is about much more. Corruption corrodes the government's ability to help grow the economy in a way that benefits all citizens. The political will to build strong and transparent institutions can turn the tide against corruption. The fiscal institutions and policies like tax administration or procurement practices, effectively used, can fight corruption in a big way. If we analyse the countries the world over we find that more corrupt countries collect fewer taxes, as people pay bribes to avoid them, including through tax loopholes designed in exchange for kickbacks. Also, when taxpayers believe their governments are corrupt, they are more likely to evade paying taxes. Statistics show that the least corrupt governments collect 4% of GDP more in tax revenues than countries at the same level of economic development with the highest levels of corruption. A few countries' reforms generated even higher revenues. Georgia reduced corruption significantly and tax revenues more than doubled, rising by 13 percentage points of GDP between 2003 and 2008. Rwanda's reforms to fight corruption since the mid-1990s bore fruit, and tax revenues increased by 6 percentage points of GDP.

Corruption also prevents people from benefitting fully from wealth created by their country's natural resources. Because the exploration of oil and mining generates huge profits, it creates strong incentives for corruption. The resource-rich countries, on average, have weaker institutions and higher corruption as revealed by an IMF study. Countries with lower levels of perceived corruption have significantly less waste in public investment projects. Most corrupt emerging market economies waste twice as much money as the least corrupt ones. Governments waste taxpayers' money when they spend it on cost overruns due to kickbacks or bid rigging in public procurement. So, when a country is less corrupt, it invests money more efficiently and fairly. Corruption also distorts government priorities. For example, among low-income countries, the share of the budget dedicated to education and health is one-third lower in more corrupt countries. It also impacts the effectiveness of social spending. In more corrupt countries school-age age students have lower test scores. Corruption is also a problem in state-owned enterprises, such as some countries' oil companies and public utilities like electric and water companies. These enterprises are less efficient in countries with high levels of corruption. Fighting corruption requires political will to create strong fiscal institutions that promote integrity and accountability throughout the public sector.

Investment in high levels of transparency and independent external scrutiny is essential. This allows audit agencies and the public at large to provide effective oversight. Colombia, Costa Rica, and Paraguay are using an online platform that allows citizens to monitor the physical and financial progress of investment projects. Norway has developed a high standard of transparency to manage its natural resources. A free press enhances the benefits of fiscal transparency. In Brazil, the results of audits impacted the re-election prospects of officials suspected of misuse of public money, but the impact was greater in areas with local radio stations.

The chances for success are greater when countries design reforms to tackle corruption from all angles. For example, reforms of tax administration will have a greater payoff if tax laws are simpler and they reduce officials' scope for discretion. Transparent, merit-based hiring and pay reduce the opportunities for corruption. The heads of agencies, ministries, and public enterprises must promote ethical behaviour by setting a clear tone at the top. Focus on areas of higher risk, such as procurement, revenue administration, and management of natural resources as well as effective internal controls are desirable. In Chile and Korea, for example, electronic procurement systems have been powerful tools to curtail corruption by promoting transparency and improving competition. Countries can also join efforts to make it harder for corruption to cross borders. For example, more than 40 countries have already made it a crime for their companies to pay bribes to gain business abroad under the OECD anti-corruption convention. It starts with political will, continuously strengthening institutions to promote integrity and accountability, and global cooperation.

That is a comprehensive perspective on corruption. It is an issue not confined to civil services. However, the role of the higher bureaucracy needs no emphasis. Besides the larger implication in terms of losses because of corruption they have to be examples of integrity and probity in public life. The society looks towards them with hope and expectation of a better India. Perhaps a structural change may be considered for better governance. The IAS for example is supposed to be having the desired expertise in every field under the sun. How can an officer who handles 15 departments at different levels in the entire career of, say, 35 years be an expert in environment, water, road construction, space, defence, law and order, finance, banking, insurance at the same time? This is a ridiculous assumption. It is humiliating to actual experts who work but the highest decision making is with the IAS officer. Why can't their aptitudes be ascertained and they are selected for one or two core areas? Why can't the equally bright guys in other more than two dozen services who missed to be in the IAS just because they secured a few marks less in a descriptive examination consisting of 1750 marks be given the same responsibility. That will reduce the ego arising from the perception that they are the masters of everything in the bureaucratic domain. Similarly I often wonder why the policemen should be recruited through the Civil Services examination. Policing is a technical job and there are nuances of Police Administration. The cadre of police officers will be more professional if the policemen are recruited young like the army officers and they reach the top without reporting to anybody except the political executive. The IRS will have better expertise if the officers are recruited separately from amongst those who have a larger exposure to Accounts and law. These are thoughts worth pondering over. One step which needs to be initiated is that a rigorous and impartial examination should be introduced which should be carried out every five years to determine competence, integrity and personality traits for continuation in service. Merely passing an examination once should not presume fitness for ever.

There is a school of thought which advocates scrapping of civil services because it has failed to deliver in the last 75 years. It is argued that it was a need of the colonial masters who had to rule and govern. But after independence the priorities changed to development and public welfare. That's an argument which can't be brushed aside. The political executive needs to give a thought to it. I am personally not against civil services. I have been a part of it for 35 long years. However, I have been an ardent advocate of the desirability of structural changes. The least that needs to be done urgently is that we stop glorification of the civil services and the examination for this forthwith. It perpetuates certain myths and has a negative impact on society in general and young minds in particular. Not all who crack the civil services exam are extremely intelligent as is often made out. Not all bureaucrats are exceptionally intelligent people. Another myth is that bureaucratic jobs are the best career options for dynamic youngsters. On the contrary, after 1992 in the post liberalization phase there are numerous career options for youngsters with adequate knowledge and skills in different fields.

8

Medical Profession in India; Need for Basic Changes

"Healthy citizens are the greatest asset any country can have."

—Winston S. Churchill

I said earlier that I have been singularly fortunate in having doctors in my life who have been empathetic, academically brilliant and great personal friends at the same time. It has been part of growing up that I learnt to respect medical professionals. But as I grew up and closely observed the way medical education is imparted in our country, the academic levels with which the students enter medical career, the options available as career as a doctor, general attitude of the doctors towards the patients and the patient's attitude towards the doctors and the worth of the profession in terms of earnings, I found there were too many distortions and shortcomings which need to be addressed.

We need to have a look at the mammoth population of our country with a substantial number of people below poverty line and widely varying economic levels even among those who are above the levels of poverty considered as poverty line. The literacy levels of the population also impinge upon the strategy to chalk out a plan for a desirable universal healthcare. The world's population continues to grow, but the pace of growth is slowing down. The world's population is projected to reach 8 billion by 2022 and 9.7 billion by 2050. By 2100 it is likely to reach 10.4 billion. India is set to become the world's most populous country by the end of the decade, overtaking China. According to the latest edition of the United Nations' World Population Prospects. India's population is set to rise to 1.515 billion in 2030 from 1.417 billion in 2022.

So the massive population is a problem typical to India. We need not go into analysing whether we belong to the First World, the Second World or the Third World for drawing a healthcare strategy based on the models followed by other nations. In any case the 'Third World' is an out dated concept since the 1990s. It has now become a derogatory phrase which has been used historically to describe a class of economically developing nations. It is a part of a four-part segmentation that was used to describe the world's economies by economic status. The Third World falls behind the First World and the Second

World but was ahead of the 'Fourth World' though 'Fourth-World' countries were hardly recognised at all. Today, the preferred terminology is a developing nation, an under-developed country' or a low and middle-income country (LMIC). There can be few ways to divide up the world for purposes of economic segmentation. Classifying countries as First, Second Third and Fourth World was a concept created during and after the Cold War, which ran from approximately from 1945 to the 1990s. In general, nations are typically characterised by economic status and key economic metrics like gross domestic product (GDP), GDP growth, GDP per capita, employment growth, and an unemployment rate. In developing countries, low production rates and struggling labour market characteristics are usually paired with relatively low levels of education, poor infrastructure, improper sanitation, limited access to health care and lower costs of living. Developing nations are closely watched by the International Monetary Fund (IMF) and the World Bank, which seek to provide global aid for the purposes of projects that help to improve infrastructure and economic systems comprehensively. Both the organisations refer to these countries as lower-middle or low-income countries.

Although not very relevant for drawing our strategies, it is worthwhile having a look at the best healthcare systems of the world. Every country has a different approach to healthcare and the medical system for prevention and cure.

While each model is distinct, most countries don't adhere singly to a single model, rather, most create their own hybrids that involve features of several. Cost of medical claims differs from country to country too. Many countries have single-payer healthcare which is funded by the government. The government removes all the competition in the market to keep costs low and standardise benefits. The National Health Service controls what "in-network" providers can do and what they can charge. Funded by taxes, there are no out-of-pocket fees for patients or any cost-sharing. This system is used by the UK, Russia, UAE, Spain, Hong Kong and other countries. Another healthcare system option is where employers and employees are responsible for funding their health insurance system through "sickness funds" created by payroll deductions. Providers and hospitals are generally private, though insurers are public. In some instances, there is a single insurer (France, Korea). Other countries like Germany and Czech Republic have multiple competing insurers. Some employer-based healthcare plans are also used in the US. A third popular option is the national health insurance model which is driven by private providers, but the payments come from a government-run insurance programme that every citizen pays into. Essentially, the national health insurance model is universal insurance that doesn't make a profit or deny claims. In this case, some citizens have private health insurance, some may receive subsidised public healthcare, while some are not insured at all. It is used in China and Japan among others. The out-of-pocket model is the most common model in less-developed areas and countries where there aren't enough financial resources to create a medical system like the three models described. In this model, patients must pay for their procedures out of pocket. It is used by Congo, Ethiopia and some other countries around the world. Healthcare will continue to be a major concern everywhere in the world. After all, there is a need to have a meaningful conversation on necessary reforms that involve providers, systems, payers and the government. That conversation should include a thorough examination of the strengths and weaknesses of these global models so that they can inform new healthcare policies and ultimately build a model that can work for everyone.

Countries around the world apply different approaches to provide medical care. Some rely on government support, as in the single-payer approach. Other nations depend on the private insurers and a third group of countries, such as the United States, have a mixture of both. The quality and efficiency of a country's healthcare system can have a massive impact on its citizens' quality of life. Healthcare is a global industry encompassing both physical and mental health. It covers a range of functions, from the prevention, diagnosis and treatment of disease, illness and injury, to long-term recovery. According to the World Health Organization, a well-functioning health care system requires a steady financing mechanism, a properly-trained and adequately paid workforce, well-maintained facilities, and access to base decisions on. Healthcare is a costly item in national budgets, but who gets the best value for money, and who has the best outcomes? The World Health Organization's last global report ranked these 10 most advanced countries in medicine with the best healthcare in the world—France, Italy, San Marino, Andorra, Malta, Singapore, Spain, Oman, Austria and Japan. Since this ranking, which analyses health system efficiency, other studies have produced slightly different lists.

India has a multi-payer universal health care model that is paid for by a combination of public and private health insurance funds along with the element of almost entirely tax-funded public hospitals. The public hospital system is essentially free for all Indian residents except for small, often symbolic co-payments in some services. At the federal level, a national publicly funded health insurance program was launched in 2018 by the Government of India, called Ayushman Bharat. This aimed to cover the bottom 50% (500 million people) of the country's population working in the unorganised sector (enterprises having less than 10 employees) and offers them free treatment at both public and private hospitals. For people working in the organised sector (enterprises with more than 10 employees) and earning a monthly salary of up to Rs 21,000 are covered by the social insurance scheme of Employees' State Insurance which entirely funds their healthcare (along with unemployment benefits), both in public and private hospitals. People earning more than that amount are provided health insurance coverage by their employers through either one of the four main public health insurance funds which are the National Insurance Company, The Oriental Insurance Company, United India Insurance Company and New India Assurance or a private insurance provider. All employers in India are legally mandated to provide health insurance coverage to their employees and dependents as part of Social Security in India.

As of 2020, 300 million Indians are covered by insurance bought from one of the public or private insurance companies by their employers as group or individual plans. Indian nationals and foreigners who work in the public sector are eligible for a comprehensive package of benefits including both public and private health, preventive, diagnostic, and curative services and pharmaceuticals with very few exclusions and no cost sharing. Most services including state of the art cardio-vascular procedures, organ transplants, and cancer treatments (including bone marrow transplants) are covered. Employers are responsible for paying for an extensive package of services for private sector expatriates (through one of the public or private funds) unless they are eligible for the Employees' State Insurance. Unemployed people without coverage are covered by the various state funding schemes for emergency hospitalization if they do not have the means to pay for it. In 2019, the total net government spending on healthcare was $36 billion or 1.23% of its GDP. India had allocated 1.8% of its GDP to health in 2020–21. Since the country's independence, the public hospital system has been entirely funded through general taxation.

The National Health Policy was endorsed by the Parliament of India in 1983 and updated in 2002, and then again updated in 2017. The recent four main updates in 2017 mentions the need to focus on the growing burden of non-communicable diseases, on the emergence of the robust healthcare industry, on growing incidents of unsustainable expenditure due to health care costs and on rising economic growth enabling enhanced fiscal capacity. In practice, however, the private healthcare sector is responsible for the majority of healthcare in India, and a lot of healthcare expenses are paid directly out of pocket by patients and their families, rather than through health insurance due to incomplete coverage. Government health policy has thus far largely encouraged private-sector expansion in conjunction with well-designed but limited public health programmes.

According to the National Health Accounts report, the total expenditure on health care as a proportion of GDP in 2018 was 3.2%.Out of 3.2%, the governmental health expenditure as a proportion of GDP is just 2%, and the out-of-pocket expenditure as a proportion of the current health expenditure was 42.06% in 2019 while expenditure of the government and health insurance funds increased to 57%.

> **"Health care and education are too important NOT to be left to the free market."**
> ***–Kevin D. Wlliamson***

Attracting 45% of health tourists visiting India and 30 to 40% of domestic health tourists, Chennai is termed "India's health capital". The Human Rights Measurement Initiative finds that India is doing 80.5% of what should be possible at its level of income for the right to health.

Whatever be the prevailing healthcare model in our country, one thing is certain, each nation-state and political system has to evolve its own policy according to acceptable norms. But irrespective of political dispensation the desirability of a healthy nation by providing healthcare to all citizens can have no debate. India's gigantic and rather worrisome population, substantial portion of population living below poverty line and a sizable portion of the population with no wherewithal to take care of their basic needs makes the task of universal health difficult for our policy makers. We need to be concerned with the incidence of infant mortality. We need to be worried about the malnutrition in rural and urban India and pathetic unhygienic conditions in urban slums. We need to feel proud of the fact that despite constraints our youngsters have been, of late, excelling in sports at international levels. Mental prowess of young Indians going abroad to developed nations for higher studies or for employment has been more than sufficiently proved the world over. That only suggests that productivity of every Indian needs to be taken to its optimum level through proper nutrition and universal healthcare. Perhaps Indians can work wonders if every citizen could be ensured his or her basic right, that is the right to health. The right could be considered granted meaningfully if access to medical facilities are ensured and the problems like malnutrition, environmental pollution, etc. are tackled. Another problem is that of potable water in several areas which needs to be addressed on a war footing. Defecation in open spaces is another unhygienic phenomenon which is a national shame.

With such an onerous task of creating and maintaining generations with good and robust health there can be no two views on the fact that we need the brightest and most contented manpower as doctors. The craze for becoming doctors and making a fortune is never going to decrease as long as the human ailments are there. But the important thing to be seen is whether the value system in the society and the comparative financial rewards are attracting the brightest. Unfortunately it is not so. When I was in college more than four decades ago medicine used to be the preferred career for eight out of ten best students. Today one out of twenty best prefers the medical career. As the Chief Commissioner of Income Tax, Uttarakhand in 2017 and 2018 I visited so many schools at Dehradun as part of my outreach programme where I used to engage with students of class XI and XII talking to them about desired qualities of good citizenship and on any issue which the future citizens of India and their young minds wanted to raise. My interactions were with students of reputed boarding schools as well as with those students who were studying in government schools. To my utter surprise, rather dismay, only a very small number of students expressed the desire and the plan to take up medicine as a career. They found the recognition and prestige attached with the medical career not attractive enough. They found the financial rewards also in the career not commensurate with the number of years of studies involved. The pressure to make it to the post-graduation and super specialization was further demotivating. Resultantly it is not the best but the much inferior flock of students who make it to the MBBS course. This is not to suggest that a number of extremely bright young minds still join the career because of their personal preference. Their numbers of course are a miniscule to a huge population.

The demand for doctors has increased multiple times since 1947. It is natural with the growth of population. Naturally the need has been met by the increase in the number of medical colleges. In 1947 there were just 19 medical colleges in the country with 1000 students. In 1976 when I was in Intermediate (12th) there were 106 medical colleges run by the government and a small number of private medical colleges. Now in 2021-22 there are 321 government medical colleges and 291 private medical colleges. India has the largest number of medical colleges in the world, both modern medicine and AYUSH. Close to 90,000 MBBS graduates in these more than 600 medical colleges of Modern Medicine (Allopathy) and 53,000 graduates in another 733 AYUSH medical colleges are produced every year. AYUSH stands for and means Traditional and Non-conventional Systems of Health Care and Healing which include Ayurveda, Yoga, Naturopathy, Unani, Siddha, Sowa-Rigpa and Homeopathy etc. The doctor to patient ratio on the face of it is not adverse in absolute terms. Assuming 80% availability of registered allopathic doctors and 5.65 lakh AYUSH doctors, the doctor-population ratio in the country is 1:834, which is better than the WHO standard of 1:1000. The ratio is inclusive of the AYUSH doctors. While there can be no objection to the recognition, promotion and expansion of traditional and non-conventional systems of health care there are divergent views whether the AYUSH graduates should be treated at par with the allopathic doctors for statistical purposes in policy making.

The statistics of doctor to patient ratio, number of medical graduates, number of medical colleges etc. actually do not address our problems so far as healthcare is concerned. What should be a matter of grave concern is why a majority of those among the best are not opting for the MBBS course and the medical career. In my view it is because of the value system which prevails and which acts as the potent demotivator for the bright to pursue a medical career. I have examples of my personal friends who were extremely bright and could have successfully made it to any career like Engineering, Civil Services, Law etc. but they opted to take up medical careers by choice. Let me cite two examples, one of a medical graduate/post graduate joining the service of the government and the other one opting to work privately. The one choosing to go for the government service joins the Government of Bihar and gets posted to a remote Block. Undeterred by the inconveniences of travelling to the place he reaches there. He is told there is government accommodation for his stay. He discovers that an ill-kept house, dilapidated to describe realistically, is there. Next morning he reaches the Primary Health Centre where he is supposed to function as the Doctor. He finds that half of the paramedical and other members of staff are either absent or late for duty. The telephone installed at the PHC is not functioning. He, therefore, cannot speak to the Civil Surgeon, the boss of the medical service, sitting at the district headquarter. Basic and essential drugs/medicines are found missing. To do justice to medical treatment is impossible. Yet he has to manage examining the patients and also be careful of the mood of the patients. Some may lose temper and even become violent at the doctor for no fault of his. In the afternoon he calls up the Block Development Officer and he is shocked to find that he speaks like a boss would speak. He further discovers that the BDO was a guy from his native village and was a very ordinary student. He is confused about his status in the hierarchy of officers at the Block. Although most of the things at the place of his work were shocking, the conduct of the BDO was kind of a cultural shock and a mockery of his education. He spends a month and abandons his job because the clerk at the Secretariat explains that the formality of resignation was going to take time. He doesn't even get his month's salary expeditiously and ultimately forgoes it. He comes back home, studies for a year for ECFMG (now USMLE). He is now a successful and fairly rich physician in the USA. He is sure that he will never come back and work in India. And I personally know his patriotism and love for India is beyond question. What a brain drain and loss to a system of healthcare.

Let us now have a look at what typically happens to a bright graduate/post graduate choosing to start his medical practice privately. Another friend, a classmate of mine from Intermediate, set up his clinic in a Tier 2 city to which he belonged. Everything was fine except that there used to be too many irrelevant questions, more often than not repetitive, by the patients irrespective of their level of education. One fine morning a belligerent patient for reasons best known to him started alleging wrong treatment and came on the verge of violence. He, whose level of education was very poor, was hardly talking sense. Later my friend discovered that he was advised by a quack whom he often used to consult. Finding private practice to be a risky affair called it a day. He then took up a job with a corporate hospital for which he had to make certain investment in their shares. My neighbour, an alumni of the prestigious Armed Forces Medical College, Pune had to recently close down his nursing home because of violence by a local small-time politician.

These are two examples of what happens to a fairly bright student who takes up medical profession for to fulfil his dreams of becoming a respectable person in the society and of being able to earn enough by his education. The initial disillusionment itself frustrates him. On the contrary, a student who took several attempts to get a seat in a government medical college finds that his plans of making money are fulfilled with enough respect because his options in terms of a career were limited. Worse still there are too many seats available to get a medical seat through payment of capitation fees. Lacking in merit they also enjoy the same status as a doctor with their counterparts having entered the profession through sheer merit. The brighter lot takes time to absorb this shock.

Another anomaly plaguing the medical education system is a mad rush for specialisation and super specialisation. A large number of students nowadays start coaching for post-graduation entrance right in the second year of the MBBS course, thus compromising with the skills basic to being a good doctor. It is high time perhaps we could think of avoiding mushrooming of specialists and training to make doctors, who are specialists in family medicine or general specialists, award them with a suitable degree and ensure proper financial rewards for their service. This would be a better model to take care of the needs of the less privileged and the overwhelming population residing in small towns and rural areas. The need for specialist and higher treatment should be referral which should be decided by the general practitioner. This will also ensure the overcrowding of the bigger hospitals and their resources. The general practitioners would treat all common medical conditions and refer patients to hospitals and other medical services for urgent and specialist treatment. One Shri J. K. Chhaparwal Assistant Professor of Medicine has written a very insightful Article on 'General Practice and Family Medicine as a speciality: key to health care in India' which I would like to extract for a perspective.

"Health is a basic need of human beings and access to health-care is a fundamental Human Right. The constitution of India charges the state with the responsibility of providing health/medical care to the people in the state in the Directive Principles of State Policy. It can be seen as a fundamental right in 'Right to life' under Article 21. The quality, quantity, distribution and availability of human resources for the health care sector is far from satisfactory, to deliver care driven, rural oriented and equitable health care services. Over the years health related education and training has become more urban oriented, doctor-centric and technology driven. Medical education is part of the whole system of education which is in crisis mode today. We are paying a high price for inadequately investing in the balanced growth for the social sector i.e. health and education. A large urban rural divide is present in terms of location of health care facilities and their quality and is increasing with decreasing access and equity of services for the rural areas and urban slums. Over investigations, over medicalisation and technology driven strategies dominate the urban rich in tertiary care hospitals.

Despite all these lacunae, impressive change in health indicators has been recorded since independence. Infant mortality rate has been brought down from 146 to 30, maternal mortality rate from 840 to 212, life expectancy at birth from less than 30 to 65, crude birth rate 41 to 22.5 per thousand population and total fertility rate 6.6 to 2.6. However, the general health indices in India are below average of other developing countries and are way below socially acceptable level. The country still carries an enormous share of the global disease burden. With 17% of the global population, India accounts for 20% of the total global disease burden: 23% of child death, 20% of maternal death, 30% tuberculosis, 68% of leprosy and 14% of HIV infection. India continues to bear a larger portion of the global burden of pre-transmission communicable diseases, acute respiratory cases, diarrheal diseases, besides other preventable diseases. Magnitude of mortality figures for communicable diseases indicate 2.5 million adult deaths, 2.5 million child deaths in a year (Task force report

"The collective principle asserts that no society can legitimately call itself civilised if a sick person is denied medical aid because of lack of means."

–Aneurin Bevan

on medical education for National Rural Health Mission, Government of India, 2006).

While the aggregate number of doctors (0.8 million doctors) is not very low for a developing country, only 28% of them are located in the rural areas. Eighty-three per cent of the total health expenditure is in the private sector and it has a dominant influence on the health system. Our doctors are mostly self-employed. The present system of medical education is not oriented to produce competent general practitioners or a family physician. The medical care in India is divided into codified and uncodified medicine. Codified medicine includes western and the Indian system. Non Codified medicine practitioners are in huge numbers such as in home medicine, folk/tribal medicine; besides the non-qualified practitioners of codified medicine. The medical profession needs to be structured like a pyramid with a base made of special trend general practitioner/family physician. Over 420 medical colleges are located in urban areas where only 25-30% of the population live. Annually we train 52,000 MBBS, 24,000 Specialists (MD & MS), 32,000 AYUSH, 60,000 nurses, 16,000 ANM and 40,000 pharmacists. Still no authentic data is available on the paramedical training facilities.

There are very few post-graduate degree programs of MCI in family medicine/general practice as a speciality. The number of specialists being trained have no relationship to the numbers of graduates, the speciality proportions, skill mix, manpower required to meet out health care and teaching, the disease profile, the emerging disease pattern, epidemiologic changes, lifestyle changes, economic development, grass root specific manpower and research requirements.

Any successful development process must have a pyramidal structure with a strong horizontal base. In terms of medical education it has to be a strong base of clinical generalists/family medicine/general practice specialists who ought to be the backbone and stability of the system. The family physicians/general practitioners of yester years are no longer visible. This needs to be urgently addressed. There is a need to introduce new postgraduate courses in disciplines such as general practice/family medicine including maternity and child health, geriatrics, specific branches of public health, emergency medicine, sports medicine, critical care, trauma care and so on to meet the actual need at the grass-root level. For example, children constitute 42% of our population whereas 40% of our doctors are not paediatricians. We must train our family physicians and general practitioners adequately, in an integral manner, to cater for this delicate population who would be the future citizens and back-bone of our nation. Same is for women's health.

Recently Dr. Devi Shetty (2015) stated that if India can initiate some radical changes in medical, nursing and paramedical education, dramatic changes would be visible in a very short period. India can become the first country in the world to dissociate health care from affluence. This can only happen by closely linking health care delivery with medical education. According to World Bank data, Cuba produces the largest number of doctors per capita (6.7 per thousand against 2.5/1000 in US and 0.7/1000 in India) and its health indices are better than that of the USA, which spends the highest on health care. India is grossly short of doctors and nurses. Its paramedical training programme is virtually non-existent. We simply do not have the number of medical specialists needed to take care of our people. For 26 million child-births per year we need to perform at least 5.2 million caesarian sections. For successful child birth following a C-section, we need over a lakh of obstetricians, specialist anaesthetists, paediatricians and radiologists, etc. We only have around 30,000 ob/gyn specialists, 20,000 anesthetists and radiologists. Only 30% of our population has satisfactory access to proper anesthetists services of which 80% are urban beneficiaries. Large number of specialist posts are vacant in hospitals all over the country. In most developed countries postgraduate seats are twice the number of undergraduate medical seats. However in India we have over 50,000 undergraduate seats and only

14,000 postgraduate seats in clinical subjects, the root cause of corruption in medical education today.

Family Medicine/General Practitioner as a Speciality

A recent survey in the USA showed that 62% of upper middle class Americans cannot afford to go to hospitals there, as medicine has become prohibitively expensive despite patients having more than one medical insurance policy. Fifty seven percent of the British do not want to go to a modern medical facility, if they could help it, despite the free National Health Service scheme. In the last half a century medicine has gone to the marketplace riding piggyback on technology and market forces act on it in a big way. Today consumerism rules the roost making doctors practice expensive, defensive medicine. Thinking people in the medical world will have to do something before it is too late. The only solution is to go back to the time tested family physician system with necessary modifications in the training period to make the family physician truly useful to the sick. After graduation one should take postgraduate training for at last three years in this speciality. The family physician should be a sort of jack of all trades and should have a good grounding on human psychology, health promotive activities, nutrition, exercise physiology, rural surgery and intense training in bedside methods of diagnosis and management are to be stressed, technology being given a very limited role.

Education and PG training for Family Practice throws many challenges. On one hand the family medicine practitioners should know how to manage common medical conditions that include communicable as well as non-communicable diseases, such as, diabetes mellitus, hypertension, cancer, emerging conditions like bird flu. On the other hand they should possess basic surgical emergency and trauma care skills. In addition, the family medicine practitioner should be well versed in five domains i.e. communication skills and patient doctor relationship; applied professional knowledge and skills and organisational and legal decisions (D. K. Srinivas, 2008). Indian medical Association's College of General Practitioners has been striving hard for nearly half a century to educate and train modern medicine graduates in family medicine practices. On completion of the course it awards Fellowship in General Practice, though not recognised by the Medical Council of India. National Board of Examinations (NBE), Ministry of Health, Government of India does offer a post graduate 3 years course in Family Medicine. However, this is not the celebrated specialty chosen by medical graduates."

There are about 600 medical colleges in India now and approximately 50% are private medical colleges. It is common knowledge that most of the private medical colleges are absolutely unfit to run like a college, leave aside a medical college which is more capital intensive. A thought often crosses my mind why the government should permit private investment in medical colleges when the private players are not able to afford it as per the norms and conditions prescribed. Why can't the government, say, for 10 years, not increase its budgetary provisions (the spending on healthcare being only little over 2%) and create a long-term infrastructure of medical institutes. Why can't it be enforced on the private players to strictly adhere to norms if they have to be in the business. The Medical council of India (now substituted by the National Medical Commission) has to honestly and effectively rise to the occasion. We hear of so many ways and means adopted by the private players to make a mockery of the inspections carried out by the Medical Council of India. More often than not complicity is alleged. Any complicity/laxity/lack of due diligence in matters as serious as medical education should not be tolerated at all. A realistic evaluation needs to be made regarding the availability of the required faculty for teaching, paramedical manpower, etc. If the required numbers are not available, strategy first has to be evolved to meet these deficits.

While mediocrity needs to be shunned at all costs in the medical profession for the simple reason that it deals with human life, a value system needs to be evolved in which the profession and the professionals receive their due place. They should not be seen as money makers. The fact remains that compared to other fields where one earns money through education, the medical field is the least rewarding financially. Even a specialist's consultation fee being just Rs 500 (even in cities) is ridiculous. A NRI was amused a few years ago when she was charged less than 10 dollars for consultation by my wife. This has nothing to do with the paying capacity of the people who prefer to go for a consultation in the private clinic of a medical professional. It is a matter of attitude to the profession. Subconsciously it also reflects scant regard and concern for health which actually should be the most important concern. People show concern with health issues only when they suffer from a heath disorder which is life threatening. I am not oblivious of the people who can't afford even the meagre consultation fees of the doctor. For that the government hospitals have to generate confidence in their treatment. The network of government hospitals needs to be larger. The doctor employed there to serve has to be a contented person both in terms of remuneration as well as social esteem. Only then he can be expected to deliver to his optimum capacity. There should be no red tapism in the functioning of the government hospital. It is the health professional who should have the final say in deciding as to how the hospital should be run most efficiently for delivering in terms of the health needs of the people. Usually it is the Government's Secretariat or similar bodies of the government, manned mostly by the people who have little knowledge of the medical aspects of the need of the hospital which makes decisions about the supplies of items needed to run the hospital. More often than not the egos of these non-medical bosses is highly inflated which cripples the hospital administration. Leave aside the medical issues like availability of drugs, the priority in terms of deciding about the provisions, I have personally witnessed how a clerk in a reputed government medical college responsible for disbursing stipends of the house surgeons and interns, and even the salaries of senior doctors acts pricey and makes them run at the end of the month for something which is a matter of right for them. Can the government hospitals deliver with this level of dysfunction? The government ought to rise to the occasion. Perhaps even for private medical professionals the government could bring a law facilitating consultation by him/her at a subsidised rate based on the incomes of the patients. That will mitigate the difficulties of the less privileged. Number of such patients can be limited to a number per day. So all this involves creation of a value system in which the medical profession and professionals are treated with respect, streamlining healthcare administration and increasing spending towards making healthcare available for all.

An avoidable harassment taking place of private medical professionals in the state of Uttar Pradesh is something the rationale of which I have not been able to understand. It is possible that the same practice might be prevalent in all the states with minor procedural differences. All medical establishments whether a big hospital, a nursing home or a clinic of an individual are required to obtain a registration every year from the Chief

Medical Officer of the district by the 30th April. The application for registration requires that the Certificate for fire safety is obtained and an Agreement for disposal of bio medical waste is made with a vendor for the purpose. The application is to be manually filed with the CMO or it can be uploaded too. Same documents like degree, medical council registration, etc. are required to be filed/ uploaded every year. The whole exercise takes hours. It is not understandable why a registration should be required every year. Corruption is often alleged in raising objections on flimsy grounds. To avoid the harassment a medical establishment should be required to register with the CMO only once. After that it should be only a periodical check that the CMO's office should exercise and ensure that all the statutory parameters are being met. The time and energy involved in the exercise of routine applications should be utilised towards a crackdown on quacks who thrive in large numbers and with brazen confidence.

An effective system of healthcare runs not only because of the doctors. A whole army of paramedical staff including nurses, compounders, ward boys etc. have their crucial role in running the hospital system. They need to be satisfied with a remuneration commensurate with their services.

Despite endless discussions on the needs of rural India's health little effective measures have been taken. The government has to take up the responsibility on this front. It will be unrealistic to expect private initiative. The vast network of Primary Health Centres in rural areas is a commendable structure created by the government. The issue is to ensure their efficient functioning to deliver the desired result. Adequate supplies of medicines and consumables to the centres are to be ensured. A motivated medical and paramedical staff working at the centres is an essential requirement. The facilities of stay at the place of working should be good enough. The doctors should be posted at the centres for a fixed period after which they should be transferred to their place of choice as far as possible. They should be incentivised properly in terms of remuneration while posted in rural areas. An efficient working of the Primary Health Centres for which the government has already created the basic infrastructure will satisfactorily take care of the health needs of rural India. Patients needing specialized treatment and care may be referred to the higher centres in the towns and cities.

The Medical Council of India for long was the statutory body for establishing high standards of medical education in India. It was dissolved on September 25, 2020 when it was replaced by the National Medical Commission. There have been controversies about various acts of omission and commission by the Medical Council Of India. The Council granted recognition of medical qualifications, gave accreditation to medical schools, granted registration to medical practitioners, and monitored medical practice in India. The MCI faced persistent criticism for corruption. The stated objective of the National Medical Commission are:

(a) lay down policies for maintaining a high quality and high standards in medical education and make necessary regulations in this behalf;

(b) lay down policies for regulating medical institutions, medical researches and medical professionals and make necessary regulations in this behalf;

(c) assess the requirements in healthcare, including human resources for health and healthcare infrastructure and develop a road map for meeting such requirements;

(d) promote, co-ordinate and frame guidelines and lay down policies by making necessary regulations for the proper functioning of the Commission, the Autonomous Boards and the State Medical Councils;

(e) ensure co-ordination among the Autonomous Boards;

(f) take such measures, as may be necessary, to ensure compliance by the State Medical Councils of the guidelines framed and regulations made under this Act for their effective functioning under this Act;

(g) exercise appellate jurisdiction with respect to the decisions of the Autonomous Boards;

(h) lay down policies and codes to ensure observance of professional ethics in medical profession and to promote ethical conduct during the provision of care by medical practitioners;

(i) frame guidelines for determination of fees and all other charges in respect of fifty percent of seats in private medical institutions and deemed to be universities which are governed under the provisions of this Act;

(j) exercise such other powers and perform such other functions as may be prescribed.

The NMC, with its stated powers and responsibilities, holds the key to ensuring a desirable and effective system of healthcare.

The National Eligibility cum Entrance Test or NEET(UG), formerly the All India Pre-medical Entrance Test was introduced in 2013 which is now the qualifying test for MBBS and BDS programmes in Indian Medical and Dental colleges. The idea of NEET is fine but it needs to be ensured that candidates securing below a minimum do not enter the portals of medical education.

9

Gitanjali

"Tumi jokhon gaan gahite bolo
Gorbo aamar bhore uthhe buke.
Dui ankhi mor kore chholo chholo
Nimesh'haara cheye tomar mukhe.
Kathhin, Kotu ja achhe mor prane-
Golite chaye se amritamay gaane.
Sob sadhana, aradhana momo-
Urite chaye pakhir moton sukhe.
Tripta tumi aamar Geetaraage
Bhalo lage, tomar bhalo lage.
Jani aami ei gaaneri bole,
Boshi giye tomari sammukhe.
Mon diye jaar nagaal nahi paai
Gaan diye sei charan chhunye jaai
Surer ghore aponaka jaai bhule-
Bondhu bole daaki mor Prabhuke".

''जब आप कहते हैं गाओ
मेरे सीने में गर्व उठता है,
दो आँखें फैल गईं
एक पल के लिए अपने चेहरे को देखते हुए।

जो कठोर और कड़वा है वह मेरी आत्मा में है
गली में चाहता है अमृत गीत,
सर्व साधना आराधना माँ
मैं पंछी की तरह खुशी से उड़ना चाहता हूं।

आप मेरे गीतों से संतुष्ट हैं।
आप की तरह
जानिए कि मैं इस गनरी को बुलाता हूं
अपने सामने बैठो।

मैं अपने दिमाग से किसी तक नहीं पहुंच सकता,
मैं संगीत के साथ उन चरणों को छूता हूं,
मैं तुम्हें राग के साथ भूल जाता हूं,
मेरे भगवान को दोस्त कहो।''

Translation by Deepankar Choudhury

"When you ask me to sing-
With pride my heart fills.
Tears in my eyes you bring-
As I look up to your face.
In my life, all that is tuneless-
To melt in sweet harmony it wishes.

Into my being, all of my reverence-
To fly like a bird-free, it wishes.
My singing, pleases you, it seems.
I know, you it pleases, it pleases.
I know, it is only for my prayers-
You feel my presence.
With reveries what I fail to reach.
With reverence that I aspire to touch.
In melodies of my prayers I lose myself-
My lord as my friend, I address."
Tagore's Translation
"When thou commandest me to sing
it seems that my heart would break with pride;
and I look to thy face, and tears come to my eyes.
All that is harsh and dissonant in my life
melts into one sweet harmony-
and my adoration spreads wings
like a glad bird on its flight across the sea.
I know thou takest pleasure in my singing.
I know that only as a singer I come before thy presence.
I touch by the edge of the far spreading wing of
my song
thy feet which I could never aspire to reach.
Drunk with the joy of singing I forget myself
and call thee friend who art my lord".

It was 1971. I was in class IX when Harananda, my first teacher and inspiration in life besides my father told me that he was going through Gitanjali, an universally acclaimed book by Rabindranath Tagore. He then recited the verses that I have cited above. He was in class XI then. I hardly understood anything, leave aside the essence. But I learnt the verses by heart. My father's Bengali speaking colleagues used to be immensely impressed by the recitation in Bengali by me. It was impossible for me to understand the connotation of the words 'mystical' or even 'religious' at that stage. Through the years I read Science, Marxism, Liberalism and practically everything that can give one a fair understanding of the realities of human existence. The Gitanjali fascinates me a lot now not just for it's lyrical marvel but it's contents. Having brooded over theistic beliefs, atheism, agnosticism over the years, I am sure that the laws of nature, the physical beauty of the universe and the innumerable variables in the creation which we see but don't comprehend can't be denied. Surrendering in reverence to these is the real respect that needs to be paid. It was not without reason that Primitive Animism began as a practice by humanity millions of years ago, as early as human history. Rabindranath Tagore's collection of poetry was first published in India in 1910. Tagore then translated it into prose poems in English, as Gitanjali, Songs-Offerings, and it was published in 1912 with an introduction by William Butler Yeats. Tagore was awarded the Nobel Prize for Literature for this in 1913. Writing a few words about Gitanjali is my reverence to Nature and the creator of this beautiful piece of Literature.

Colleen Hoover writes 'you'll never be able to find yourself if you 're-lost in someone else'. Some other thinker says, 'It's okay if you fall down and lose your spark. Just make sure when you get back up you rise as the whole damn fire'. The answers are all in the surrender to Nature. The 'Songs-offerings' have been expressed through the simple use of the simplest conceivable language. Through the simplicity of language and the intensity, Hinduism found humanist expression. Sincerity of the feelings expressed is one of the reasons for the universal appeal of Gitanjali. I recently came across a Critical Study of Tagore's Gitanjali in evaluating Indo-Anglian literature. I found it a very apt appraisal of the great work. The Gitanjali has the very spirit and essence of Tagore's philosophy of life. Here is Tagore's unique blend of romantic longing and a simple love of created things and also of course his devotion to God. The book is a collection of impressions of personal religious moods, and it is free from all kinds of dogmatism. All the poetry in this book is in the feeling and the tone, and in the prose-poetry which is simple, fluid and has just enough formal organisation to hold the book together. In the opinion of Williams, Tagore was wise in avoiding metre and rhyme. The imagery, pervasive but not startling, is taken from Nature and from Indian classical mythology. The one hundred and three poems of this book are unified by the poet's search for God and for his happiness in his love for the spirit which lies within Nature and Man; and the search is expressed with wistful melancholy in a sustained minor key.

As Williams points out, Gitanjali certainly contains the most obviously religious of Tagore's poems, though the religion is lyrical and vague, a type of pantheism, with echoes of Hindu Vaishnavite poetry and of Christian religious feeling for God as Father and Redeemer. The image of God as bridegroom and lover is common to the New Testament and Vaishnavism. But H. M. Williams does not agree that Gitanjali shows any mysticism; and in this connection he writes: "Unfortunately the exotic flavour of the poems and the vagueness of European knowledge of Indian religion led to their being labelled as mysticism, with exasperating results for the poet who was embarrassedly his new-found reputation as an Oriental Guru".

Williams regards Tagore as a lyric poet of shifting moods and a poet of Nature, and certainly no mystic in the technical sense in which the word is applied to Shri Aurobindo Ghosh. According to Williams, Tagore had wrongly been regarded as a mystic, and some of the blame in this connection rested upon W. B. Yeats who praised Tagore for many of the wrong reasons. A more perceptive evaluation of Tagore as an English poet, says Williams, came from Ezra Pound who accurately pin-pointed the chief literary interest of Gitanjali. This literary feature of Gitanjali, according to Ezra Pound, was the use of prose-poetry as a new medium. Williams further says that although Tagore was never completely at home in the English language, his mastery of it as a literary medium was an amazing achievement for a middle-aged foreign poet. Some of the finest hymns are those in which the poet's longing for the divine to refresh his 'arid heart' is clothed in the metaphor of the Indian seasons as in the following verses;

"The rain has held back for days and days, my God, in my arid heart. The horizon is fiercely naked—not the thinnest cover of a soft cloud, not the vaguest hint of a distant cool shower. Send the angry storm, dark with death if it is thy wish, and with lashes of lightning startle the sky from end to end. But call back, my lord, call back this pervading silent heat, still and keen and cruel, burning the heart with dire despair."

(Poem No. 40)

Tagore's Gitanjali is a perfect example of the view that the best poetry aspires condition of prayer. In Gitanjali, the tradition of Indian bhakti poetry of Mira, Kabir and others, takes a new birth. Yet, Tagore expresses himself in such a way that the poems have a universal appeal. The philosophy of universal love and acceptance harmonizes very well with Christianity also. There are various things which have made Gitanjali an appealing work universally.

10
Musings

“Tomorrow, and tomorrow, and tomorrow,
Creeps in this petty pace
from day to day,
To the last syllable of recorded time;
And all our yesterdays have lighted fools
The way to dusty death.
Out, out, brief candle!
Life’s but a walking shadow,
a poor player,
That struts and frets his hour upon the stage,
And then is heard no more.
It is a tale
Told by an idiot,
full of sound and fury,
Signifying nothing.”
—William Shakespeare, *Soliloquy from Macbeth*,
Act 5, Scene 5

Since the book starts with my encounter with the life-threatening Stroke and it’s substantial portion takes the form of a memoir, I thought it worthwhile to share some 'musings' since my age of 14, duly preserved in old notebooks. These are some quotes and some compilation of thoughts that I came across here and there, in some books that I went through at different stages and newspapers and magazines. These are as old as 1972 and as recent as 2020.

1. **Random Thoughts. NOW IS ALL. 10.09.2020:** "As each day passes by, most of us wonder whether life is on the right track, whether we shall feel when we are, say, 50 or 60 or 65 or 75 in terms of age that we lived life to the fullest. With each morning routinely spent, with each day lived for earning livelihood and deriving a sense of power or importance or feeling wealthier by what we do, and with so many evenings of well-mannered frivolities, the secret of Living Life to the Fullest still eludes us. It is not that I have unravelled the secret, but some thoughts often come to my mind which, for me, are worth penning down. So, I do. As human beings, we are probably constrained within time, which contains past, present and future (or so we think). The truth seems to be that there is no such thing as the past or the future, these are creations of mind. It would necessarily mean that time, in a psychological sense, is an illusion. There is only NOW. There is only THIS moment. Life is happening through the NOW. Let us look at small children. Let us look at animals. Let us look at Nature in general. They are all rooted in NOW. Most of us are not here, most of us are stuck in our heads

thinking about the past or anticipating the future. And that disables us to act effectively in the present which probably is the only way we can live through life. Long ago, we used to look towards the future as salvation from our present unsatisfactory life, When I top in the school, I will be happy. When I get out of college with flying colours, I will have a better life. When I fall in love with someone, life will make sense. When I have children, that would be blissful. When I make a certain amount of money, all my worries would disappear. All these things, in varying degrees, happened with us. But still there is a gnawing sense of unease. More projections for the future keep happening. It inevitably means that we are mortgaging our happiness in the present for some future that may or may not happen. We may fall ill tomorrow. We may die because of age or illness. We probably are so dissatisfied with what is going on NOW that we need an escape. We could probably be happier by accepting our feelings instead of trying to bury them. We could probably be fine with whatever happened NOW. Some day it will become RIGHT NOW eventually. Let us, therefore, embrace the NOW. Let us feel the entirety of our situation. Let us not run away from it. Situation will change, as the weather does.

Depressed—let us embrace the sadness.
Heartbroken—let us embrace the anguish.
Elated—let us enjoy it coolly.

These are all the tides of life. The NOW is the Gift and the Doorway. The NOW is the opportunity to become 'One with Life'."

2. Emotions of a Marxist; Antonio Francesco Gramsci: I read Gramsci in 1980 first. He was an Italian Marxist philosopher, journalist, linguist, writer and politician. He wrote on philosophy, political theory, sociology, history, and linguistics. He was a founding member and one-time leader of the Italian Communist Party. A vocal critic of Benito Mussolini and fascism, he was imprisoned in 1926 where he remained until his death in 1937 (born in 1891). Gramsci attempted to break from the economic determinism of traditional Marxist thought, and so is sometimes described as a neo-Marxist. He held a humanistic understanding of Marxism, seeing it as a "philosophy of praxis" and an "absolute historicism" that transcends traditional materialism and traditional idealism. I quote from him what he wrote to his Mother from the prison. It is an outpouring of emotions, overwhelming to the core.

"A few days ago, I had news-about Giulia and the children. Please believe me that I am serene whenever I think about them. Each day I grow stronger and more resistant to inner agitations. As you know I have never been excessively sentimental. This apparent insensitivity of mine must have sometimes caused you pain. Today I feel I have lost even the remnant of sentimentality left in me. Like flint, I need to be struck by steel in order for sparks to fly out from me. Only you and a handful of other persons possess this steel-like quality. Mother dear, I'd like to hold you close, very close, so that you'd know how much I love you and regret the unhappiness all this causes you. There was no other way to act. Yes, life is difficult, and sometimes sons, for the sake of their own honour and dignity, have to make their mothers suffer".

3. Friendship between Marx and Engels (from his biography): The day Marx's son died in his arms, he wrote to Engels; "I shall never forget how your friendship helped us through this terrible time." After his son's funeral he added in a letter, "In all my terrible torments of these last few days I have always been sustained by the thought of you and your friendship, and the hope that we still have something sensible to perform together in the world".

4. Quotes from the Godfather: Crime in any form can never be justified. So I have no comments on the thematic content of the novel. Essentially a crime novel by American author Mario Puzo published in 1969, The Godfather details the story of a fictional mafia family in New York City (and Long Island), headed by Vito Corleone. The novel covers the years 1945 to 1955 and includes the back story of Vito Corleone from early childhood to adulthood. I had first gone through the novel in 1973 when I was in class XI. The book fascinated me. I have, during the last 50 years, read the book several times. Some of the sentences and dialogues by the characters, mainly Vito Corleone, have been my favourites. I am just listing a few as part of 'musings'.

(i) "He had long ago learnt that society imposes insults that must be borne, comforted by the knowledge that in this world there comes a time when the most humble of men, if he keeps his eyes open, can take his revenge on the most powerful. It was this knowledge that prevented the Don from losing the humility all his friends admired in him."

(ii) "You thought the world was a harmless place where you could take your pleasures as you willed. You never armed yourself with true friends. You did not need Don Corleone. Very well. My feelings were wounded, but I am not that sort of person who thrusts his friendship on those who don't value it—on those who think of little account. Now you come and ask and don't ask with respect. You don't offer me your friendship. What have I ever done to make you treat me so disrespectfully?"

(iii) "It is good you wish to be a father to your children. A man who is not a father to his children can never be a real man. But you must make their mother accept you."

(iv) "He found it inconceivable that a grown man of substance would let such trivialities affect his judgement in an affair of business, and one of such importance."

(v) "Accidents don't happen to people who take accidents as personal insults. There are things that have to be done and you do them, and you never talk about them. You don't try to justify them. They can't be justified. You just do them. Then you forget it."

(vi) "Did Jack Woltz have the balls to risk everything, to run the chance of losing all on a matter of principle, on a matter of honour for revenge?"

(vii) "It was from this experience came his oft-repeated belief that every man has but one destiny."

5. Reflections by Regis Debray: Jules Regis Debray is a French philosopher, journalist, former government official and academic. He is known for his theorisation of 'mediology', a critical theory of long-term transmission of cultural meaning in human society, and for associating with Marxist revolutionary Che Guevara in Bolivia in 1967 and advancing Salvador Allende's presidency in Chile in early 1970s. He returned to France in 1973 and later held various official posts in the French government.

Regis Debray's lesser known book is Prison Writings. I had an occasion to go through this book in 1979. Some of his reflections in the book are very nice in terms of thought and expressions. I am just quoting one for 'musings.

"I realise I must not let this heaviness take possession of me, that these vivid sensations from the past barele deserve a moment's regret." And "At the mercy of my own confused memories drifting about in a senseless, shapeless time, in which minutes would seem hours and then hours would seem minutes, I realise that total isolation makes one lose all sense of time. Either it passes too quickly in moments of fevered delight, or it passes far too slowly as in those periods of exquisite bitterness when you try to gather up every detail of your memories with a morose fascination, going back again and again over the same ground, reviewing the sequences from the past, re-arranging past plans, rectifying past mistakes, endlessly reviewing your least movements."

6. I was in school. I used to learn new words with interest and excitement. In my enthusiasm to use the words I used to write sundry things. Not that I am any poet of significance, but once I wrote a few lines which I have preserved as a memory of growing up with vocabulary. Just reproducing as written. Not very apt or even wrong use of some words may be ignored considering age (only 14 when it was written)

"Her liliaceous beauty
unveils her virginity.
And astounded I am
Lost in ecstasy
wrapped in fantasy.
I have seen her
when the trees lie defoliated by the gale
when the leaves are flagelling
when the rainbow struts.
The cherished touches,

the hungry adolescence,—
All get tantalized.
There is no end to it.
The solitude gnaws at the heart.
My existence mocks me.
But sometimes
when the clouds shed tears,
when she walks across the foliage,
when the sylvan environs await her,
I am reminded.
I am reminded of the fathomless pangs.
Pangs of separation.
Pangs of untold love.
And also the pathos of the destitute,
the trauma of the indigent,—
their abyss of gloom,
miseries and labyrinth of existence.
My poet dies.
We are foolish mortals
screaming in rage
like a bird in a cage.
Never realising,
that time moves and alters.
Beauty perishes and fades.
Pleasures decline.
And life decays.
That life transcends philosophy.
Beauty transgresses life".

11
Convalescence

I came across this poem recently—

"I counted my years
and realized that
I have less time to live by,
than I have lived so far.

I have more past than future.

I feel like that boy who got a bowl of cherries.
At first, he gobbled them,
but when he realized there were only few left,
he began to taste them intensely.

I no longer have time to deal with mediocrity.

I do not want to be in meetings where flamed
egos parade.

I am bothered by the envious,
who seek to discredit the most able,
to usurp their places, coveting their seats,
talent, achievements and luck.

I do not have time for endless conversations,
useless to discuss about the lives of others
who are not part of mine.

I no longer have the time to manage
sensitivities of people who despite their
chronological age, are immature.
I hate to confront those that struggle for power,
those that 'do not debate content, just the labels'.

My time has become scarce to debate labels,
I want the essence.

My soul is in a hurry …
Not many cherries in my bowl.

I want to live close to human people, very human,
who laugh of their own stumbles,
and away from those turned smug
and overconfident with their triumphs,
away from those filled with self-importance.

The essential is what makes life worthwhile.
And for me, the essentials are enough!

Yes, I'm in a hurry.
I'm in a hurry to live with the intensity that only maturity can give.

I do not intend to waste any of the remaining cherries.

I am sure they will be exquisite, much more than those eaten so far.
"My goal is to reach the end satisfied
and at peace with my loved ones and my conscience."

As per Confucius "We have two lives
and the second begins when you realize you only have one."

Mário de Andrade—The Valuable Time of Maturity

I don't know what Confucius meant by two lives but one thing is sure that it becomes very important to remember that life is only once whether it has begun now or whether it was always so. Obviously we will remember this only when we realise this. There can't be a more important moment to realise this than an escape from a life threatening event. You can only thank Providence if you come to a situation of 'total health' or a 'near total health' after such an event. There may be a difficult situation if

Convalescing (2022)

Convalescing, Lucknow (2022)

you survive but develop medical complications to battle with them for a long time. There may be total permanent disability, partial permanent disability or total temporary disability or a partial temporary disability. It may be a difficult life in such situations. A stroke that I had is fatal in about 10 to 20% cases, and among survivors, it can cause a host of disabilities, including loss of mobility, impaired speech or cognitive problems. These trends have made stroke the third leading cause of death behind heart disease and cancer and a major cause of disability. There has been a plethora of research and studies about the factors that may cause a stroke. It may be high blood pressure or diabetes or even stress. But indeed all of us see so many getting a stroke without any of these and many don't get it despite all these. So with all the advancements in Medical sciences the inscrutability of nature can't be defied.

It has been a year and nine months now since the stroke that I had when I am penning down these words. I plan to publish my book soon, hopefully by Ninth of April, 2023 which will mark the second anniversary of the fateful day. The whole idea of writing a book with the stroke as the central theme came after I learnt that Sharon Stone, the elebrated movie star of Hollywood had a stroke in 2001 and she later wrote a book 'The Beauty of Living Twice.' I have now read that book. She took about three years to recover by her own admission. She has also said that a total recovery as such took almost seven years. She has been in the thick of things, however, after 3 years of the stroke and during the next ten years she again rose to stardom and fame. She had lost almost everything in terms of fortunes and relationships after the stroke. She, however, regained everything, more than substantially. At more than 64 now she is not only active socially, she retains the glamour she was synonymous with. Her story has been really inspiring and motivating. It should remind you that something like a stroke spared you, and, therefore, you should be stronger. You should also remember that time flies but at the same time you are the pilot and you should regulate the flow.

I have been in a bad shape till the end of May 2021. I struggled with my speech and my memory. These two disabilities were very depressing for me. I had developed serious problems with my right limbs, particularly my leg and the hand. I was not in a position to go to the toilet myself. Yet there was a vague optimism which was bothering me only for my memory and the clarity of speech. But the providence was kind and my memory was alright within two months and the speech also improved substantially. After that it was the right leg and the right hand which I had to struggle with on a day to day basis. That struggle continues. It is a situation which is mysterious and funny at the same time. It is so from the fourth month onwards. Each morning I have this feeling that I shall start walking normally, if not running, within the next one week but it does not happen. By the evening it becomes all the same.

Of course there is improvement but that can be discerned only on a close observation. My physiotherapist and my wife are the only people who can do that. And now after one year and a half nine months I still wait for a total recovery.

My physiotherapist keeps changing his treatment patterns. After a year he introduced exercises through Theraband. That still continues. Then for about a couple of months he administered TENS which is basically the use of electrical stimulation using skin surface electrodes which have the purpose of stimulating nerves. Now he is in a different mode of exercise. He finds gradual improvement and often explains to me. Basically he is concerned with a total correction of the Calcaneus (the heel bone). I find Indrajit, my physiotherapist to be a very sincere and hardworking person. The sincerity and discipline with which he devotes almost two hours every day with me and at my home is something I will never forget. As a matter of habit I have started waiting for him every day. He has become a routine. I am sure when I become fine and he stops coming, I will take time to adjust to a new pattern in my diurnal setting. Besides being my physiotherapist, he is young, smart and good looking. He is an interesting talker with fair knowledge of contemporary issues. He particularly follows Sports with an avid interest in football. He finds time to devote a few hours in a week for voluntary services as a physiotherapist in the local Gurudwara which has an equipped clinic where patients with all kinds of ailments are treated free. He has been shortlisted for the award of Padmashree this year presumably for his services. It is by all means a great achievement particularly in the present regime when the process of Padma awards has been made transparent and it is merit alone which is the prime consideration. I felt privileged when he told me to write a testimonial for him. I did that. I will really feel great if he finally gets the award. I pray for that. As for me he has generated the hope that he will take me to a full recovery. I have gone through articles on recovery after stroke. It does take time. So I have to keep patience and follow what Indrajit says and does. I have to make myself the priority. I have to remember that little things and developments make big days.

My elder son Prerit staying in the USA has fair knowledge of Yoga and has deep trust in the power of Yoga. He often tells me that I should be learning breathing exercises which might help quicker recovery. So I decided to give it a try. We have a Yoga expert near our house who is closely known to our entire family from Bhagalpur. He is my son's namesake. I called him and he readily and happily agreed to give me the required lessons. For the last three months he comes home every Thursday for an hour and I think I have learnt the basic breathing exercises well. I don't know whether it is aiding recovery from the effects of Stroke but it makes me feel happy.

I regret having wasted a lot of time on acupressure and acupuncture. Acupressure was still fine because it was like an exercise with no external intervention. But two months of acupressure had hardly any effect. Acupuncture was cumbersome because it involved visiting the centre of the leading acupuncturist Dr. Raman Kapoor at Greater Kailash every day. The time taken in commuting and the therapy everyday was more than two hours. I won't advise acupuncture to anybody who has suffered a stroke. I found that in three months' time acupuncture didn't have an iota of positive effect. Dr. Raman Kapoor is a glib talker but is hardly able to convince and deliver. So I decided to continue with the Physiotherapy only with trust in God and Dr. Indrajit for a total recovery.

The Strokes can be classified into 2 main categories:

(1) Ischemic strokes; these are strokes caused by blockage of an artery (or, in rare instances, a vein). About 87% of all strokes are ischemic

(2) Haemorrhagic strokes; these are strokes caused by bleeding. About 13% of all strokes are haemorrhagic. Haemorrhagic strokes are extremely dangerous because the blood in the brain can sometimes lead to further complications such as hydrocephalus, increased intracranial pressure, and blood vessel spasms. If not treated aggressively, these conditions can lead to severe brain damage and even death.

The stroke I had was a haemorrhagic stroke. I am told the bleeding stopped soon enough. Sometime in July 2021, my physician friend in consultation with the treating neuro physician suggested that an MRI should be done to see the condition of the bleeding that had happened. It was done at the Yashoda Hospital. To our great relief everything was found to have settled. For further satisfaction a repeat MRI was done after a month. I was told that everything was fine and that neurologically there was nothing to worry. I was also told that I was responding well to my physiotherapy because things inside the brain, by God's grace, were alright and in order. That was a great relief. A greater relief was that Indrajit always used to tell me confidently that I would be 100% fine in the long run. He of course never gave me a precise time frame. That was fine. I decided I should be patient because the destiny which had kept me intact could not be cruel for all times. There was something in the providence which had prescribed this suffering for me. I could only take care of my body because it was the only place where I lived. After all, everyone on this earth is fighting a battle we know nothing about.

I have not been a very keen watcher of television, but this period of convalescence, at least in the first twelve months, forced me to be around it for substantial time. I watched the news channels for most of the time and was always updated with the going ons around the nation and the world. Sometimes I used to switch on the movie channels and watched a host of movies. One particular movie which I watched was the Hindi movie Baghban starring Amitabh Bachchan and Hema Malini. It is a

2003 movie directed by Ravi Chopra and co-written and produced by B. R. Chopra. Although I had seen the movie earlier, I must have done it casually. I must say I found it to be one of the finest movies in terms of it's thematic content and a very superior acting by the lead actors. Basically a family drama it portrays the role of unkind and ungrateful sons. Amitabh Bachchan and Hema Malini as parents are portrayed as great lovers for their children besides being quintessential lovers between themselves. After retirement the parents reunite with their four sons to discuss who will support them. None of the sons want to take care of both parents causing them to live separately. On the other hand another child, an orphan, who has been supported by Amitabh Bachchan to come out of his poverty and grows into a very successful man longs to live with the persons who were instrumental in making his life worthwhile. The dialogues at the end of the movie are too powerful. I watched the movie more than once later.

I have always been crazy for good music. Two other programmes which I enjoyed to my heart's delight and waited each weekend for these were Indian Idol and Super Star Singer. Listening to the accomplished singers made my whole week. Week by week the whole year became musical. A new season of Indian Idol is on the air. I must say that Sony Entertainment Television is doing a great service to the cause of music.

An unexpected crisis arose in the month of February, 2022. For an investment in the SBI a mandatory health check was required for Mridula. A technician came who herself panicked and made us worried too with her observation that there were certain cardiac problems that she could see. We had to go to the cardiologist who also was of the view that there were cardiac problems. With my state of health it was unbearable. I cried within myself. Then I recalled that we had got our citi angiography done in 2017 and Dr Harsh Mahajan, the reputed radiologist had said that there was some enlargement in Mridula's heart which was nothing to worry about. The citi angiography was perfect otherwise and he had said that it was advisable to do it every five years after the age of 50. With 5 years already completed we again went to Dr. Harsh Mahajan for a citi angiography. It all turned out to be fine and we heaved a sigh of relief.

Neurological well-being was fine. There is a hope that with sustained physiotherapy a day of total recovery will come soon. But to undergo such a long period of recovery with a smile would not have been possible without one person who was always the most loved person in my life. The unnerving crisis unleashed by the stroke made me see a different Mridula. It was almost unbelievable to see that she could have so much patience, physical stamina, devotion in terms of physical care of a husband in bad shape and an extraordinary level of empathy. For the initial three months she shut her clinic and was always around me. The saying goes that some people come in life as lessons and some come as blessings. She definitely was the greatest blessing for me and I could not have asked for more.

In a phase of illness of this magnitude it's a great gift of providence when the medical stability is achieved. But that is not enough for a meaningful survival. In a prolonged illness the attitude, even of the people considered very close, may change. The love and concern of many others taken for granted may vanish. It is in such times that you actually see who stayed with you with genuine and true empathy. Although it is often said so but the fact is that time does not heal. But it definitely teaches how to live with the pain. What becomes most important under such circumstances is that one retains emotional sanity. The person who facilitates the required emotional security actually is the most important person. It is possible that you discover that person only in the situation of adversity. I must say the stroke and the period of convalescence acted as a good teacher to me. I realised Mridula was my greatest blessing. She was a loving wife, a career woman and a very caring and loving mother and a humble socialite always, but the stroke showed the extraordinary endurance that she could have. She actually meant more than what she ever said even in youthful and romantic moments. She made me emotionally secure. We always define an emotionally secure person to be the one whose general happiness is not shaken even by major disturbances in the pattern or fabric of life. With Mridula around me the adversity dissuaded me not to dwell on the past. It facilitated for me to be my true self. I did not require constant validation. I always felt saw, heard and understood. I never overreacted to stressors or challenges or took things personally. I never got stuck in patterns of worry or rumination. I never let bad moods or difficult emotions get in the way of what was crucial. I was just fortunate.

So the period of convalescence continues with no major regrets. It is exactly a year and nine months today on the 9th January, 2023 when I am penning down these words. Hopefully when I launch a book that I plan, I would be much better. I have been taking care of mundane affairs of life for the last more than a year, spending and enjoying my moments with Mridula, handling life's issues in the best possible manner and trying to be sure in the meaningfulness of relationships. Even some perceivably close friends have been disappointing. I hold no grudges against them. I feel thankful for the good times I had with them. But now I don't want to waste my emotions. It's a short life and I don't believe in a life after life. One must keep living till one is alive with all the life's happinesses and trials and tribulations.

Acknowledgements

1. Wikipedia.
2. Shri N. C. Asthana, IPS (Retd); His Article in the Wire on Civil Services/IAS (Seen on internet).
3 William Russell; His discussion on healthcare models (Seen on internet).
4. Dr J. K. Chhaparwal; 'General Practice & Family Medicine as a speciality: Key to health-care in India' (Seen on internet).
5. Anurag Mishra and Kritika; for the Cover design of the book. The bird in the picture is Golden Bosun.
6. Anurag, Anil and Prashant—for valuable help in operating the computer application.